LAKELAND

LAKE

Journeys into
the Soul of Canada

ALLAN CASEY

 David Suzuki Foundation

 GREYSTONE BOOKS

D&M PUBLISHERS INC.
Vancouver/Toronto/Berkeley

For Marlene, Esther, and Lewis

Greystone Books
A division of D&M Publishers Inc.
2323 Quebec Street, Suite 201
Vancouver BC Canada V5T 4S7
www.greystonebooks.com

David Suzuki Foundation
219–2211 West 4th Avenue
Vancouver BC Canada V6K 4S2

Library and Archives Canada Cataloguing in Publication
Casey, Allan
Lakeland : journeys into the soul of Canada / Allan Casey.

ISBN 978-1-55365-308-0

1. Lakes—Canada. 2. Canada—Description and travel. I. Title.

FC223.L35 C38 2009   551.48′20971   C2009-901027-5

Copublished by the David Suzuki Foundation.
Includes bibliographical references.

Editing by Susan Folkins
Cover and text design by Naomi MacDougall
Cover photograph by Daryl Benson/Getty Images
Printed and bound in Canada by Friesens
Printed on acid-free paper that is forest friendly (100% post-consumer
recycled paper) and has been processed chlorine free.
Distributed in the U.S. by Publishers Group West

We gratefully acknowledge the financial support of the Canada Council for the Arts,
the British Columbia Arts Council, the Province of British Columbia through the
Book Publishing Tax Credit, and the Government of Canada through the Book
Publishing Industry Development Program (BPIDP) for our publishing activities.

The best remedy for those who are afraid, lonely, or unhappy is to go outside, somewhere they can be quite alone with the heavens... amidst the simple beauty of Nature.

ANNE FRANK, *The Diary of a Young Girl*

CONTENTS

ACKNOWLEDGMENTS

As with many works of nonfiction, the front cover of this one is make-believe in that it credits only one person. These pages could not have made the journey to completion without the participation of many people, literally from coast to coast.

I am grateful to Rick Boychuk, who was enthusiastic from the concept stage and kindly assigned me to write feature stories for *Canadian Geographic* magazine that would become the raw material for the Lake Okanagan and Lake Winnipeg chapters. I wish to thank the entire CG team, and in particular Elizabeth Shilts for her brave editorial work. It was Jim Sutherland of *Western Living* magazine in Vancouver who sent me over the ice of Lake Athabasca—just one of his many bold departures from editorial orthodoxy in a career that has produced so many informative, entertaining magazine pages. Thanks also to Sheila Hansen of *Westworld* magazine, who has published much lake-related material of mine over the years, research that has helped shape this work. A version of the Ajawaan Lake chapter first appeared in *Reader's Digest,* for which I would like to thank Liz Crompton.

Significant financial and logistical support for the travel described herein came from the agents of several government tourism-promotion departments. Many of them bent their own rules to accommodate a book that might or might not promote tourism in a measurable way, but would address conservation issues of increasing importance to that industry. From west to east, I wish to thank Catherine Frechette, Miles Prodan, and Kelly Reid in the Okanagan Valley; Daryl Demoskoff in the rectangle province of Saskatchewan; Cathy Senecal and Colette Fontaine in Manitoba; Helen Lovekin and Claude Aumount in Ontario; Isabel Gil, Sophie Bouchard, and Nancy Donnelly in Quebec; Randy Brooks in Nova Scotia; and Gillian Marx in Newfoundland.

Further support for the research came via an expedition grant from the Royal Canadian Geographical Society and from a science journalism award from Genome British Columbia and the University of British Columbia School of Journalism. Crucial support with expedition equipment came from Evan Froom, Chad Pysden, and Aeneas Precht.

As to sources, I am indebted to many scores of people, not all of whom I can thank by name. Often the briefest casual encounters yielded valuable information. My deepest thanks go to all those people who shared their knowledge and passion for *their* lake. They took time from busy lives, took me aboard their boats, took me under their roofs. The list includes all those named in the book. Others, who do not appear, nonetheless gave just as generously. In particular I would like to thank Chris Purton at the Dominion Radio Astrophysical Observatory, Penticton; Wayne Roberts, Silver Star; B.C. Parks interpreter Scott Alexander; Eileen and Mark Sadlowski, Kelowna; Barney Reeves and Rob Watt in Waterton, Alberta; Lorelei Ford of the Saskatchewan Watershed Authority; James Sanderson, Prince Albert; Morris

McLachlan, Waskesiu; Ellen MacDonald and Brett Purdy, University of Alberta; Garth van der Kamp at Environment Canada; Heather Hinam of Hecla Oasis Resort; Al Kristofferson, Alex Salki, and Len Henzdel of the Lake Winnipeg Research Consortium; Gary Forma from Ontario Parks; Doug Harvey of Parks Canada; Lori Nelson at the Lake of the Woods Museum; and Anna McCrory of the Bras d'Or Lakes Preservation Foundation, and a special thanks to the friends and family of Don and Pat Clysdale who gathered for a lakeside brunch on Callander Bay, Lake Nipissing.

I wish to thank Rob Sanders and his team at Greystone Books for their partnership in this adventure. In particular, thanks to: Susan Folkins of Toronto for helping me wrestle a book out of a manuscript that was, once upon a time, half again as long; and to Michael Mundhenk of Vancouver for bringing grammatical law and order to these pages. Thank you to Laurie Anderson and Marc Pelletier, who provided invaluable input on the Lac-Saint-Jean chapter.

Without the advice and support of family and friends, I could not have finished this task. Thanks to Mark Nicholson, Karin and Gabe Tate-Penna, and Dean Hoscheit for travel companionship, ongoing research perspective, and sympathetic ears. Thanks to my neighbours at Emma Lake, especially Ivy Robertson and Judee Ens. Thanks to Max Yuzak and Lee Forand for encouragement and an always-warm welcome on the west coast.

Most of all thank you, sunny Marlene, for muffins and raw pumpkin seeds, for recruiting Kali and St. Paul to the cause, for bottomless patience, for your unfailingly generous wisdom.

ONLY IN CANADA

The Proximate Wilderness

A LONG TIME ago, I was lying on a black-sand beach on the
Greek island of Santorini with my beautiful fiancée. Every-
thing was perfect. It was June. The Mediterranean was so clear it
seemed you were flying when you opened your eyes underwater.
We had brown skins from easy days under the sun, Marlene and
I, and the beach was populated by carefree backpackers like us.
In those days travel was still cheap in the Greek isles, and we had
enough money to eat well most of the summer.

Inexplicably, though, I wanted to go home. Back to Canada. I
could not stop thinking about the lakes of northern Saskatchewan
and how the aspen leaves would have reached their fullness by
now. I pictured chokecherries and deep green moss and orange
lichen. With pleasure I imagined flipping over my canoe and
dragging it into the water. I was homesick.

My future wife was amused. "You want to leave *here*," she said,
gesturing at the cosmopolitan scene around us with a swirl of her
hand, "to go sit by that cold puddle?"

The cold puddle was called Emma Lake, a small lake on the fringe of the northern bush where my family had a cabin. I had never failed to spend some part of the summer there. Marlene was more indulgent of my quixotic whims back then, and a week later we were home. Still punchy with jet lag, I stood on our deck at Emma, swatting mosquitoes and watching my father burn hamburgers on the barbecue. The water shimmered coquettishly up at us through the birch trees, and I had a great sense of belonging.

Like a lot of Canadians, I have been drawn irresistibly to lakes my whole life. Access to pure lakes is fundamental to my quality of life in my home and native land. I love them all. Vast, wild, labyrinthine ones with granite islets carved into whorls like glacial fingerprints. Lakes in dizzying profusion seen through the windows of a floatplane. Turquoise pools held tight in the arms of the Rocky Mountains. Reedy, shallow reaches where jackfish prey.

I love everything about lakes. The quickstep music of whitecaps splashing ashore, the scents that carry off a northern bay like waves of memory—of fresh-caught fish and spruce and smoke of distant forest fire. The vivid blue paint of damselflies hovering over the water, or the wavering green of minnows moving into the shade under a boat dock like suspended jade pieces. Or the walkie-talkie magic by which water transmits the voices of swimmers far down the shore on a still morning.

Somehow, I even like what is disagreeable about lakes: being caught under a thunderhead in a small sailboat, the existential plague of black flies and mosquitoes, and the melancholy light of late August at high latitudes that hints too early of winter.

Affection is one thing. The hard work of writing a book is another, and I might have been happy to leave the story of the greatest lake country in the world to other writers. Only none had bothered to tell it. Or scant few. I discovered this one day a couple of years ago. I was about to leave on a trip to Lake Athabasca,

Canada's eighth-largest lake—one you can learn more about in a later chapter. Wanting to read up on the lake in advance, I went down to the Saskatoon Public Library to find a book. On the way, it struck me that I could not recall ever reading a book about any lake. There was probably a whole branch of classic literature on Canadian lakes just waiting to be explored, and I relished coming home with an armload of good reading. But what ought to have been a fertile region of the Dewey Decimal empire turned out to be a barren shelf.

Finding not a single volume on Canadian lakes in the public library, I searched the local university catalogue, then the National Library—efforts that revealed the literary gap to be system-wide. There were a tiny handful of books on individual lakes, mainly local history, and some nineteenth-century monographs long out of print. There were many scientific works under the heading of "Limnology"—the study of lake ecosystems—but none were accessible to the general reader. That was about it.

In stark contrast to this near-total information vacuum, there were thousands of published resources on the Great Lakes. They are certainly an impressive spread of fresh water, a fount about the size of the United Kingdom in area, and good books about them are published regularly.

I knew, though, that Canada's lake-greatness stemmed not from the sheer size of five titans, but from the great sprawl and density of its three million other lakes. Having lived in three provinces and travelled in the rest, I knew firsthand that lakes are relatively common in almost every part of the country. They are dizzyingly numerous across vast inland areas, as anyone who has ever flown in the North can attest. I knew from Mrs. Lorna Zat-lyn's grade eight history that Canada's entire fur trade past could not have unfolded as it did without the presence of countless lakes, one spilling into the next, that allowed Europeans to hopscotch deep inland to the remotest corner. Without lakes, Canada might have remained a closed world much like Siberia still is today.

Most importantly, I knew that ready access to lakes for pleasure is one of the great perks of citizenship in this country. Relatively pristine lakes remain within easy distance of every urban centre, and recreational use of lakes—for cottaging, camping, boating, swimming—is *the* national pastime. I knew that bounteous fresh water makes us the envy of our southern neighbours. American tourists spill over their northern border each summer, not in search of back bacon or 5 percent beer, but for access to clean, pure, quiet lakes where the fish are biting.

Taken for granted though they may be, happy associations with lakes are part of the Canadian collective unconscious. The proof is there in beer commercials. Advertising copywriters, our modern priests of unspoken desires, sell not only beer but coffee and doughnuts, weed whackers, capri pants, bug dope, and patio furniture against a lakeland backdrop. That the whole nation is stuffing picnic coolers into the trunk for a weekend at the lake is an assumed cultural norm.

The initial disappointment in finding so little writing that celebrated what I considered to be Canada's defining landscape feature soon turned to a sense of intriguing possibility, like a fresh trail leading north into virgin territory. In so many ways Canada is still an undiscovered country. Though we have mapped every inch of it from space, we have hardly begun to gather the truth of this land we have caught in a great lasso of borders and called a nation. It is a delightful thing to be reminded that your own country is still young and innocent, the work of imagining it still not fully done.

Upon this realization, the seed of a long-dormant quest sprouted—one I had been waiting a lifetime to make. I went out upon a series of interconnected journeys through lake country, to figure out the role of lakes in our lives and in the great cycles of nature. I wanted to see how we use lakes, what we demand of them, and what they may require of us in return. I came to call this watery country of mine Lakeland because something so vast, so unique and magnificent in the world—and as yet so unsung—deserved a name. I wanted to see lakes in as many parts of the country as time, money, good luck, and the patience of my family would allow, to see them in all the seasons and from many perspectives, to ride in as many kinds of boats, with as many kinds of people, as possible. Mostly I tried to approach Lakeland as if it were a country unto itself. Where I went and what I saw is the subject of these pages.

Most of these lakes are accessible destinations not too far from the populated pavements of southern Canada, the lakes people use. The northernmost point I reached was about 59 degrees north latitude, which is to say just shy of the territories. Beyond the provinces lies a deeper wilderness of roadless, uninhabited lakes, the true North. But that is another world, another story.

All of the chapters embrace a wider geography than merely the water circumscribed by the shores of the destination lake. Just as a gull or a robin is the product of the migration route along which it feeds, a river is the sum of many streams, a lake is the offspring of its watershed. It would be an academic exercise, for example, to look at Lake Okanagan without considering the beguiling, beleaguered valley that contains it. Lake Winnipeg cannot be understood without the context of its vast watershed, which runs from the Rockies to within a whisker of Lake Superior. Ajawaan Lake, though not much more than a pond, lies at the end of an international pilgrimage.

These journeys can be read as simple travelogue, but real work gets done too. For the sake of economy a particular theme, or related set of themes, is explored at each lake destination—for example, fishing, algae, international tourism, waterfront fashion—but most of the themes are relevant to all the lakes. The approach is as much about finding commonalities across Lakeland as it is about celebrating variety. And so with the people you meet herein. I hope readers will see their own lake experience reflected in other lives, other lakes. Many Canadians feel a profound personal connection to one lake or another. But I think we have hardly begun to articulate our lakes' importance as a whole.

That work begins with seeing the land as it truly is, with the immediate physical realm, with the here and now. As the American iconoclast Edward Abbey observed, there is an elegant truth in the physical surface of things, especially when those surfaces have been shaped to intricacy by nature. That seemingly rudimentary step—awareness of what is right before our eyes—often gets overlooked in our rush to "higher" knowledge, in our attempt to tidy the world into clever patterns, orderly schemata. I hope that along the way of these travels, the reader will gain a satisfying number of higher insights—into lake history and natural history, lake ecology, lake politics, even lake psychology. But the first task of the journey is gaining an awareness of the land itself and the ways we use it. As we struggle toward a balanced and sustainable role within the biosphere, all our theories are wobbly if we fail to see the very earth under our feet.

ARE THERE really three million lakes in Canada? This plausible figure is borrowed from some lake scientists at the University of Guelph. But the number depends on your definition of *lake*. Some definitions specify an arbitrary square area. Some add a water depth requirement. If you include every little kettle hole, bog swamp, and seasonal prairie slough, then the number grows to fanciful orders of magnitude. Yet regardless of how you define them, the remarkable fact remains that about 60 percent of the world's lakes are found in just one country: Canada.

We may have a vague idea that lakes were formed by glaciers, but that tells us little in a land where *everything* has been shaped by ice sheets. These have spread over the territory currently known as Canada dozens of times in the last two and a half million years. At first they followed a forty-thousand-year cycle, later slowing to hundred-thousand-year periods between glacial maximums. In between, there have been warmer, relatively ice-free eras like the one we are currently witnessing. Until the theory of human-driven global warming came along quite recently, it was commonly understood that the next glacial winter was imminent. How much human-driven climate change will alter the pattern—or halt it altogether—is now the overarching question of earth science.

Canada's lake-rich landscape is born and reborn of ice. Each time the ice advances, it erases the lakes and watercourses of the land like a child's hand sweeping away a sand picture. When it retreats, a lot of water remains pooled, willy-nilly, on the surface, what geologists call a deranged drainage, a wet, youthful world where the water has yet to be coaxed down to sea by erosion and time. It gathers in gouges—called ice scours—cut by the relentless ice into the exposed bedrock parts of the country, creating the familiar Canadian Shield lakescape that surrounds Hudson Bay in a great ring. In areas of land covered by loose till, sand, and gravel, great pieces of stranded glacial ice left surface depressions when they melted. These are kettle lakes. Ice scours and kettles—these two types account for the vast majority of Canadian lakes.

The sprawling Lakeland of northern North America is surely one of the great life zones on earth, defining this part of the world as the rain forest defines South America and the savanna does Africa. Certainly lakes are quintessentially Canadian in a way that the country's other signature tableaux are not. The Rockies are stunning but, let's face it, hardly unique. Similarly, Canada's slice of the Arctic, including both its indigenous culture and its iconic sea mammal species, is cut from a most international pie. The great boreal forest rings the entire Northern Hemisphere like a green cape pinned at the Bering Strait. My own beloved prairie is but an antechamber of the great grasslands that run almost to the Gulf of Mexico and echo around the world.

No, there is nothing so uniquely Canadian as a lake.

The 40 percent of lakes not crammed into Canada are spread thinly over the rest of the world. They are virtually absent over much of Australia, Oceania, South America, Asia, Africa, and Antarctica. There are, of course, exceptions. Africa has lakes Victoria and Tanzania, the magnificently large rift lakes, so called because they lie over fault lines. There are mountain lakes in the various ranges.

As for northern landscapes with a glacial geology comparable to that of Canada, Finland achieves a similar lake density, but on a much smaller scale. Apparently the efficient Finns have made a careful count and find they have precisely 187,888 lakes, if you define *lake* as any standing water over five hundred square metres in size. As you might expect of the world's largest country, Russia has plenty of lakes as well. Lake Baikal in southern Siberia, another rift lake, is so deep it contains a fifth of the world's fresh water. But Russian lakes do not approach the number and density found in Canada.

Lakes are not only rarities, but oddities on a global scale, associated with fluke geologies, imbued with magic. There are volcano-crater lakes, coastal impoundments and everglades, *cenotes*, oxbows, meteor-impact lakes. In Antarctica, buried under thousands of metres of ice, scientists appear to have found some large lakes, possibly kept in a liquid state by geothermal heat.

Let us pay respect, briefly, to that elephant in the living room . . . Of the Great Lakes a great deal has been said. Those inland seas are a world and a culture unto themselves, storied and sung in works from *Paddle-to-the-Sea* to "The Wreck of the Edmund Fitzgerald." They are qualitatively unlike any other lakes in North America. They cradle massive populations, great smoking cities, heavy industry. They have their own economy, their own weather, their own wars, their own diplomacy. They are shared by two countries. On the American side, they are sometimes referred to as the Third Coast, an apt nickname for what is effectively a maritime region. The Great Lakes are really an extension of the St. Lawrence Seaway, bringing worldly goods off the salt water and deep into the continent. Through that open door an ocean of troubles has entered. Zebra mussel and sea lamprey are among dozens of invasive foreign species that have permanently altered the lakes' ecosystems. From within, pollution is the most indelible human imprint on the Great Lakes, and issues from both sides of the border.

None of that is in this book—because it is in so many others. In these pages, I refer to the Great Lakes only as a point of comparison.

Scientists refer to the Big Five as the Laurentian Great Lakes, a good hint that there are others. Indeed, the Laurentian ones are really just the southern terminus of an extended great-lake chain that cuts diagonally across the map in a line longer than the distance from Halifax to Vancouver. Lake of the Woods, with a convoluted shoreline said to be longer than Superior's. Lake Winnipeg, nearly the size of Lake Ontario, far larger than Erie. Reindeer and Athabasca Lakes, sprawling, nearly uninhabited. Great Slave, the deepest lake in the country at 614 metres, enough to swallow the CN Tower with room to spare. The largest lake wholly within Canada is Great Bear.

Back to Lakeland . . . Canadians have so many fine lakes we do not compute them a particular value. We once felt the same way about the bison, the Carolinian forest, the tallgrass prairie. It is difficult to prize a surplus. Elsewhere in the world, much more fuss is made over far fewer lakes. It took an American to observe that "the lake is nature's most beautiful landscape feature." The words belong to Henry David Thoreau, writing in *Walden*, published in 1854, one of the few sustained meditations we have in North American literature on the subject of lakes. For the record, New Englanders use the word *pond* in the same way as do Newfoundlanders, so Walden Pond is, in fact, a lake. But not much of one.

The English Lake District has been a tourist draw in northern England for nearly two centuries now and is protected as a national park. It is celebrated in the work of William Wordsworth and Samuel Taylor Coleridge, Beatrix Potter and Arthur Ransome, to name a few. Yet the wee ponds that compose the Lake District would disappear into Lakeland like a twist of lemon in a cup of Earl Grey.

In contrast, lakes seldom appear in Canadian literature. When they do, they never play themselves, but serve as a metaphor for unconscious stirrings, mostly of the dark and murderous kind. Literary lakes are psychological stages for felony, death, and madness.

In her mordant guide to Canadian literature entitled *Survival*, Margaret Atwood has a lot to say about nature, lakes included, and the reason it attaches to dark themes. Whereas to Wordsworth and the English Romantics nature was a warm, kindly female divinity, out on the lonely Canadian frontier she shows her fangs. In fact, *she* becomes an *it*, genderless and shadowy, indifferent to the human cause. Nature will, given a chance, kill you. It's nothing personal, mind you, just business, the enterprise of recycling nutrients—eat and be eaten. The whole thrust of Canadian literature, says its poet laureate, is about survival in the face of this omnipresent threat of nature as predator.

The two favourite *natural* methods Canadian novelists and poets use to dispatch their characters, Atwood says, are drowning and freezing. And so Canadian lakes are literary murder weapons for all seasons. We have the old Chippewa woman in Duncan Campbell Scott's "The Forsaken," left to die out there on the ice, because she has become useless like a broken paddle. We have the protagonist of Earle Birney's poem "Bushed" going insane in a cabin by a haunted mountain lake. These poems are standard reading for Canadian high school kids.

The nature-as-indifferent-monster theme is potently distilled in Atwood's own brilliant short novel *Surfacing*. It is the story of a young woman's search for her father (or his corpse, or his ghost) on a lake in northern Quebec. The characters are effectively imprisoned by the water until the climax, and the lake swims with portentous meaning. At one point, the heroine even dives beneath its inscrutable surface to find submerged Aboriginal pictographs, hoping to find clues in the lost art of a vanquished people. Like its lake setting, *Surfacing* is deep, cold, and archetypal, a forbidding territory of the unconscious.

While I choose to run with Wordsworth and the Romantics and ascribe friendly motives to Mother Nature, I grudgingly admit that she can be a little scary. And yet we possess a deep desire to touch the wild, to be at home in it at some level. This fear-love push-pull has plagued humanity since the Fall. We thirst as deeply to be intimate with nature as we do with other people. Both these objects of our desire are likewise prickly, intimidatingly complex, and sometimes even deadly dangerous. And so we search for safe points of entry, where we may reach past the brambles and find the fruit.

In Canada, this brings us to lakes. Upon their shores we find nature at her most accessible and inviting. This is the great gift of Lakeland: the ready interface it provides with wilderness. Ice fields, mountain faces, swift north-going rivers, the open tundra, uninhabited coastline, the great tracts of forest—Canada has all these aplenty, but they are not easy places to visit. The lakeshore, by contrast, is an open door. Linger on the threshold, with your pail and shovel. Or go deeper. Walk the shore until the sounds of the parking lot no longer follow. Paddle around the bend until the world is out of sight.

Lakes are our proximate wilderness, that piece of untamed biosphere from which average people can take a bite. That we do continue to obey an innate call to feed there is another great paradox of wilderness access—hope and threat combined. We consume wilderness even as we seek to take part in it, for consume is what we do. No matter where we go, we bring the ecological threat of our own presence along with us. This would seem an insurmountable problem. Increasingly, the message from the environmentalists is that this earth would be an absolute paradise if only we ourselves weren't in it. *You human beings are the cancer of the planet,* says a computer program named Agent Smith in the cyberpunk action film *The Matrix.*

Even if we are the rogue cells in the superorganism called Gaia, are we not still a *rightful* part? Cancer may play a positive role in evolutionary terms, devastating though it is to individuals. Cancer or no, I go to Lakeland as much as I can. I wish we had a different transportation paradigm so I did not have to burn a tank of gas to get there, but I *have* to go nonetheless. There seems little hope of accomplishing our great task as a species—of achieving a harmonious place within nature—if we do not possess an intimacy with it. The paradox again: to fall in love with nature, you must trample it a little. Walk a half-hour down a trail at first light, and you destroy the night's work of a hundred spiders. A child wading in the shallows with a dipping net will catch a sense of wonder, along with some minnows. If a few of the minnows do not survive their imprisonment in a bucket on the end of the dock, has it been a fair trade? For good or ill, it is up to us to decide. "You humans shall have dominion over all the fish and birds and animals," says God on page one of the book of Genesis.

As will become apparent, I have concerns beyond spiderwebs and minnows. Runaway development, driven by the great economic boom that accompanied the end of the last millennium, has threatened many areas of the proximate wilderness, including my own cherished corner at Emma Lake. At stake is not the wholesale destruction of Lakeland but the easy and close relationship with the natural world in the lucky land called Canada. It is increasingly difficult to get into the lake country—that is, increasingly expensive. In my lifetime, the proximate wilderness has been aggressively bought up, and urban standards of affluence have been imported like rolls of lawn turf. Humble cabins with families of eight sleeping in bunk beds have been replaced by sprawling retirement homes with two occupants and three bathrooms.

The new tourism has grown in step, and its infrastructure is a heavy industry. Probably it wreaks more permanent disruption of sensitive and accessible wild places than logging or mining. Roadside motels with small, efficient, and affordable rooms have been scraped away to build landscaped resorts. Nine holes have become twenty-seven. The vanishing practice of car camping in the public grounds with a tent, the lowest-cost, lowest-impact means we have of visiting lakes, is doubly stigmatized—both by the culture of affluence and by those who presume to say that the "real" wilderness cannot be found in a cul de sac of tents. No wonder visitation numbers are dropping in national and provincial parks.

The transition from seasonal use to permanent colonization is another force of change in the proximate wilderness. This is where people of sufficient means, liberty, and free time set up house in beautiful places of which they know little except the view. They build palaces in villages, and their weighty urban capital transforms rural communities forever.

We are moving toward a place that, in the short history of a young hinterland country, was unimaginable only a generation ago. In this place, the proximate wilderness is a gated enclave, an upper tier, where standards of affluence and expectations for consumption are sky high. It is nature at a price. I hope that we have not already "won" Margaret Atwood's survival game, not yet completely beaten wilderness back with our capital and fenced it in with wrought iron. I hope that the next literary chapter we write as a country will not be called "Paradise Lost." We risk raising the first generation of Canadian children to grow up without any particular attachment to wilderness because their families cannot afford membership.

As I write these words, the country is reportedly on the brink of hard times after a long run of good fortune. Such things come and go—booms bust; bulls hibernate. When the markets receive their inevitable corrections, however, there are no corresponding rationalizations on the lakeshore. Oversized houses do not get smaller. Ill-conceived subdivisions do not revert to woodlots. Only their market prices backslide for a time, waiting to catch the next wave. Development is a one-way track.

Still—and this is where things get interesting—some of the wealthy and influential people colonizing Lakeland become its most capable defenders. They are lawyers, publishers, city planners, deputy ministers. The irony is, they mainly come around to this wilderness advocacy after they have bought a fine house from which to view the wild. But they do come around. I say *they*, but I really mean *we*. I come to Lakeland by the same route. The question is, from what peril shall we defend the proximate wilderness? Is it merely about keeping newcomers out after we ourselves are in?

The task is really the opposite: to steward and retain the

near-wilderness and keep it accessible and pertinent to a whole people. We need to discover sustainable use on a far wider front than the scattered patchwork of national parks can provide. Anyway, park officials have largely given up trying to protect our near-wilderness because they cannot afford the real estate prices either. We must dig deep into the roots of our own acquisitiveness. This means *not* building, *not* buying. It means visiting versus colonizing. It means rethinking exclusivity. We need to protect not just diversity of wild species but diversity of viewpoints, diversity of people in the proximate wilderness.

Our greatest *need* . . . is to *want* less. Living more simply used to be the whole point of lakeside culture. Let us reacquire the skills there on the still generous margins of the Canadian bush. Let us gather this knowledge where and when we may. Let us succeed, with new ideas, at rethinking our place as a species on this forgiving scale. For there are dark clouds gathering on the wider horizon of the world. If we stand still and allow them to overtake us, the problems in Lakeland will be remembered as summer storms in comparison.

THE HOME PLACE

EMMA LAKE, *Saskatchewan*

Summer cottages beginning to sprout here . . . it must be the paved road.
MARGARET ATWOOD, *Surfacing*

MAY THE first. Early in the year to be crawling out of a bed at Emma Lake. And cold.

I woke to what sounded like someone pounding a metal stake into the ground somewhere across the lake. Such insistent clamouring of progress carries far on dense morning air and enters through the drafty windows of an old cabin. But it was only the ticking of the stovepipe, thank God, and the fire going out. Whatever time it was, it was time to get up. I pulled on my clothes and stepped outside into the deep bright silent morning. Except for one pair of crows there to help me kick off the season, I had the lake to myself.

The other birds had not yet arrived. The previous night on the drive north I had seen migrating canvasbacks, biding their time in the ditches and ice-free sloughs, looking like white shoes tossed on the water. I saw the northern flicker on the edge of the prairie too, pacing the grass in his black-and-tan waistcoat like an Englishman waiting for a tardy train, and flashing his absurd painted tail. In the city I had left behind thousands of robins, held up by a spring snowstorm like holiday travellers stuck in an airport.

Somehow they all knew that the ice still kept its firm, white grip on Emma Lake.

Perhaps not completely firm. Taking an axe and bucket, I went down to the water's edge and saw that the season was shifting. Trapped sunlight in the shallows had melted the ice down to a thin, clear watch glass. Under it were dozens of beetles sunning themselves like microscopic sea mammals upon the stones of the bottom. They scattered sluggishly in the cold water when my axe broke through their sunroof. A large water boatman rowed up from the bottom to see what in hell was going on.

So, this was how the lake ice was vanquished, hunted from the pack margins by a hungry wolf sun. In truth I have never had the luxury of time to watch the lake ice go out, from start to finish. Or the complete arrival of spring in the lake country. Or many such stately marvels of nature. Even when you are lucky enough to own a cabin, you mostly catch these things in installments, on weekends. It can take years to piece together the full story.

Anyway, this year I was going to watch the whole play of spring unfold from start to finish. Every scene.

Using a few concrete blocks, I built a little pier to deeper water to fill my bucket. Until the ice went out and the intake line could go in, I would haul lake water to wash dishes. Drinking and cooking water I would buy down at Ambrose grocery. Otherwise, there was an outhouse—a rare breed on this high-priced road nowadays. I set the full bucket on the sand behind me and placed both hands into the lake, trying to hold them there. The icy burning was so intense I yanked back in a few seconds, laughing. You would not laugh long if you went in for the full baptism this time of year.

Looking north toward the point, I spotted the inevitable blight. Another Super-Size-Me cabin was going up. A Vinyl Villa. A Taj McMall. A Plastic Fantastic. I invent many names for such places. But as architecture they say just one thing: *look at me.* So I looked. The blond particleboard expanse of the new behemoth could swallow three of the old cabins. The newspapers all said the economy was on the brink of collapse, but fools with more money than sense were still plentiful.

One of the first super-sized places appeared just up the beach from us a few years ago, built by a wealthy retired couple. They tore down the sixties-era bungalow that had served a family of five for many happy years and cut down every tree on the lot. Then they put up a house so large, so out of proportion to the other cabins on the beach, that boaters out on the lake steered a course for it all summer, mistaking it for a commercial building, a new place to buy ice cream or gasoline. This was supposed to be the couple's retirement dream home, but they lost interest after a few seasons and sold it. The little cabin next door was left permanently in the shadow of its hulking neighbour. Such is the march of progress.

A succession of ever larger mansions soon began eclipsing one another around the lake. The Super-Size-Me cabins are easy to spot, not only because they are comically large, but because they do not leave any room for trees. I suppose the Super-Size-Me owners enjoy a treed view as much as the next person—they just do not feel obliged to contribute any trees to the commons themselves. What they do with their own damn property is nobody else's business, after all.

Carrying my water back up to the cabin, I noted flecks of orange lichen on the bronze skin of the alder. I passed the saskatoon bush that would kindly proffer, come July, a few cool clutches of berries. I saw how the club moss had thickened alongside the stepping stones. To rediscover this small corner of the world anew each season was to experience the great, slow beat of a still wild heart. I left the bucket outside the door and went to sit on the deck in the morning sun.

The Rural Municipality of Lakeland, as land around Emma is called, is covered by mostly aspen and birch, a transitional zone between prairie and boreal forest called parkland. Once the leaves unfurl, you are cloistered for the summer behind plush green curtains. But early in the year when the branches are stark, you can see through the neighbouring yards and down the Carwin Park road, or far uphill through the bush. It is like looking at an x-ray of a loved one.

In fact, I had come to our cabin in the clear light of early spring to make a kind of diagnosis. I wanted to understand my connection to this small, overbusy lake. What was its magnetism that had drawn me to it for a lifetime? Despite traipsing all over the wide world, I have somehow managed to spend at least part of every summer here. Even most winters, I have made a pilgrimage or two.

Otherwise Emma Lake follows me. It is a recurring setting of my nocturnal dreams, its vivid waters stirring with totemic life forms and Jungian symbolism. Even by day I can close my eyes and imagine every curve of the road leading to it from the city, each stand of tamarack or spruce, every creek and marsh, the ditches full of alfalfa and goatsbeard and tiger lily. I can reproduce, just by thinking about it, the feeling of sweet calm that has never failed to meet me when I arrive. I shut off the engine, step into the lake-cooled air, glimpse the water through the trees, and feel my blood pressure ease.

Such experiences are common in this sprawling country of mine, where clear, pure lakes are so plentiful we do not even bother to name them all. Canadian lakes cast a spell. A certain lake will lay a hold upon you, begin to flow in your veins. If this happens in childhood, as it did for me, you are imprinted for life, like a Canada goose that knows how to find its way back to its nesting ground from Texas or the Baja. This is no exaggeration, no idle anthropomorphizing. One fellow I know who moved to Hawaii years ago still keeps a cabin on the Carwin Park road. A woman I knew in high school migrates with her kids from Chicago each summer. We return from afar.

You do not need to own a cottage to be caught in the spell. Campers haul their trailers, and tenters pitch their canvas, on the same lakes year after year, often on the same campsite. You do not even need to be a Canadian. A whole industry of angling tourism caters to Americans who want to fish the same Canadian lake every summer holiday.

But it is cottagers who demand the most from the lake country. Our imprint is more permanent. When I first knew Emma Lake and the Rural Municipality of Lakeland, there were about fifteen hundred small cabins. Even then it was commonly understood that there was room for no more. Yet despite calls for development moratoriums going back through many municipal governments, the number has since doubled, and will eventually double again. There is now talk of condominiums.

Emma Lake has become just the kind of place I would normally avoid. Too many buildings, too many roads. Outdoorsy acquaintances sometimes wrinkle their noses when I admit my family has a cabin on Emma, which has become an unhappy symbol of overdevelopment. In recent years I have found it disheartening to look upon, so I escape nearly every day on my bicycle down the peaceful backcountry trails of nearby Prince Albert National Park.

Unlike the newcomers, I have been here long enough to remember when bears, lynx, herons, river otter, and deer came right down to the Carwin Park beach, remember the sanctity of the bush before the invasion of all-terrain vehicles, remember when huge families squeezed every ounce of pleasure from tiny cabins. Yes, it is tempting to blame these interlopers for ruining paradise. I admit that when I go past their outré mansions, I do sometimes curse them.

As much change as has come to Emma Lake, it was still quiet as all eternity in the early season. The great houses had not stifled the enigmatic beauty. I felt the heat of the sun where it struck my shoulders. In the bare branches there was some movement. A pair of juncos appeared in their little hooded travelling capes, leap-frogging through the canopy. One perched on top of the shed door I had left open. She kept darting into the darkened building. *Do not think to build your nest in there, sister, for I must lock the door to protect my lawn chairs.* Both the juncos and I belonged to this place. Whether it belonged to us in turn was not a question that worried the juncos. Real estate was a human problem.

Like the juncos, I keep returning here, keep using this lake, consuming its pleasures, right alongside everyone else. And how can I begrudge my neighbours what comes to me by divine good fortune? The newcomers' appetites for comfort might eclipse mine—but then mine eclipses that of the juncos much more. Our basic capitalism and our hunger to belong in nature are philo-sophically the same. If I am honest with myself, I remember that *my* family pioneered the Carwin Park road along this shore of Emma Lake. *We* were the interlopers once. We opened the door. If anyone is responsible for what has happened here, we are. *I am.*

MY PARENTS built this place in 1960, for $2,500, land included. Faux log siding painted cherry-red, red shingles, white trim. It resembles the chief's house at a rural fire station. The little cot-tage still belongs to my mother, but she is too old to manage it alone, and my father is passed on. Eventually it will come to my wife and me. And from us to our children. No, it is not for sale.

Such waterfront properties today are only available to the well-off, and even they have to fight for them tooth and nail. I am fortunate to have such a coveted place. In fact, you might say I am a Genuine Lucky Bastard.

I was born to an unwed teenager somewhere in far southern Saskatchewan, a dry, lakeless country where cactus grew on the south-facing slopes. My young mother was destitute and had no choice but to sign me away to the judge. As a ward of the state, I spent the next two years in a series of French-Catholic foster homes, eventually fetching up in a town whose one claim to fame was a giant who lived there—though even the giant ran off with the circus as soon as he could. My only words were in French, then a second-class language. I was to have been deposited in an orphanage as soon as I was out of diapers. I bided my time and my bladder control and waited for luck to arrive.

One day it did, in a long green car. A handsome couple got out. He was very tall and dark and wore a long cashmere coat and a wide-brimmed hat. She too was tall, a Nordic blond. The pair embodied the very style of the Kennedy era, which otherwise might never have arrived in that dusty town. Somehow, I was scooped up from among a whole houseful of unwanted progeny and shouldered out the door, rescued from a Dickensian fate at the age of two.

We went north out of that dry country. My mother, as the yellow-haired lady became by order of the provincial court the moment we crossed over the threshold, recalls that I cried most of the way. This was a formality on my part, for I had nothing to lose but two government-issue stuffed toy animals.

Olive and Bob Casey, my new parents, lived in the small city of Prince Albert, "Gateway to the North," on the North Saskatchewan River where the prairie ends and the boreal forest begins. They were by then already in their forties, radically late by then-current standards to take on parenthood. They had recently bought a real estate and insurance business and worked like dogs to make a go of it. They also worked for charities and service clubs, sat on hospital boards and school committees. They square danced, played bridge, and went to costume parties. They were the two most social people I have ever known, and thought nothing of inviting thirty people to dinner. Their home was rarely without visitors and was the centre of gravity for both sides of the family.

Very best of all, they—we—had a small cabin on a lake.

Although I've pieced together the preceding bits from others' reminiscences and mom's Kodachrome slides, my own solid memories begin at the cabin. We first went to Emma Lake as a family in the spring of 1964, and it was like finding the thread of my own existence after a wandering start.

The cabin was a plain rectangle with a gable roof. Inside, it had a woodstove for cooking and heating, a wood floor, no telephone. Everything was half-finished. The bedroom "walls" were bare studs with old bedspreads pinned to them for privacy. In anticipation of a veranda not yet built, there was a front door that opened over a precipitous drop to the rocks below. Afraid of me falling from that doorway, my mom was fastidious about keeping its high latch fastened, and wedged an old knife under the door trim for good measure. But she would open it to toss out old dishwater with a great war whoop, then let me lean out for a look while she kept a protective armlock around my belly. The woodstove was a marvellous fire beast my father tamed. I fell asleep to moths circling bare bulbs. In the morning, sunlight reflecting up from the lake danced under the roof boards, and the sound of lapping waves permeated the place.

Outside, three pathways led from the door. A set of crooked steps went up to the road. Another went to the outhouse, a two-hole privy over a pit in the rocky soil, the ghastly contents of which were perennially fascinating. The third went down to the water.

The lake. Its face is as evocative and difficult to describe as those of my children. You felt its coolness, smelled its fresh-fish scent, gauged its breeze by the shivering of the aspen leaves overhead. Each whitecap played a tune, from the throaty splash of landing to the hiss of the water percolating back through the sand. When calm, the lake became a mirror of the moment—of sun and cloud, of speedboats, of teals jetting over its surface, of your own freckled face hanging over the dock. When the morning breeze arrived, a dazzling pathway of reflected light ran across the water to meet the rising sun.

Emma and the lakes around it had been named, like so many places in western Canada, by an employee of the Dominion Land Survey. Christopher Gravel called one lake after himself, one for his brother Oscar, and a third for his sister Emma, who today lies in Notre Dame Cemetery in Ottawa. Modest resort beaches arose, serving budget holidayers from town with rooms, beer parlours, marinas, and dance halls. By my time, the halls had been taken over by hippies. On a Saturday night you might hear "Bad Moon Rising" booming over the water from MacIntosh Point, "Magic Carpet Ride" coming from Sunnyside. Emma Lake is actually three interconnected lakes that wind away to the north. But we felt we had the best spot. Through our windows, the scene was always intimately familiar yet somehow never quite the same twice. One does not tire of a water view.

That simple truth was already beginning to put great pressure on the tiny lake by the time I got there. All the lakefront lots on Carwin Park were built upon, and there were already the beginnings of a second row on the back side of the road, about ninety cabins in all in our subdivision. And there were many subdivisions. People gave cute names to their places—"Skunk Hollow," "Life begins at 40," "La Dolce Vita"—and we knew nearly every owner by first name. We were entitled. We belonged.

The problem with newcomers is that they arrive blind to local history, the environmental truth of a place. To us, the road and the cabins had *always* been there. There had always been this store, that gas station. In fact, most of the visible development was quite recent, created by the very demand we brought. To pioneer farm families in the area and to the handful of rugged types who had tiny log cabins on the shore of what was up to then almost a wilderness lake, we must have seemed an invading horde. We were the Super-Sizers then. It would be many years before we entertained any thought that we ourselves might be a threat to this pretty place. For a period of blessed ignorance that coincided with my childhood, it remained an uncomplicated paradise within a thirty-five-minute drive of the city. And we used the hell out of it.

The family business was beginning to sprout profit, enough to let Olive quit working and even buy her a used car. For the first time in her life she had leisure and a bit of pin money. As soon as school let out, she and I decamped to our summer palace like a pair of Indian rajas, far from the heat and the tedium of the city.

Of Icelandic descent, Olive grew up on a farm on the muddy shore of Little Quill Lake in southeastern Saskatchewan and was not afraid to get off the pavement. We'd jump into her old white Comet that always seemed in need of a new muffler, and made it our business to know every cart track within fifty kilometres of Emma Lake. My wife today would not dream of traversing these rutted backwoods roads with only a boy for a copilot. Sometimes we'd come to a mud hole spread across the whole road. "Look at that big *lake*," Olive would say with a whistle, surveying the obstacle, her sandalled foot on the brake. She'd let the tension mount for half a minute, then gun it. The noise from the tailpipe would shatter the stillness, and the mud would fly into the bush. She had Viking blood.

It was rarely just the two of us. The cabin at Emma exerted its magnetism over many, and across a great distance. My friends from town without cabins jockeyed to be invited there. Cousins arrived by the half-dozen all summer long, from both sides of the family, from Toronto and Los Angeles, from England and Morocco. The lake left a lasting imprint on many people. My cousin Dan Casey, who was close to me in age and whose visits were always a highlight for me, would one day name his daughter Emma, after the lake.

The lake seemed to unlock a sense of capricious fun in every city-weary visitor who found the way there. We took them to see the bison in the national park, or up the steep approach to the Anglin Lake fire lookout, where we climbed the thirty-metre tower. We took my grandmother and her sisters—all of them wearing cotton shifts the size of pup tents and insisting on carrying their enormous black purses into the bush—out to pick Saskatoons. One of my cousins painted a mural on our fence entitled *The Emma Lake Monster*, a local landmark for years. We had epic badminton tournaments, and one summer Bob and Olive introduced the game of *pétanque* to Carwin Park after having learned it on a trip to Guadeloupe.

But mostly we swam. Adults and kids alike spent all day in bathing suits, dunking sandy feet in a sun-warmed pail of water before entering the cabin. The only reason to be inside in daytime was to cook and eat. Even when it rained or the wind blew whitecaps we swam. On truly cold days we wore out board games or played hide-the-shell, a deceptively difficult game invented by my parents. It involved hiding a small seashell in plain view among the bric-a-brac of the cabin, and then someone had to find it, aided by shouts of "Hotter!" or "Colder!" if needed. People wrote stories and plays, painted the lake view, fell into books they would never read in the city.

We went to sleep in unison. The cabin was too small to do otherwise. Once the sun went down, we unfolded pullout beds or spread sleeping bags on the floor, and living room became bedroom. The night was a varied adventure of snores and being stepped upon in the dark by people en route to the outhouse. It was unfeasible to sleep in.

My father arrived in a hail of gravel every Friday night. He always drove like the devil, bringing the excitement of the city with him, and the tension. By then he managed a stable of high-strung real estate salespeople. On his doctor's advice, he took up smoking in order to relieve the stress. Still, he loved the buoy-ant times he found himself in. He wore expansive sideburns, wide ties, and loud polyester beachwear. By the weekend, he was ready to enjoy himself at the lake, which he did—like everything else— rather furiously.

He and Olive knew many people, and there was always a party somewhere around the lake. Having no siblings to babysit, I mostly tagged along. Before I was ten I had been to more happy hours, brunches, mixers, wind-ups, fondues, badminton and bridge games, fish fries, and 19th holes than most adults would see in a lifetime. I got used to the ways of middle-aged adults, their politics and prejudices, their bellowing voices, their booz-ing. These potbellied businessmen in loud shirts, these women in paisley dresses and metallic lipstick, were riding a wave of eco-nomic good times they did not wish to question. They had all come through the war, and some had caught the tail end of the Depression. Now they just wanted to enjoy the good life—which in Canada meant having a cabin on a nearby lake.

Emma Lake, at least our recreational version of it, was created not by God but by John Diefenbaker. The thirteenth prime min-ister was elected in our riding of Prince Albert and was a friend of my parents. Dief saw that lakefront lots could be used as political capital in the postwar boom. Indeed he tied his folksy political image to the wholesome backdrop of northern lakes. He loved to be photographed in his siwash sweater standing beside a float-plane, holding up a nice catch of trout.

So it was that in repayment of political debts to the Prince Albert citizens who elected him, Diefenbaker dedicated a small dam on the Spruce River just inside Prince Albert National Park. I stop to read the little plaque whenever I pedal by on my trail bike. The dam provided water to supply the hitherto rather swampy Emma, Anglin, and Christopher Lakes, making them much more attractive to people, if less so to mallards and pintails. Voilà, cottage country!

With Dief's help we had enough water to float a boat. The weekend of my ninth birthday, Dad roared in as usual, but pulling a trailer. On it was a new aluminum skiff, shining silver through the fence. I flew up the six steps. Dad had the trunk open, and in it lay a six-horsepower Evinrude Fisherman and a fuel tank. I saw at a glance that this beautiful little boat was sized just for me. My head swam. Dad always became formal when giving presents, doubly so when conferring responsibility. A transaction on this scale was unprecedented, and he acted as though he were ceding Hong Kong back to the Chinese. *This boat would be mine only as long as I operated it in a manner such that... I should not expect any childish presents later on, just a piece of birthday cake... If I was ever seen aboard without a life jacket, it would be my last voyage...*

"I swear," I whispered. I wanted to hug him, but we shook hands as the legality of the transfer required.

So began one of the happiest chapters of my life, with a command of my own, on waters ripe for exploration. From Sunset Bay to the reedy north end, Emma stretches scarcely ten kilometres. Within these prescribed bounds I skippered my silver boat hundreds of hours a summer. Each spring, a forty-five-gallon drum of fuel would be delivered to our cottage, and believe me when I say it takes a determination to empty one of those into a six-horsepower motor.

Running that boat was like a job. My little air-cell life jacket became faded and grimy from heavy use. I had an oily streak tattooed on my left bicep from the starter cord. I trained dozens of kids how to drive. It was always fun to hand over the tiller to a new apprentice, go sit in the bow seat, and watch the delighted expression that only a small boat can bring to a face.

Each morning before the shore breeze came up, I went on salvage patrol. Overnight calms would always draw an assortment of flotsam into the centre of the lake, whatever junk irresponsible adults let loose. Into the bilges of my little boat went stubby beer bottles, paddles, orphaned water skis, lengths of rope, boat fenders, air mattresses, toy boats, inner tubes, chunks of styrofoam. I took in tow pieces of dock that had parted from shore. Several times I found boats adrift and tugged them back to their owners. Adults were careless fools.

Small two-stroke gasoline engines exert a heavy burden on the biosphere. A few years ago, the U.S. Environmental Protection Agency famously announced that annual spillage from America's lawnmower gas tanks alone eclipsed what the *Exxon Valdez* disaster had loosed into the Gulf of Alaska. Given the sensitive freshwater environments in which they operate, marine outboards like my Fisherman are among the most harmful and have been outlawed in many areas. They direct their exhaust—a mixture of combustion gas, unburned fuel, and oil—straight into water, which serves doubly as filter medium and sound muffler.

But I would not learn all that until later. I remember the pleasure of seeing that fuel rainbow spread on the water behind an outboard on a cold start in the morning—like the harbinger of good times just ahead.

The little Fisherman was just the first in a line of powerboats we owned as I grew up, each with more horsepower than the last. People all over the lake were doing likewise, and the water became treacherously busy on weekends. With some new friends from down the beach, I took up waterskiing. We got pretty good. We'd ski tricks in the morning calm—sideways, backwards, on one ski holding the rope with the other foot—and carve slalom buoys in the evening. It takes a lot of gas to improve a little, and in one day we could have run through the forty-five gallons that used to provide a whole season's motorized amusement. We were prevented from doing so only by Jimmy Carter's energy crisis and the first big spike in fuel prices. It was our first hint that the world was not limitless after all, and, looking back, it arrived in the nick of time.

A NEW decade was beginning, my innocent youth at the lake ending. Being a teenager in the seventies meant watching the Age of Aquarius skid into the Age of Irony. Rock-and-roll and bell-bottoms were just two more things to buy at Sears. Over in London, punk was being invented—though we were too far back in the jack pines to hear about it. Meanwhile, there was Elton John. The seventies were the sixties recut in polyester. Even the lustrous moon, that great prize of the dead Kennedys, had been found quite worthless—except as a viewing platform for earth's fragile, threatened beauty.

The consequences of using that thin blue biosphere as a dumping ground were just beginning to be understood by the populace. The media gathered all threats into one convenient catchall word—pollution—and terrorized us with it to sell their newspapers and broadcasts. Our teachers, parent councils, civic leaders wrung their hands helplessly for a while. Then they set up wastebaskets from coast to coast and admonished us schoolchildren to fill them. The message was clear: the earth was officially a mess, and our generation was going to clean it up. I seemed doomed to pick up after my elders forever.

The future looked bleak on TV. A new Canadian show called *Here Come the 70s* packaged all my worst nightmares into a weekly half-hour. Its opening theme music played over a montage of distressing images: water birds expiring in spilled crude oil, mountains of garbage being bulldozed into the ocean, spewing smokestacks, famine bellies. These were rapidly intercut with shots of a naked young woman wading into dark water until she submerged in a ritual suicide. The sight of her lovely blond hair floating on the surface of the water was devastating.

On the drive in from the lake one Sunday night, I hung over the front seat of the car and confessed my fears to my father—that I had been born just in time for the apocalypse. "Rubbish!" he cried. He was now trying to quit smoking and always irritable. "This is the most exciting time of all." Dad basically reiterated Woody Allen's theory that being born anytime after the invention of penicillin was good. He had survived the Depression, the war, and the Bomb. What was a little smog? Adults, when it suited them, liked to believe that pollution was a far-off, abstract problem, a disease of big cities, like crime.

In fact, we were keeping up with the times at Emma Lake. To combat mosquitoes, my uncle would come with his fogging gun. It resembled an automatic weapon and emitted a white pall of insecticide. One year there was a dramatic boom in the forest tent-caterpillar population. People fought back with Malathion, filched agricultural pesticides, even grandfathered DDT. We demanded that the municipality oil the Carwin Park road to keep the dust down, though the waste oil used for the job would eventually all run downhill to the water. Like most owners, my dad hauled in tons of beach sand, which silted up the lake when the waves got rolling. He rigorously uprooted any shore vegetation, the lake's natural buffer against uphill pollutants. One day a friend of Dad's surveyed our stubborn beach grass and decided to wield the Final Solution. He splashed buckets of gasoline across the sand and, brave fool, lit a match. One of the neighbour kids and I had swum out to watch from the water. The fireball went higher than the cabin, a blast of heat hitting our faces. Dad's friend singed his eyebrows, but the beach grass remained.

Innocence is fleeting, and there came a time when I preferred to remain in town, staying out all night with friends. We were now denizens of the adolescent world of smoke, drink, and jejune chaos. We wrecked cars and played cat and mouse with the cops in the bush north of town. One night before a party, we went to see the new film *Apocalypse Now*. We thought it was brilliant. That wall of cleansing napalm fire on the screen caught our mood. It was time to put aside childish things.

DESPITE MY best intentions to watch the unfolding of spring at the lake down to the last detail, I let myself be drawn back to the city at the crucial moment. Warm days arrived, and I hoped the ice would hang on. It did not. On my return a week later, through the trees along Carwin Park, I saw the lake was born again. Water.

The birds were already there. Noisy gulls bobbing, a loon calling, three mergansers going by like jets at an air show, a pair of buffleheads. Dan from Danny Boy Plumbing had been here, had dragged my water line into the lake, primed the pump. No more bucket and ax this year. Sitting on the shed roof was the junco with her bead eyes upon me. *See all that you have missed?* Yes, I see.

There was a period of a dozen years when I did not get to Emma Lake so much and nearly lost touch with it for good. I travelled all over the world, studied at four different universities, got married to my hometown girlfriend Marlene Yuzak, began a career as a journalist. By then we were living in southwestern Ontario, where I had a comfortable job on a newspaper. My daughter was born, and her brother was about to arrive. We were ticking off the milestones of a middle-class life at a furious clip. Emma Lake was three thousand kilometres away.

Around that time, the media had invented a new catchall word for a suite of old problems. What was called pollution in the 1970s was now subsumed, in the last decade of the millennium, into a broader conflict zone called the environment. As always with these media fashions, coverage of environmental issues combined sensible practical information with manufactured hysteria. One of the most lucid voices emerging from the background noise came from Canada's west coast. It belonged to scientist turned journalist Dr. David Suzuki.

In 1990, Marlene and I read a line of his, tossed out in an interview, that was to alter our future. Suzuki remarked that the major threat to the environment was simply that people moved so much. It was the new economy. Where previous generations held the same job for life, now people moved across the country at the drop of a hat, to earn another five thousand a year, to flee downsizing, to chase booms. And in so doing, they lost track of nature. Parachuting into a new place, we cannot know what the natural space is supposed to be like, or how fast it may be changing, or what burdens we ourselves are placing upon it. True stewardship of wild and semiwild places is borne of long familiarity with their innate patterns and rhythms.

Suzuki was describing Marlene and me precisely. We always felt detached from the Ontario landscape we had adopted. In the way of blessed ignorance, it was comforting. We did not mourn the loss of Carolinian forest because we could not remember it. People said Lake Huron, Lake Erie, and the Thames River were heavily polluted. But they looked all right to us. We had not known them as children.

Meanwhile, the landscape we knew so intimately back in Saskatchewan was already starting to slip from familiar touch. As for the cabin at Emma, once my parents were too old to use it, there would be no point hanging onto it. My place of deepest acquaintance with the natural fabric would fade into memory like an old tune.

So it was that not long after our son was born, we four migrated back across the country, returning to what the great western essayist Stan Rowe called our "home place." As we travelled down the long boreal corridor of Ontario, up the Manitoba escarpment, and onto the Saskatchewan plateau, I watched the natural world through the window sort itself into a familiar beauty.

It was like falling in love. The natural world that had up to then been backdrop for pleasant adventures now seemed to hum with purpose, meaning, and pattern, from the dragonfly's wing to the rhythm of sand dunes. As a homecoming gift, my dad gave me a coffee-table book of Courtney Milne's landscape photos from around the world. Seeing my own home place pictured among those international Edens, I was hungry to learn all I could about the one in my own backyard. I began what Sharon Butala has called an "apprenticeship in nature."

I watched birds. I made a plant press and collected specimens, cast impressions of animal tracks, photographed mushrooms. I acquired a telescope and learned the constellations and the motions of the planets along the ecliptic and the reason the moon danced through her phases as she did. From plans in a book, my son and I built a remote-controlled submarine from a plastic crate and several bilge pumps. It carried a black-and-white video camera and brought back images from the bottom of Emma Lake comically similar to Apollo lunar footage. I took up flying gliders, learning to ride aloft on the invisible currents of the lower atmosphere. I bought the first of many small sailboats, the sole purpose of which—I once read—is to observe the weather.

I canoed a lot. From Bill Mason's books and films I picked up not only paddling tips but a way of relating to nature, of hearing what he called the "song of the paddle." Mason said that in order to hear this music, you had to be physically comfortable. Thus, knowing how to keep warm and dry in the bush was not only a practical skill but a spiritual one.

The canoe makes a fine altar. One gorgeous night around the summer solstice I went paddling alone on Moon Lake, an oxbow just south of Saskatoon. It must have been nearly eleven o'clock, with twilight glow still in the sky and the stars winking on. In a trance, watching the vortices spinning off my blade across the dark water, I had an idea that came to me straight from the collective unconscious—that long ago the creator rode a great canoe over the night sky and that the whirlpools that danced from his almighty paddle became the galaxies. And so the universe was spun into being.

Out of such revelatory moments, I came to see that the natural world was an earthly perfection, heaven made manifest. It was unfair, perhaps, that a profane schmuck like me had found a way to view the face of divinity anytime he liked, but that is what may be called grace. I was delighted to learn that precontact North American Aboriginal cultures made little practical distinction between heaven and earth. Each contains the other. In *Sleeping Island*, his book about paddling through northern Saskatchewan in 1939, American Prentice Downes transcribes a telling conversation between a Dene man and an Oblate priest on the subject of heaven:

> Tell me, Father, is it [your Heaven] like the land of the little trees when the ice has left the lake? Are the great musk oxen there? Are the hills covered with flowers? There will I see the caribou everywhere I look? Are the lakes blue with the sky of

summer? Is every net full of great, fat whitefish? Is there room for me in this land, like our land . . . ? Can I camp anywhere and not find that someone else has camped? Can I feel the wind and be like the wind? Father, if your Heaven is not like all these things, leave me alone in my land, the land of the little sticks.

As much as possible I shared this path of discovery with the family. We covered a lot of happy miles together from our home base at Emma Lake, and the kids got to experience the lake much as I had. Lewis played with my old Lego. Esther harvested clay from the lake bottom to make beautiful, fragile sculptures of snakes and salamanders. We swam and played hide-the-shell, watched the bison, and climbed the fire tower. The lake had seen us full circle, one generation to the next. It was a good thing we followed David Suzuki's advice, for it had taken me that long to really *see* the place for what it was.

ALL THIS newfound awareness of nature had the corollary effect of making our impact on it that much more plain to see. The Rural Municipality of Lakeland bears the scars from decades of haphazard, ill-conceived development. The sheer number of cabins—three thousand and growing—and their grand scale are only the beginning.

With the lakefront lots taken ages ago, many of the newer places are built on lots so steep they should never have been surveyed. To gain access, the new owners must devote a large portion of their property to road work. Even the best of such roads turn into water chutes in heavy rain, and the mud flows down to cloud the lake. The worst are so steep they render the cottage useless, and so where once you had trees, now you have an empty building traded from one naive buyer to the next.

Many owners excavate their entire property. With the thin topsoil gone, local native plants will not grow for decades, opening a door to invasive weed species. It is difficult for me to comprehend people who would willingly turn treed property into an open-pit mine and then build a house in the middle of the wasteland.

Whole new subdivisions have been razed down to bare clay. This is how neighbourhoods get built in cities—for the developer, it is cheapest just to bulldoze everything. Once another matching house goes up, suburban-style landscaping with lawns and shrubbery goes in, sentencing the hapless owner to a lifetime of mowing and weed killing. One Lakeland development on a golf course is so perfectly suburban it could be in Edmonton, Saskatoon, or Mississauga.

The lakes are caught in the self-aggrandizing web of roads that chokes natural spaces wherever it spreads. The route around the south end of the lake has been recently widened and paved into a speedy thoroughfare. The old road belonged mostly to barefoot children carrying ice-cream cones from the store or wobbling along on their bikes to the beach. Its narrowness and potholes kept drivers in check. People in a hurry could always use the provincial highway, which runs parallel just three hundred metres away. But taxpayers have blind faith in pavement that hurries along to nowhere.

The real pressure to upgrade roads in Lakeland is owing to the earth-shaking tandem-axle honey trucks that maraud everywhere. Sewage holding tanks were wisely mandated here a generation ago. But no one foresaw the amount of sewage-truck traffic it would take to service the ten-room houses replacing the old cabins, with their multiple bathrooms, dishwashers, and laundries.

All-terrain-vehicle enthusiasts have carved an illegal, expanding road network of their own. The unstoppable scourge of these powerful machines has turned game trails into muddy gorges, cut the bush around Lakeland into tiny blocks that have ceased to function as wildlife habitat.

Local store owners sell thousands of fireworks, which disturb the peace every weekend night. Unregulated light pollution is beginning to obscure the starry night sky. Much of the municipality has been logged. The number of golf holes continues to grow despite the shrinking golf market.

To its credit, the municipal government has tried to curb development with a new land use plan. The developers have hit back with lawsuits in the cynical knowledge that the local government has neither time nor money to fight. Last summer I met the Lakeland reeve for coffee at the Yellow Fender Café over in Christopher Lake town. He is an affable fellow who comes to meetings in suspenders and plaid shirts. But there was a strain in his voice. "So many people are threatening to sue us now, I tell 'em 'Get in line!'" Serving on council is such a thankless, high-pressure job that good people refuse to seek election, leaving seats vacant. He was not sure if he would run again himself.

Even if the council did manage to halt all development entirely, their own neighbours across the highway in the Rural Municipality of Paddockwood were approving new subdivisions at a frightening pace, indifferent to the pressure they were putting on Lakeland.

So goes the conquest of capital over community. Over on Christopher Lake there is a stretch of mansions people now call Millionaires' Row. But of course that is only proverbial—you need much more than a million to belong there.

Awareness is meaningless without action, to borrow from Che Guevara. But it was difficult to know, idling there upon my deck chair, how best to do my part to remedy matters. Should I stand up and run for one of those empty council seats? I could fetch the big framing hammer from the shed and begin to pull our cabin down board by board, let it all go back wild. *What would you say to that, pretty junco?*

Whatever would happen, I was aware that stewardship of something beautiful and precious, this little silver square of land, had passed into my keeping for the wink of time that is one life. By the time my children had kids of their own, it seemed impossible the lake would have anything left to give. But it is hard to assess one lake in isolation. I lacked solid reference points, the framework of comparison. Perhaps what seemed like a local catastrophe was merely a national average.

Wielding Emma in my mind like a measuring stick, I determined it was time to go take the length and breadth and depth of the wider country one lake at a time, to see if three thousand cabins was a little or a lot, to observe how people used other parts of the lake country, how the near-wilderness looked after them, and how they looked after it.

The season for that was just beginning. Warm days lay ahead, a delicious prospect in the Canadian bush. Like money in the bank. My first destination lay just over the horizon in the national park. Each summer I cover a lot of miles along its backcountry trails. This year it was time to follow one of those routes to the lake of the grey wizard.

THE GREY WIZARD

AJAWAAN LAKE, *Saskatchewan*

This wall, which was really a dam, seemed as if it were holding
the lake in place: which is really what it was doing, for without it there
would have been no lake at all, only the stream running through.
GREY OWL, *Sajo and the Beaver People*

AT THE top of a rise where old birches grew, my wife stood in the warm afternoon light against the silver backdrop of Kingsmere Lake, looking north, waiting for me to catch up. Normally, she does not like to backpack, Marlene. She takes no pride in standing up to heavy loads, exposing the body to risk and sweat, the mind to ennui—all those inevitabilities of wilderness travel on foot. So mostly, when I go off on such adventures, it is in other company. But for journeys of the soul she has more willing legs than most, and the little cabin called Beaver Lodge at the end of the trail held out some kind of promise for her.

The cabin lay on a tiny lake called Ajawaan, near the northern boundary of Prince Albert National Park. It was home, briefly, to one of the most enigmatically glamorous couples of the 1930s. He was an author, conservationist, and con man from England named Archie Belaney who masqueraded as a Canadian Aboriginal called Grey Owl. She was his true-Iroquois wife, Anahareo, who shaped him into a brand that sold throughout the British Empire.

Beaver Lodge was built in 1931 to house not just Grey Owl and Anahareo but also their two adopted beaver kits, Jelly Roll and Rawhide. The installation of this photogenic quartet was all a publicity gambit to promote Canada's fledgling national parks. A happy account of how it came about is provided in Grey Owl's masterpiece, *Pilgrims of the Wild*, one of three international best-sellers he wrote in the little cabin.

Though Grey Owl—I will call him by his nom de plume—was a celebrity in the wide world, at home he was a desperate alcoholic who patronized bootleggers. Local people did not buy Grey Owl's Indian act. Even if they appreciated his conservation message, seeing him passed out on the sidewalks of Prince Albert or Waskesiu did not bolster his credibility at home. My grandfather Allan knew Archie Grey Owl from former days in northern Ontario and had nothing kind to say of him—he was a drunk, an impostor, and a bigamist, and that was that. Even so, Grandad and some of my great uncles were not above drinking and card playing with a famous author at backdoor speakeasies down on the East Flat.

Even his celebrity was precarious. When he died and the *North Bay Nugget* newspaper revealed that he was an Englishman posing as Aboriginal, the Grey Owl name went down like a drowned muskrat. I think that it was not the charade itself, but the role he played, that drew indignation. Western Canada was effectively an apartheid society in Grey Owl's day and long after; to pretend to be Aboriginal was an affront to the establishment in a time and place of systemic racism.

Against the standards of debauchery achieved by modern celebrities, Grey Owl's little foibles hardly rate. If he lived today, he would have gone to rehab then gotten back to writing. His fancy for aboriginal ways would be mere fashion in these days of cultural free-borrowing. In Germany, there are social clubs for people who dress in buckskins and live in tipis on the weekend.

Although Grey Owl's messy biography rides the changing times, his message is perennially worthwhile. He wrote *lovingly* about the wilderness. The bush was not a fearful and capricious foe, nor a field of conquest. Rather, it yielded a simple living along with spiritual solace. It was heaven incarnate, a practical divinity you could simply touch. Here was a figure who stood apart from Margaret Atwood's literary survival motif, who wrote about nature as a trusted ally.

During his heyday, Grey Owl inspired a generation to take to the wild country with reborn gaze, to find in nature what the machine age could not supply. He spawned a recreational approach to the proximate wilderness that persists to this day, and the new national park system provided the playground to practise it. Each summer an enterprising number of Grey Owl readers travelled to Prince Albert National Park and made the forty-kilometre walk to the author's lakeside cabin. Hundreds still make the pilgrimage to Ajawaan Lake every year. Pilgrimages have a way of becoming recurring, and I had made the trip a few times before. This was Marlene's first, and I found her eagerness a little mysterious. Of all the trails in the wide world, why *this* trail, why *this* cabin? Why *this* man? Well, she has a certain instinct for things.

So we found ourselves at the trailhead, two pilgrims of the wild. Getting to Grey Owl's cabin on tiny Ajawaan means first legging it around massive Kingsmere through the up-and-down of its eastern shore. You can take a powerboat, if you are willing to transport one over the railway portage below Kingsmere Lake and can abide the noise and stink. On a fair-weather prospect, you can canoe Kingsmere instead. But the route across the wide-open lake is fully exposed to the prevailing northwesterlies, and it is possible to become wind-bound on the shore for hours or days.

Opting for the certainty of walking—and of hard labour—we hoisted our packs and stepped under the canopy of the forest, on the sphagnum floor made lush by a wet summer. The white petals of bunchberry bloomed in the warm shade. At this latitude, the boreal forest still contains vestiges of prairie: grass on south-facing slopes where tiger lilies grow. Tracks of elk, of deer, pocked the trail. In creek vales and low places the route was flooded. Some of these wet spots had been bridged by deadfall, and we took up sticks to balance our way across. Twice we had to remove our boots and wade. The trail emerged onto the Kingsmere Lake shoreline, and when we reached the sand, our voices disturbed a bald eagle atop a black spruce. She screamed at us once, then flapped away north in the direction of the cabin.

In appreciation of Marlene's rare company, I gallantly offered to carry nearly all the gear to keep her pack light. While she skipped along daydreaming, I plodded with my nose to the uneven ground, my feet hurting already. My old Vasque hikers were no longer comfortable, as they once had been. We stopped often—to examine burls and pick strawberries, to marvel at those streaks of purple sand that accumulate where the waves break, to drink and snack until the chirring squirrels drove us on. It was a fine summer afternoon to walk—cool under a high overcast—and we had the trail completely to ourselves.

Camping is not allowed on Ajawaan Lake itself. We would drop our packs at a campsite at Kilometre 13 and make what mountaineers call a dash for the summit. We would be unencumbered, but it meant backtracking further to camp—twenty-seven kilometres in one day. The drive from the city had made for a very late start, so we were unsure if enough daylight remained. Once we reached our campsite, I set up the small tent and put most of our things inside. After rooting for the flashlight, we continued down the trail.

Grey Owl's background is well-known to many, and there is no point competing with his many biographers. But for those wanting a brief version . . . An unwanted child born to a dreary urban life in 1888 in Hastings, England, Archibald Stansfeld Belaney had a boyhood fascination with Canada, with its wild-life and indigenous culture. These dreams propelled him over the Atlantic before he was fully a man. He adopted his Aboriginal identity shortly after arriving in this country in 1906, and soon most people knew him as Archie Grey Owl. He was a good piano player, a lively raconteur, and extremely adept at throwing a knife.

Though his story would vary slightly over the years, he claimed a Metis (Scots-Apache) ancestry; Hermosillo, Mexico, as his birthplace; and the Ojibway as his adopted people, and the last part was true. His first and only legal wife was an Anishinabe from the Lake Nipissing area, and through his in-laws he learned his way in the bush. For two decades, he made a quiet living as a trapper and guide in Ontario—interrupted only by a tour of duty as an infantryman in World War I.

Archie was hardly alone in reinventing himself upon arrival in the New World—no crime in that. The real victims of his lies were his many abandoned wives and children.

Had it not been for his third wife, the one he called Anahareo, he might have spent his days in obscurity. Gertrude Bernard was her real name, though she also went by Pony, and she came from Mattawa, at the confluence of the Mattawa and Ottawa Rivers. If he was the actor, she was the impresario. With Archie's knack for storytelling, she encouraged him to write of wild Canada for the English magazine market. Moreover, she got him to stop trapping and supplied him with the conservationist ideas that would later make him famous. Trapping was getting to be a thin living anyway. Archie was a fine prose stylist of the period—another truth about him—and soon had a book contract. *Men of the Wild Frontier* was published in 1931, and Grey Owl was launched on a bright, short trajectory of fame. From that point he had seven years to live.

His work came to the attention of the Canadian Dominion Parks Service—the world's first national parks agency—which engaged him as a naturalist. His first posting was to Riding Mountain National Park, an upland on the Manitoba escarpment, but there was not enough lake water there to suit the couple, let alone Jelly Roll and Rawhide. Six months later that same year, the unusual family moved west to the 3,900 square kilometres of Prince Albert National Park.

"Far enough away to gain seclusion," wrote Grey Owl of his new cabin at Ajawaan, "yet within reach of those whose genuine interest prompts them to make the trip." When Grey Owl and Anahareo first came to these woods, there was no Kingsmere Lake road. Visitors who wished to make the hike first had to paddle the twenty-five-kilometre length of Waskesiu Lake and then ascend the creek between them. Travelling alone, Grey Owl could make the entire journey to town in a day—often driven by the fury of alcohol withdrawal. Despite the distance, Grey Owl and Anahareo were *the* couple to meet in the summer of 1936, when more than seven hundred people visited the cabin described in *Pilgrims of the Wild*.

Grey Owl and Anahareo were celebrities in the modern sense of the word, and cameras adored them. He, a lean, dark, square-shouldered six-footer with a fiery gaze and a flowing mane, was a dashing and still virile fortysomething. She, racy in her slim-fitting breeches and high boots, nineteen years his junior, was as smouldering as any Hollywood screen idol. The couple played versions of themselves in films that circulated widely in the hungry thirties, feeding a generation rich only in imagination on images of a mislaid utopia. It was the best of times for the couple, and their daughter, Shirley Dawn, was born.

In Canada's national parks, meanwhile, the Grey Owl name was having the desired effect as an advertising tool. Visitor

numbers were climbing across the board—though not everyone came on foot. Ironically, as the automobile was coming
into its own, national parks were a mainstay destination. Six car-
accessible new parks were opened between the wars. The
mandate of park administrators was to supply parks for people;
conservation was secondary. Citizens demanded cheap access
to wilderness for recreational purposes, and the new park system
delivered this economic good.

Just like Emma Lake a generation later, Prince Albert National
Park was entirely a political invention, a payoff to the citizens of
Prince Albert who had a knack for getting prime ministers to the
capital. When William Lyon Mackenzie King had lost his own
seat in the 1925 general election, Prince Albert had provided him
a safe-seat by-election and restored him to Ottawa. In return, the
local Board of Trade demanded a national park named after the
city. King delivered. When he arrived in the park resort town of
Waskesiu in the summer of 1927 for the grand opening, King
received a fine log cabin as a bonus. The tubby Prime Minister
made his speech, donned a woolen singlet for a quick dip in the
lake, then retired to his new place. He would never spend another
night there.

Most visitors stayed at the campground, and Grey Owl fondly
referred to Waskesiu townsite as a "tent city." At summer peak,
so many families crowded in that there was no room to walk
between the tents in the campground. As with most new parks,
the large majority were from the region, from Prince Albert or
Saskatoon; which was about as far as you could drive a car with
spoked wheels over rough, narrow roads.

Campers in Waskesiu were mostly mothers with great broods
of children. They tended to stay all summer, the husbands joining
on the weekend. Out of this happy matriarchal minisociety, certain local customs emerged—including a distinctive style of tent

house. It had a canvas roof to meet the park definition of *tent*, but a wood floor and walls that gave more comfort, cleanliness, and security. "Shack tents," as they were called, had to be removable to comply with campground rules. By tradition, they were put up the Victoria Day long weekend in May in a great communal work bee that anticipated the warm days ahead, then dismantled in a more wistful mood and stored away by Labour Day in September.

Shack tents spoke of our innate hunger for a simple life in nature and for sharing in community. Although nearly all were an identical 21 square metres in size, with a small stove and an icebox, each was unique in decorative touches. Serious cooking was done in the communal camp kitchens, where excellent fires were kept going all day. Women traded stories and fed each other's children from the tops of large cast-iron stoves shared by all. Mainly the shack tents were bunkhouses, and the diminutive buildings could swallow surprisingly large families into cozy comfort when night fell.

Even in the depths of the Great Depression shack tents were affordable. They were still plentiful in the seventies, and many of my parents' friends had them. Some of these people had plenty of money; some had little. But in the context of the shack tent village of Waskesiu, for the brief Canadian summer, class privilege took a holiday.

One day a fellow down on his luck came into my father's office in town and offered his shack tent in payment for some insurance. Dad took it, though we already had our place at Emma. That afternoon, the fellow's wife and children came into the office, some of them in tears, begging Dad to undo the deal, which of course he did.

For snobbish reasons, park officials abhorred shack tents. They hated the name, which smacked of shantytowns. They argued that shack tents constituted private property, contrary to the spirit of public land. This was absurd in that, like many another national park townsite, Waskesiu had subdivisions of large private cottages monopolizing the best viewpoints. It had pricey hotels, bungalows, restaurants, and shops all making profit. A succession of plans to get rid of these popular "eyesores" was hatched from Ottawa over three decades, but the feisty shack tenters always fought back. Ultimately, the park got rid of shack tents by the cunning stratagem of allowing them to stay up year-round and to have fixed roofs. They soon evolved into just another subdivision of expensive, if small, permanent cabins. They are now tiny works of art only the wealthy can afford.

A few years ago, a local history group set up two of the old shack tents as outdoor museum pieces in downtown Waskesiu. The little houses are a beautiful evocation of a small-footprint sensibility we had not long ago and need to reacquire now. In recent years, national and provincial parks have begun to offer similar small dwellings, especially yurts, for rent in campgrounds.

The role of national parks is being rethought in many ways. They are important preserves of sanity in the overdeveloped proximate wilderness, but they alone cannot compensate for our greedy proclivities as once was thought. Parks, in some ways, promote the very uses of nature they nominally stand against. Their attractiveness only makes real estate prices in surrounding areas that much higher. And as long as wardens are keeping a chunk of bush down the road safe for the fox and heron, I feel free to landscape my beachfront lot. Indeed, parks themselves are artificial landscapes. Fire protection alone has made the forest unnaturally old, interrupting its natural cycle of rejuvenation for the sake of the nice view I wish to enjoy while riding my bike down the trail. Park administrators know these things, know that the future of conservation is more complex than we ever thought. We citizens must rediscover economy, modesty, and simplicity not just within the bounds of a government map, but in our own families, house by house, a shack tent at a time.

THE SUN was slanting precipitously by the time we got to the north end of Kingsmere, and we picked up our pace as best we could on tired feet. The trail crossed an old spruce bog. The wind had uprooted many trees in the uncertain ground, giving a sullen air of destruction. When I came through this Mirkwood a few years before with a friend, the musician Gabriel Penna, we were startled by a great red deer. Which is what *waskesiu* means in Cree: red deer. In the half-light I looked for animal shapes ahead, but this time we were alone.

We reached a stream I could not remember: Ajawaan Creek. Perhaps it had been dry before. Now it was swollen, and again we had to pull off our boots and wade. Underway again, we climbed away from Kingsmere, deeper into the bush. We were retreating to our own thoughts. Marlene had said little all afternoon. In the melancholy twilight that hinted of fall, mine turned to the loneliness of the artist.

When summer ended and the visitors retreated from Ajawaan Lake, so did Anahareo. She didn't mind wintering in a tiny cabin, but not with a crabby, alcoholic writer. She would wander months alone in the bush, obeying a lifelong obsession with gold prospecting, leaving young Shirley Dawn to be raised by friends in Prince Albert, and Archie to his work. Grey Owl sacrificed his happiness to his books, summoning his happy family only through his art: "I am lonesome for them all, and so I spend my time with them on paper."

Soon he embarked on the first of his hugely successful lecture trips through England and North America, which he did without Anahareo but with a new companion he dubbed Silver Moon. Grey Owl fretted about his performance in advance of these tours, about how to impress people in the Old Country. His act was by all accounts transcendent. Wearing an elaborate beaded costume he had made himself, he delivered his lines before projected photographs of the primeval forest, a multimedia show ahead of its time.

The pace was gruelling. Lovat Dickson, Grey Owl's English publisher, reported that the star performed 88 times in 138 days and travelled 7,000 kilometres through the small country. Gruelling too was the weight of deception. Archie had to travel with a sun lamp to maintain a swarthy complexion. Whereas back home he could drop into the anonymity of Prince Albert speakeasies, on tour he had to maintain his act around the clock. The English bought him wholeheartedly. King George invited him to an audience so that the child princesses Margaret and Elizabeth—the latter the future monarch—could view the noble savage of Canada.

A subsequent tour of more Indian-savvy North America met a cooler reception, and Grey Owl returned home exhausted and sick. He came down with mild pneumonia and had to be taken from Beaver Lodge to hospital in Prince Albert. Weakened by a lifetime of hard drinking, he slipped into a coma and died shortly thereafter, on April 13, 1938, at the age of fifty.

AND YET there we were, seven decades later, two new visitors beckoned by words that had outlived the darkness of controversy that followed. On beaten legs, we entered the little valley of Ajawaan and glimpsed the cabin. A boardwalk was laid over the picturesque approach along the west shore of the lake, which is small enough to lie glassy most times. Like Grey Owl himself, Beaver Lodge is visually striking—it is more a stage than a home. Like a real beaver lodge, it is perched proud on the foreshore where no one in their right mind would build. This allowed the beaver inhabitants immediate access to the lake through a plunge hole in the floor. It was cute in pictures; in practice, the cabin was bug-infested and damp. At Anahareo's sensible insistence, a second cabin was built on higher ground, for people to inhabit.

We clunked onto the small stoop at last and entered. Beaver Lodge was still the same stark room with a crudely built bed and a kind of platform table. An official guestbook had been filled to the very margins, and an overflow started in a wire-bound notebook left by some visitor. The entries were from all over the world but also from people we knew from Prince Albert. Tokens were left about: a small drum, a bit of tobacco, a feather, even a pair of crutches.

Three simple graves lay among the willows and dogwood. Grey Owl, Anahareo, and their daughter, Shirley Dawn, together in eternity as they seldom were in the land of the living.

I felt a twinge of disappointment mixed with fatigue and thirst. There was a funereal air to the place. It was already full dusk and we had many kilometres to backtrack. If the spirit of Grey Owl was about, I could not spot him.

"It's just a shell," Marlene said where she sat on the stoop, purposefully retying her boots for the continuation of the walk. She uses this same expression to describe the human body in a spiritual context, the corporeal vessel that we occupy for a fleeting time. She spoke the words when my father died, as a comfort, to remind me not to hang on to trappings. As for Grey Owl, she had not marched twenty kilometres to see a log house, but to take that first step past it, to reach the beginning . . . of awareness.

When you trade the city for the wild, it takes time to acclimate to a new way of seeing. Often, this does not begin to occur until we turn for home. We create objectives to occupy the restless human mind: to see a cabin, catch grayling from a certain stream, bag a summit. With our task achieved and the mind satisfied, the heart may be freed to roam where it may.

Similarly with Grey Owl; you begin to understand what he

stood for when you let the trappings of identity, deception, and cultural appropriation fall away. Grey Owl understood nature and our bittersweet relationship with it, that mix of yearning and fear.

British director Richard Attenborough failed to understand this in his unsuccessful 1999 film *Grey Owl*. Not even Pierce Brosnan in the title role could save the feature, which did not even open in the United States. Attenborough chose to shoot the Canadian scenes in Quebec, which is why the Laurentians are visible from his version of Ajawaan Lake—though that is not what hobbled the film. It was easy to capture the drama of self-destructive genius, of doomed lovers, of multiple identities. As for nature, though, the prime mover, the great cause of the main character, Attenborough did not know where to point his camera to frame this elusive god.

Some truths can only be reached on foot. As soon as we departed from the cabin, our mood lightened. Though the sun had gone down and darkness filled the wood, somehow we began to see more, to feel it, hear it, scent it on the wind. On the way back down to Kingsmere, a warm breeze was coming up from the south and laying whitecaps into the beach. When we again reached the swollen creek, Marlene said, playfully, that it only made sense that one of us should carry the other across, so that one pair of feet at least stayed dry. I hoisted her piggyback, the wind whipping her hair across my face, and her laughter in my ear.

Soon it became pitch-black, and we had to feel our way along. Our flashlight held two near-dead batteries and gave only a decorative glow. By the time we had crept the seven kilometres back to camp, we were giddy with exhaustion. I lit the stove, and we feasted on a packaged curry, noisily, the food tasting as it only can when you have gone over the ground all day on foot. We were not alone. A woman with two quite small children had arrived while we were on the trail. It was an adventurous outing for such a trio.

But a woman travelling alone was safer here in the protective wrap of a national park than upon any street in Saskatoon. We raised our tea mugs to Grey Owl, to Anahareo, to our neighbours, to each other, and to the night. Then we slid into the tent mumbling that in three minutes we would be deep asleep. It took less. Sometime in the middle of the night I woke and crawled out. The overcast that had made it so dark earlier was blown away, leaving a sky so star-heavy it seemed to pulse with energy and purpose.

AS MARLENE said some time later, when I asked her why she had taken that trip, Grey Owl changed the way people felt about nature, and that is not an easy thing to do. "He had some difficulties, but I knew he had a good heart. I knew if you walked his path you would feel it."

During his time, faith in progress had fallen hard. The monstrous destruction of World War I, the moral turpitude of the Roaring Twenties, the utter collapse of the economic system that underpinned a new society in the thirties and a return to militarism—it was an uncertain century.

"You are tired with years of civilization. I come and offer you what?—a single green leaf." This was the central message of Grey Owl's lectures abroad. People were spiritually hungry for simple, pure things, the reacquisition of lost knowledge.

Grey Owl was a careful and patient observer of nature and its fractal, intricate beauty. Owing to his long residence in the bush, he could trace the interconnectivity among species and their environment that has eluded our reductionist modern science until recently. He campaigned to save the vanishing beaver not simply because it was cute or because trapping it had devolved into a cruel, unneeded vestige of an outdated industry. Rather, he was probably the first observer to note that without the beaver, the forest itself would cease to function properly.

Today they call the beaver a "keystone" species, one upon which other organisms up and down the food chain are highly dependent. Grey Owl saw it vanishing. At the commencement of the fur trade that followed the creation of the Hudson's Bay Company monopoly in 1670, there were perhaps 200 million beaver in what is now Canada. One beaver pelt yielded sufficient felt to produce eighteen hats of the kind desirable in Europe then. This economic demand opened Canada like no other wilderness, lake by lake, from one beaver colony to the next, until the history of the country was written and the beaver was all but gone.

In *Pilgrims of the Wild*, Grey Owl contemplates the transformative effect of the beaver's extirpation across so much of its range: "Was this then, to be the end? Beaver . . . *were* the wilderness. With them gone it would be empty; without them it would be not a wilderness but a waste."

If you went to school in Canada, you have done a unit on *Castor canadensis*. The beaver is—how very Canadian—the second-largest rodent in the world. Like the panda, it eats shoots and leaves, and also the bark of deciduous trees. More massive than they appear, larger individuals can top thirty kilograms. A multifunctional animal, it is foremost an aquanaut. It dresses sensibly in layers of coarse and fine hair, which it grooms assiduously and keeps oiled. Its coat is a diver's dry suit. The beaver can deploy little swim goggles over each eye for underwater viewing. It can seal off ears and nostrils, and it can close its mouth behind its incisors to allow it to gnaw underwater. The black, muscular tail provides both steering and propulsion. The beaver has a prodigious lung capacity, allowing it to stay under for fifteen minutes. If you ever get the chance to hear the sound of a beaver catching its breath, you will swear a human swimmer is near.

In terrestrial mode, the beaver is a tireless logger and earthmover. Someone has calculated that on average, a beaver chews down 216 trees a year with its ghastly yellow incisors. It transports and shapes tonnes of mud and sticks into extensive earthworks. Grey Owl described beaver dams "one hundred feet long and over four feet high" that looked like they were built by a gang of men, an entirely accurate description. It is fun to canoe down the kind of meandering creeks beavers inhabit to examine their engineering. Dragging the occasional keel over a beaver dam will do little harm, though the furious owner will be on the scene to assess damage before you are even around the bend.

Beavers obtain security by building lodges with underwater entrances. They only make dams if the water depth is insufficient to cover their front door, or to gain access to a wider underwater area. In winter, they stay mostly iced in, keeping warm in their lodges by body heat and feeding from the cache piles set aside the previous summer near their home entrances.

Like fire, the beaver is a rejuvenating force in the life of the boreal forest. Through flooding and tree cutting, the little fellow opens up a system that otherwise moves toward closure and monoculture. Lakes, ponds, wetlands, and marshes are at the busy end of the biodiversity spectrum. They support aquatic plants, insects, fish, kingfishers and ducks, loons and mergansers. When beavers eventually abandon their dams, the dry flats sprout grasses that feed deer. Beavers are not just adapted to lake environments, they manufacture them.

For accuracy in giving these few facts about the beaver, I have leaned upon the fine materials published under the *Hinterland Who's Who* program of the Canadian Wildlife Service, a staple of Canadian television in the sixties and seventies that has since been resurrected. Grey Owl knew all these things from direct observation and was able to set down the information fancifully, yet with great precision, throughout his books.

The Canadian Wildlife Service credits Grey Owl for bringing the symbol of a country back from the brink. And so we are indebted to a hard-drinking, knife-throwing cad. I like the humanity of that. It reminds me of a story the late Anthony de Mello told. In Ireland, a girl who got in a certain kind of trouble did not bother to ask advice from the parish priest installed in his cathedral. Better to seek the fallen priest living alone on the margins of the wild, who actually knew a thing or two about the downside of things. If it is a wizard you seek, find one who has seen enough for his hair to go grey.

In the brightness of morning we walked out of the bush, going slowly on legs stiffened by the previous day. For a game we tried to count every animal sighting, but soon lost track of the squirrels and smaller birds. A pair of whitetails looked up at us, then bounded off noiselessly. An elk stood calmly in the sun, showing his muscled flank like a Paris runway model while I took his picture. When we reached the parking lot, the grouse were pecking for gizzard stones and displaying their plumes. As we drove back along the Kingsmere Road, just before the place where it becomes pavement a lanky, grey-coated wolf stood on his great paws watching us approach, then loped away into the diversity of the beaver-tended forest.

THE CITIZEN SHIP OF SCIENCE

LAKE WINNIPEG, *Manitoba*

A running river can almost, or quite nearly, escape pollution,
whereas an enclosed pool is easily sullied.

CICERO, *De Natura Deorum (On the Nature of the Gods)*

THE BIG ship was easy to find in a small Manitoba town on a dead-flat lakeshore. The highway through Grand Rapids rises onto a high, curving bridge over the river, and from it could be seen the MV *Namao* stemming up the current. She made a pretty picture in the gentle light of a late September afternoon, gleaming in her new coat of paint, blue and white. She idled to a stop and began to come about, the words "Lake Winnipeg Research Consortium" were billboarded across her topsides, and the green-grey horizon of the lake's north basin spread behind. The ship was aiming for a tiny wooden dock, and I turned from the highway down a gravel road to meet her.

Namao is Cree for "sturgeon," a sluggish, inscrutable fish rarely seen in action, and it seemed a fitting name. I had been waiting all summer to meet this slow ship, the only Canadian vessel outside the Great Lakes dedicated to lake science. Back in April, I had received an invitation to cruise aboard the *Namao* and learn about this work firsthand. The only proviso was that I had to be ready on short notice, since the sailing schedule was "tentative." In fact, the *Namao* spent the whole summer in dry-dock for repairs. It seemed odd that the cruising calendar of a thirty-four-metre vessel and crew would not be known far in advance or that her mainte-nance work would not be done in the ample Canadian off-season. I had all but given up on the ship when the call came to meet her in Grand Rapids, where the Saskatchewan River empties itself in the north end of the world's tenth-largest lake.

Lake Winnipeg, though vast, is only a remnant of Glacial Lake Agassiz, which once covered much of Manitoba. Eight thou-sand years after Agassiz roared down to the sea in one calamitous torrent, the province still resembles a recently drained bathtub, a flood-prone flat of many shallow lakes, small and large, and not much elevation in between. Or, to use an old joke, Manitoba is 55 percent land, 45 percent mosquito larvae.

The deck crew no sooner made the ship fast than a wiry fellow in orange fleece climbed over the rail and strode up the gangway, fixing me in his sights. Mike Stainton, a chemist with the Depart-ment of Fisheries and Oceans, had a head of unruly grey curls, like carded wool, and a bluff manner. With over three decades at the agency, he was among the most senior scientists on a federal payroll anywhere. But that did not necessarily make him a Gov-ernment Man.

"Canada has spent more money understanding Lake Malawi in Africa than they have on Lake Winnipeg," he said, helping me toss my gear aboard over the port rail. It was true: Canada has spent millions on studying African lakes as a form of international aid. Lake science at home was a different matter, apparently. He explained that the ship had languished all summer because money could not be found to operate her. Funding for this voyage had been cobbled together only days before. "I am sure the public thinks someone is minding the store, but the kind of work we are doing on this ship is extremely low budget."

This was a disturbing assertion, given the heavy stream of alarming reports coming out of Lake Winnipeg in recent years. An American-planned water diversion in North Dakota was probably going to flush nonnative species into Lake Winnipeg via the Red River. There were persistent rumours that heavy metals and polychlorinated biphenyls (PCBs) had been released into the lake by the great Manitoba flood of 1997. The Manitoba Hydro dam on the Nelson River was preventing the lake from flushing itself free of pollutants.

But it was the lake's growing summer algae blooms that concerned people most. Across Canada, algae are a familiar nuisance for beachgoers in the dog days of summer. But the thick green mats coating Lake Winnipeg were so big they were being picked up by satellite imaging. Commercial fishers were getting rashes from handling their algae-clogged nets, and swimming bans were common.

Before I could quiz Mike further, he handed me off to a woman with a clipboard and disappeared. The science coordinator was, among a hundred other duties, responsible for orienting greenhorns. She assigned me to a berth, pointed out the heads and the emergency muster station, then wrote my name at the bottom of a list of all souls aboard, making fifteen in all. Then she, too, vanished. I tossed my duffle into a surprisingly inviting cabin, warm and softly lit, and went to explore the ship.

The *Namao*'s main deck held a dozen cabins off a central passageway. Companionways led up to the bridge and down to the galley and mess, the latter a small room at the ship's water line, with the chilling air of dusk coming through an open porthole. There was a large chart of Lake Winnipeg and a schematic drawing of the *Namao*. She displaced 380 tonnes at full load, operated at a maximum speed of 11 knots, and was built at Riverton Boatworks in 1975. She was a Coast Guard buoy tender until

the government outsourced her job. The *Namao* was oddly similar in size and layout to another environmental science ship, the
Calypso of Captain Jacques-Yves Cousteau, made famous on television in the seventies and lovingly parodied in the 2004 film *The
Life Aquatic with Steve Zissou.*

But there were no Frenchmen cavorting on the *Namao* in
watch caps and bathing briefs, nor anyone else aboard. I went out
the starboard hatch, aft to the stern, up to the bridge, and down
to the foredeck—all empty. There was a gathering of people down
on the dock, and I climbed down to join them.

"Hey, you got a truck, right?" said a voice, one of the deck
hands, his mischievous face catching the yard light of the fish
plant. Crew and scientists had been aboard a week since leaving the home port of Gimli down in the south basin, and they
were trying to mount a beer run to the hotel off-sale. I offered
my services with a smile; hands were dug in pockets and purses,
arithmetic done and redone. The junior scientist aboard, a young
woman from Newfoundland, rode shotgun with the money
while I drove into town. At a roughneck bar, we loaded cases of
a discount brand called Lucky for the crew. The young scientists
drank a little upmarket, in Labatt or Molson territory.

The party that followed back aboard the *Namao* was a floating
microcosm of the shores that surrounded her. The crew hailed
from the Aboriginal and Icelandic fishing communities around
the lake. The bo's'n and his two deck men did the heavy sailing
work: anchoring, docking, making fast. The ship remained in the
good hands of her officers during libations. The mate looked in
on the party for a while, but did not imbibe. The captain stayed
aloof in his cabin, high on the bridge deck.

The chief engineer, a lugubrious fellow in a soiled blue officer's shirt, kept relentless watch. Like the *Namao* herself, the
chief once belonged to the Coast Guard, and he missed the old

navy discipline, still wore his stripes. Alcohol was still officially forbidden, and the chief scowled disapproval whenever he passed.

Still, the *Namao* was the last big ship on Lake Winnipeg, and all the crew were happy to be part of a long lake-mariner tradition. They took other jobs—framing houses or fishing—but this was the role they liked best.

As for the scientists, they were divided into two distinct camps. The first demographic was young, female, and marginalized. Studying wildlife, ecosystems, nature for its own sake—that is the hungry end of the science world. It is much easier to attract funding for research that can lead to corporate profits, like herbicides, biotechnology, new drugs. The science coordinator, who had traded her clipboard for a can of Pilsner, said she had done enough field work aboard the *Namao* to get a master's degree three times over, but could not get funding to work up her data for publication.

"Every time I work on this ship, I lose money," she said wearily, her younger colleagues listening intently. "If I wanted to work in Africa, I could get funding."

Mike Stainton represented the other stripe of scientist aboard. Which is to say, male, established, financially secure, born of an era now fading fast, when unfettered research money still flowed freely, steered by simple curiousity and public good. He could retire comfortably any time he wanted. He was not smug about it.

"It's a problem," said Mike. "Who is coming up to replace my generation?" He was drinking red wine from some stash he had brought aboard, and he tilted a stemmed glass toward the young women scientists down the hall in a gesture of salute. "I wish them luck. But they won't be given the opportunities I got. Science has changed."

The long drive off the prairie, a time zone change, the late hour, and so many new faces finally caught up with me. I went off to my cabin, crawled into the warm cocoon of a curtained bunk, and fell asleep as fast as any watch-weary sailor.

AFTER WHAT seemed the merest flicker of time, a new day was signalled forcefully by the ship's engines roaring to life. I put on several layers topped by rain gear and made my way below for a danish and coffee. The fluorescent-lit mess was small, so the crew ate first and then readied ship while the scientists took their turn. Both groups had come and gone before I straggled in, though full darkness still showed through the porthole.

Reaching the deck, I found my pickup truck was once again in demand. Len Hendzel, a senior colleague of Mike Stainton's at the Department of Fisheries and Oceans, had completed his work aboard. He now wished to return to Winnipeg with his collected samples, arrayed on the dock in a dozen picnic coolers. I was glad to turn over my keys. I could just as easily retrieve the truck from Winnipeg as backtrack here, for the boat would not return to Grand Rapids in any case. But I wondered how the fellow would have made the seven-hour trip had this means not been available. What kind of shoestring science was this for a lake that produced hundreds of millions of dollars annually in hydroelectricity, fish, tourism?

All hands now aboard, the lines were were drawn up and the *Namao* set off down the last short stretch of the Saskatchewan River to where the big lake waited. We slid close along the bank, where small houses lay in quiet yards under school-bus-yellow aspen leaves. For a September morning it felt warm, the lake giving away its vast stores of summer heat to the air.

Of all the watery places on maps to lure my eye on winter nights, Lake Winnipeg is the great jewel. Also the most unattainable. Cottagers from Winnipeg keep to the smaller, more protected south basin with its sandy beaches and little resort towns. The much larger north basin, a dangerously open great lake unto itself with neither bays nor islands for shelter, is not for pleasure boating. In the days of the fur trade, voyageurs greatly feared even the short traverse along the shore between the mouth of the Saskatchewan and the headwaters of the Nelson. Behind the bulwarks of the *Namao*, I would gain access to a wild place rarely seen by Canadians even today.

Lake Winnipeg can blow into huge, steep-fronted waves. It is prone to seiches, tidelike swells that flood ashore. I always imagined setting forth in a cold tempest, upon ocean-sized waves. The lake that now opened to the misty eastern horizon, under a just-risen sun lighting the underbelly of a half-formed high overcast, was the picture of calm and warmth. Mike Stainton joined me on the foredeck, just to share in the pleasure of the morning light. It was like steaming out to sea, and soon there was only the water all around, slightly turbid, a pale green tinge suggesting much life.

"Less than 1 percent of the Manitoba population has ever seen this," he said softly. A scientist to the bone, he added that the number was merely hypothetical, but certainly accurate as to order of magnitude. He began to explain the research equipment rigged on board.

A boom bolted to the ship's bow, like an insect's proboscis, pierced the lake ahead of the ship and picked up surface water before it was disturbed by the hull. This sampling stream was pumped through a variety of sensors housed in watertight cases. Among the measurements of interest to lake scientists are water temperature, clarity, pH, salinity, and levels of key organic elements, such as oxygen, nitrogen, phosphorus.

The system was visibly makeshift. Many of the fittings hailed from a hardware store. There were lengths of garden hose, crude plywood housings, even bicycle inner tubes. It reminded me of the leaky basement setup I had built in the days of brewing my own beer.

Limnologists, as lake scientists are generally called (from the Greek root *limne*, or "lake"), are specialists that Canada produces in abundance, like hockey players. While there are many different flavours, lake scientists can be grouped into those who study the open water or pelagic zone and those who study the bottom mud, the benthic zone. The *Namao* was a ready platform for either one. A third area, the *littoral* zone, is the shallow perimeter of the lake where you find minnows, leeches, and the "weeds" that tickle the toes of swimmers, but that is best studied from a pair of hip waders.

Scientists rank lakes according to their overall productivity, a relative measure of an ecosystem's ability to support life. Some waters contain a great deal of nutrients and support a rich, diverse food web. Others are relatively nutrient-poor and sustain little life. As with rivers, altitude has much to do with it: water picks up nutrients as it flows over the ground. So lakes get warmer, muddier, and more fecund along the road to sea level. Unproductive lakes are called oligotrophic or even ultra-oligotrophic; productive ones are called eutrophic.

Lake Winnipeg is naturally productive, supporting a large commercial walleye fishery. But man-made nitrogen and phosphorus were, it was generally accepted, driving the lake to unnatural eutrophic levels. As every gardener knows, nitrogen, phosphorus, and potassium—scientists call them N, P, and K for short—are the three primary plant nutrients. Unfortunately, excessive amounts of N and P are byproducts of human enterprise. And so, like carbon in the atmosphere, these vital elements for life on earth are turned into pollutants through oversupply. Livestock manure, agricultural fertilizers, and municipal sewage are major sources of nitrogen. Phosphates are in many common detergents, household and industrial.

"The lake simply reflects the environment it drains," said Mike, looking out at the mute grey expanse. "If you put a molecule of fertilizer on your farm, if you wash your car in Winnipeg, flush a toilet in Calgary, you are changing the lake."

Lake Winnipeg acts as a storm sewer for nearly a million square kilometres of Canada and the United States. Its catchment area runs from the Continental Divide to the Great Lakes watershed. It includes every major western city and one of the most intensely farmed regions of the world. It drains parts of four provinces and three U.S. states, home to 6.6 million people and 20 million live-stock. Hugging the edge of the barely sloping prairie, every square metre of the lake represents a drainage area the size of three or four urban lots. The surface-to-catchment ratio of 40:1 is the larg-est of any major lake in the world.

Given such topography, Lake Winnipeg is extremely vul-nerable to nutrient overload, and it is now considered the most eutrophic of the world's major lakes.

With a few minutes until we reached our first sampling point, I climbed up to the bridge deck to pay respects to the captain. Mervyn Sinclair was a big, quiet-spoken man from Selkirk, greet-ing me with an enormous warm hand through the sliding hatch and pulling me inside. Two storeys above water, the great sweep of the lake seemed much larger than it had down at the rail. The bridge was heated, the radios crackled their reassuring counsel, the blond wood panelling added to the feeling of warmth. The captain commanded from a swivel chair abaft the helm. The bo's'n gently played the wooden wheel and watched the compass; the mate plotted at the chart station. There is no workplace so fine as a ship's bridge, and this one felt like a cozy cottage perched at the end of a narrow island. It gave a lazy feeling, like being at the cabin on holiday.

But my place was down on deck, where a twelve-hour day of science was beginning. With the ship idling forward, all hands worked together. A big trawl net was lowered by crane to collect fish species at the surface. Meanwhile, a smaller, fine-mesh plankton net was cast from the stern rail. These nets would be towed for thirty minutes. From bins and boxes the scientists drew the appurtenances of their business: ropes wound on wooden hand reels; coiled hoses and electrical cables banded together to form multiveined umbilicals; and innumerable sample bottles and jars, every size and shape, plastic and glass, each neatly labelled in advance.

When the trawl nets came aboard, we made a full stop and set anchor. Now the *sondes* went overboard. A catchall term for any kind of electronic sensing apparatus dropped into the water, sondes sampled the entire water column between surface and bottom. The diminutive science officer wielded the largest of these, one resembling a futuristic hand weapon, and I took a picture of her holding it à la Arnold Schwarzenegger. It was the only time I saw this fiercely hardworking woman smile.

One of her young colleagues sorted the net catch of fingerlings, which were taking a last swim in plastic tubs of lake water before they were sorted into species, placed in small plastic bags, and entombed in the banks of freezers below deck. Some trawls netted an adult-sized walleye. The entrails would be kept for examination while the fillets were saved for a fish fry—the *Namao*'s only job perk. When one did come in, a deck hand who doubled as a commercial fisherman was summoned. Drawing a well-used knife, he produced two perfect fillets in seconds, deft as an executioner. I've watched people in a swarm of black flies spend half an hour to fillet a fish.

Other sampling was done from the afterdeck. A young woman whom I never once saw in anything but oilskins and deck boots hauled up bottom mud with a small double-jawed shovel like a Tonka toy. Thereafter, she would sit on an upturned plastic bucket and painstakingly sift the mud to find the benthic invertebrate species. Their small bodies were nearly invisible to my eye and very fragile. It was cold, wet, and tedious work, and I thought it the worst job aboard.

The final task was mine. I hauled in the small plankton net, its mouth somewhat bigger than a basketball hoop, and collected its plankton catch. After its thirty-minute tow, it appeared empty. But if one gently flushed the mesh sides with water, a green mass would accumulate at the bottom, perhaps a cupful of plankton. A marvellous and diverse bestiary, these drifting, mostly single-celled organisms are usually too small to see, but are stunning gems of infinite complexity through a simple microscope. Some produce through photosynthesis, some consume other plankton, some are decomposers. Together with ocean plankton, they are the great base of the global food web.

I thought the chlorophyll-rich, fresh-smelling aggregate looked almost appetizing, like pesto or some sort of health food. When I made this observation to Mike Stainton, his stricken look suggested he had overesteemed my intelligence. He warned me sternly that there were probably enough toxic blue-greens trapped in the filter to do me mortal harm.

The blue-green algae in my net were at the heart of Lake Winnipeg's problems. They belong to an adaptable group of species that defy classification. Producing their energy from photosynthesis like plants, they are also considered a form of bac-teria. Cyanobacteria, as they are called in taxonomists' Latin, are mostly aquatic, but are also found in terrestrial ecosystems. To defend themselves against predators, blue-greens can produce potent liver and nerve toxins. Livestock that drink from affected sloughs can die, as every rancher knows. Likewise deer and other wildlife. Swimmers, or commercial fishers handling clogged nets, can suffer rashes and nausea. It is even possible, in windy, turbu-lent conditions, to inhale the single-celled creatures.

While blue-greens are just as much rightful citizens of lake ecosystems as loons or perch, eutrophication can shift the food supply unnaturally in their favour. Toxicity is not the only problem with great algal blooms. Anything that lives in a lake eventually dies and sinks to the bottom, where decomposer species go to work on them. The benthic mud is analagous to a forest floor, a place where nutrients are recycled. But the process consumes oxygen, and if algal blooms are too large, deoxygenated areas can spread through lakes, driving away anything that can swim and killing everything else. This process has produced persistent dead zones in the Great Lakes, especially Lake Erie.

After each stop, all the bagged and bottled samples were muscled down a ladder through a narrow hatch in the deck to the field laboratory in the ship's main hold. Some were stored in the refrigerators for later study, while others needed immediate processing. The tiny plywood lab was crowded for two, and someone had jigsawn a map of Lake Winnipeg in the door.

Everything was then squared away up on deck, the anchor hauled, and it was off to the next sampling point. One stop kept a dozen people fiercely occupied for an hour, not including the time it took to actually process the samples. And this was just one of sixty-five such points the Lake Winnipeg Research Consortium hoped to sample at least three times a year—if it had the money.

DURING LULLS, as we steamed between positions, Mike Stainton would find me at the stern rail and offer installments of his views on what was happening to Lake Winnipeg, the arc of his own career, and the failings of government science. Eutrophication, he said, was hardly a new problem. Nutrient overload from anthropogenic sources was all too common in both marine and freshwater ecosystems worldwide. It was the scourge of the Great Lakes, and I would be seeing more of it in my travels to come.

The deeper question was why, in the backyard of the Canadian government's most prestigious lake-science facilities, Lake Winnipeg went unstudied for nearly thirty years. And why, even now, the critical environmental science needed to protect what is sometimes called the Sixth Great Lake depended on a volunteer organization, a hand-me-down boat, and scientists working on their holidays.

Recognition of the eutrophication problem on the Great Lakes in the 1960s was the birth of modern lake science in North America, and Mike Stainton was there. He came west from Hamilton, Ontario, in that momentous year, 1968. A social revolution was in full flower, research money flowed freely, and science was going to help bring in the Age of Aquarius. The Freshwater Institute was established in Winnipeg by the Department of Fisheries and Oceans, one of many government agencies tripping over each other to study something new called the environment. Saving the Great Lakes was *the* top priority, and the best minds in limnology were recruited from the world over. Mike remembered it as a time when government research was entrepreneurial, with hotshot young Turks competing for advances and scientific curiousity setting the agenda. Mike worked extensively at the Experimental Lakes Area research station north of Kenora, Ontario, an internationally renowned outdoor "laboratory" of fifty-eight small lakes. There, he helped tackle one lake threat after another: nutrient overload, acid rain, endocrine-disrupting compounds, the impact of aquaculture and invasive species.

And the Freshwater Institute was not alone. In a classic example of government double-spending, the newly created Department of Environment Canada built its very own National Water Research Institute in Burlington, Ontario, and commissioned the *Limnos*, a custom forty-five-metre Great Lakes research vessel. With millions of voters inhabiting their shores, the Laurentian Great Lakes were—and continue to be—an easy spending target in Canada. To date, the country has spent some eleven billion dollars on Lake Erie alone. Under the terms of the Great Lakes Water Quality Agreement signed by Richard Nixon and Pierre Trudeau in 1972, American agencies responded in kind.

Unfortunately, the bioscience revolution Mike joined in the late sixties veered away from its youthful promise. As the Kennedy afterglow became a Reagan-Thatcher hangover, Mike watched as government agencies began to reel in their budgets and their borders of influence. It was no longer scientists who set the agenda, but managers, and administrative gaps opened up among them.

One of these gaps was wide enough to admit Lake Winnipeg.

Officially, neither the Department of Fisheries and Oceans nor Environment Canada takes responsibility for Lake Winnipeg. The DFO is mandated to monitor only the commercial fishery. EC, with a staff of 6,500, contends that management of the lake is a provincial responsibility because the lake lies fully within the province of Manitoba. It is true that since 1930, Canadian provinces have enjoyed the right to be stewards of their "own" natural resources. But it remains a federal responsibility to provide the necessary science for the provinces to steward these resources effectively. Just what constitutes "necessary" science is perennially debated, and the environmental consequences of this Orwellian arrangement have been catastrophic not just for lakes.

Moreover, water defies placement in a single management category. Relevant departments include Health, Agriculture, Utility Power, Economic Development, Forestry, Transportation, Sewage Treatment, and Recreation, to name but a few. Such players are spread across three levels of government. And because Lake Winnipeg receives its water from four Canadian provinces and three American states, this confusion is multiplied to absurdity.

Somehow, none among this great swarm of agencies has bothered to study Lake Winnipeg for a long, long time. During Mike's entire career, federal research spending on the lake was essentially zero. As a very junior scientist, he made the last research cruise on the lake back in 1969 aboard the MV *Bradbury*, which now sits on the lawn at the Selkirk Maritime Museum. Federal scientists would not venture onto the lake again for twenty-nine years.

Mike, who had been gazing aft over the *Namao's* wake as he finished up this history, now turned to me. "What I always ask people is, whose responsibility is the lake? It's everyone's. That's why we formed the consortium."

In 1999, Mike Stainton and several colleagues from the Department of Fisheries and Oceans took matters in their own hands by founding the Lake Winnipeg Research Consortium. Though they started with little more than a name and a mailbox, they hoped to do what layers of government bureaucracy could not: bring real stewardship back to the lake. The approach was grassroots. The scientists enlisted citizens who lived and worked on Lake Winnipeg: cottagers, sailing club people, commercial fishers, pig farmers, First Nations band councils, citizens of Winnipeg, Gimli, Selkirk, and other municipalities. Though funding was spotty and the scientists were doing Lake Winnipeg research on weekends and holidays, the goodwill was nonetheless universal. At least *somebody* was doing *something*.

Ironically, the very government agencies that eschewed formal responsibility for the lake wanted to be included, in a low-profile way, in this communal effort. Instead of having it busted for scrap, the Coast Guard donated the *Namao*, provided only that she be painted any colour but their own red. The Department of Fisheries and Oceans began to allow Mike and his colleagues to use "discretionary time" on Lake Winnipeg research. Yet the scientists continued to wear their own hats, beholden to no one. They were citizen scientists, not G-men.

Whether this citizen science had come in time to avert a repeat of the Great Lakes debacle was yet to be seen. Not long after my voyage, Environment Canada would announce some eighteen million dollars in funding for a Lake Winnipeg watershed study, and enough federal funding for the ship was secured to achieve the Lake Winnpeg Research Council's goal of three full sampling tours a year. These were very modest contributions compared with what governments had spent on the Great Lakes. Perhaps the greater hope was in having found a source of lasting environmental stewardship. Leaving such things to distant bureaucracies, to mercurial governments with four-year visions, had not worked well, and government science had not saved the Great Lakes. Maybe citizen science would save Lake Winnipeg.

AFTER FOLLOWING the routines of the *Namao* for two more days, I left the ship at a lonely dock below Matheson Island, where we had berthed overnight in a dense fog. I did not want to overstay my welcome on an underfunded boat, but I hated to leave the great green horizon of water, the fireball sunsets, the sound of waves washing down the hull at night as we swung to anchor. The ship would pass to the south basin through narrows that were said to be beautiful. But Lake Winnipeg is too big to know in its entirety even over a lifetime. Besides, Mike Stainton's battered Toyota was parked there, and I could be helpful by driving it south for him.

The route wound on for two hours through poplars where migrating bald eagles roosted, hunting their way south along the lakeshore, pursuing the great vees of geese moving with the season. A few rustic buildings appeared, the remotest cabins kept by southerners. Eventually the bush began to show clearings and the first strings of barbed wire. The boreal forest gave way to parkland prairie, bur-oak pastures and saskatoon patches. With finality, the dead-flat land turned to grain farms, dotted by small Lutheran churches and motels called Valhalla.

The populated southern shores of Lake Winnipeg were ahead. This was the Republic of New Iceland.

About 75,000 Canadians are of Icelandic descent, about one-third of them Manitobans with ties to the big lake. In a wave beginning around 1870, many Icelanders settled the inland sea of Lake Winnipeg, believing it would allow them to live the life they already knew, to fish and farm in season. Though little known outside Manitoba, the lake society they built was a unique experiment in Canadian confederation. Virtually a country within a country, the Republic of New Iceland was duly recognized by the Canadian parliament as a self-governing, self-adjudicating territory. Officially, New Iceland lasted only a few years before it was swallowed by an expanded Manitoba, but the Icelandic character of Lake Winnipeg's south basin remains.

I detoured onto the marshy, wild peninsula that separates the north and south basin, today called Hecla-Grindstone Provincial Park. It protects a richly biodiverse wetland, low limestone cliffs along the shore, some parkland forest. The northernmost district of New Iceland, it was home to a small fishing village called Hecla. Fishing as a sole occupation did not continue long after World War II, and Hecla was all but abandoned by 1970. The New Icelanders left this stretch of shore much as they found it. As a legacy of their one hundred years of good lake stewardship, the departing residents cleverly persuaded the Manitoba government to create a wildlife refuge and to preserve the village itself. The park road climbed slowly out of the marshes onto the low limestone plateau that forms the north end of the island. The village houses were separated by large lawns that once were produce gardens, each home bearing a heritage name, like Birkiland or Breida. The houses may still be used as summer places by legal descendants of the pioneers. Old wooden vessels were hauled up for show; modern Gimli-styled commercial fishing skiffs made of fibreglass were tied at the government dock. The gravestones north of the church were covered in lichens that require clean air and undisturbed decades to grow.

Today the regional economy is based on catering to Winnipeggers who use the south shores for pleasure. Back on the main highway, I found the town of Gimli already busy on a Friday afternoon with city people arriving for one of the last weekends of the season. Gimli was the *Namao*'s home berth and the headquarters of the Lake Winnipeg Research Council. It was still warm, though the light felt faded now in the way that makes September both beautiful and melancholy. The great arc of beach was empty, but there were people strolling on the breakwater. I stopped for lunch at Amma's Tearoom, where they serve the kind of Icelandic fare you otherwise can only get at weddings and funerals—the *vinatarta* was almost as good as my mother's. Still reacquiring my land legs, I felt the phantom swaying of the ship as I sat at the table, my grubby-sailor appearance drawing sidelong glances from the aged ladies filling the restaurant.

Whether it was the comforting food or the warm fall day or just my own cultural pride, I felt increasingly good about the future of Lake Winnipeg in light of its Icelandic past. I was encouraged that care of this lake was finally in the hands of the people who actually lived by these waters, who had a personal stake in their future. This seemed a good place to stand and fight.

I passed south through the resort villages that were mostly all the same: small grids of cottages on streets that dead-ended on the lakeshore. Sometimes there was a beach. In places there were steep banks and muddy waves lapping right into the shrubs. In such spots there were often precarious, spidery lookout platforms built of rough sticks standing high over the water. Elsewhere the shore stood only a little above the water and sandbags were left to guard against storm waves and seiches.

Over the Toyota's AM radio came a story on the CBC about the record walleye catch being enjoyed that year by the Lake Winnipeg commercial fishery. Some happy fishermen were interviewed. They could not explain the good fishing, but one said it proved the lake was healthy. No scientists were interviewed, but they would have said what I had learned in the previous days: that eutrophic waters are known to produce some years of abundant fishing as a precursor to collapse. But even this did not cloud my newfound optimism in citizen stewardship. Besides, the lake was just giving fair warning—nature's distress signal—and there was still time to respond.

It was nearly evening by the time I reached Winnipeg, fought my way across town in Friday rush-hour traffic to the Department of Fisheries and Oceans, and found my truck in a parking lot just where Mike Stainton had said it would be. I traded his keys for mine via a commissionaire inside the door, feeling I had done my little part for the big lake, at least for one week. I still had an eight-hour drive home across the prairie, but there would be due payment. The sky was clear and would soon be full of stars. Venus was still up. The moon would appear by midnight.

ALMOST THE SEA

BRAS D'OR LAKE, *Nova Scotia*

The Millionaire had built himself an elegant summer palace at Baddeck,
with striking views of the Lake and the beautiful bordering countryside.
NEIL MACNEIL, *The Highland Heart in Nova Scotia*

COMING UP from the south, you first catch sight of Bras d'Or
Lake at a rise near the turn to Iron Mines. It sounds like
bruh-doo-ers when Nova Scotians say it, pluralized because its
convoluted surface is divided into different arms joined at a central narrows, so that it feels more like a collection of lakes. The
name is a French corruption of the Portuguese *lavrador*. Like
the Labrador coast, it derives from the title of the explorer João
Fernandes, who charted this part of the coast in 1498 and was a
landholder, or *lavrador*, back home in the Azores.

Stopping in a small pullout along the road, I shut off the
engine and walked down to the margin of sparkling blue water
I had crossed a continent to see. An apple tree growing on the
shore was dropping its ripe, red progeny directly into the waves. I
bent, put my hands in the clear water, and tasted a fingertip. Salt.

After the best days of fall have passed on the prairies, there
is often another full month of decent weather waiting in other
parts of southern Canada. That was reason enough to take a seat
on a WestJet flight to Halifax, then strike north to the end of the
mainland and across to Cape Breton Island. While my trees back

home were already stark, the hardwood forests of these ancient mountains were just beginning to don their tartan of fall reds, oranges, golds.

Then there was Bras d'Or. In many ways this island lake is unique in the country. A catchment for the runoff from most of Cape Breton, it is one of the largest gatherings of fresh water on the eastern seaboard. Yet it retains narrow openings to the sea. That makes it an estuary, but just barely. The tidal pulses of cold sea water flowing in do not mix readily with the relatively warm fresh current, which leaves some arms of the lake much saltier than others. With a foot in both camps, the waters are home to both marine and freshwater species. The temperature extremes bring subarctic species into proximity with subtropical species. In all it is one of the most complex aquatic ecosystems on earth.

Bras d'Or is also a culturally deep lake. The first people of Cape Breton are the Mi'kmaq, the easternmost Algonquian-speaking group of North America. Over the last thousand years, the lake has been visited in turn by every major European exploring and colonizing power. Norse sailors likely entered these waters. Giovanni Caboto, whose name adorns the strait between Nova Scotia and Newfoundland, may have anchored in Bras d'Or Lake as early as 1497. French traders settled soon after. But it is the Scots who settled in the nineteenth century who imprint this island lake most.

The Scots-Gaelic flavour of the area is nowhere more on display than in the resort town of Baddeck, on the west shore. Like Jasper, it is one of those sensible tourist traps that retains small-scale charm. The pace is *slow*. The tallest buildings are little wooden churches. In the high season, a nightly *céilidh* takes place in a hall across from the convenience store, the come-and-go crowd spilling onto the sidewalk along with the music. I walked along the waterfront and down to the government dock. The toy

harbour, the little lighthouse on the point at the mouth of Baddeck Bay—my mom has a refrigerator magnet she bought here
three decades ago, and the scene has not changed.

A little building the size of a child's playhouse served as the
customs office, a reminder that foreign vessels make landfall
here. Taking a seat on the bench, I surveyed the fleet swinging to
their anchors in the southeastern breeze. Among the usual plastic
sloops was a sturdy-looking blue-hulled cutter named *Atlantis*. A
wind generator spun in the rigging, lights glowed in the cabin,
and a string of laundry flapped along the deck. From the stern rail
flew a flag I could not place.

"Know where she's from?" said a voice from behind. A dark,
lanky fellow of twenty dropped onto the bench beside me and
began to roll a Drum cigarette. Michael was on his way to work an
evening shift at a tourist pub. He had his choice of such jobs during summer. But once these crimson leaves of October fell, town
would empty out. Besides mining, some perennially unprofitable
steel milling, and a few uncertain maritime jobs, Cape Breton
has little industry. Farming was mostly abandoned decades ago.
As it has always done, Cape Breton still exports its young people,
and Michael was going to Poland to teach English.

"I think that flag is Russian," he said. It was a good guess—
three horizontal stripes, red, white, and blue. The windmill
should have given a clue, however. As I was soon to learn, *Atlantis*
sailed from the Netherlands.

I ambled up to the local library, a one-room place with ship
models and a view of the water from the windows. Baddeck was
the kind of place where one could while away a winter reading
books about the sea, a tempting idea it seemed just then. A librarian wearing a tag that said "Laverne" slid me the sign-in binder
for Internet access as I approached the desk. Most tourists came
in to check their e-mail.

"Actually, I'm looking for a boat ride," I smiled at Laverne. She was a calm creature with a head of thick silver hair.

"Have you noticed the schooner?" she said with professional straight face, gesturing out the window. Tied to the Baddeck pier below us, impossible to overlook even for tourists, was a garish sailing vessel that noodled around the bay every few hours with a load of visitors strapped on deck. I explained that I hoped to get out with somebody local who worked on the water, be it fisherman, scientist, or pirate.

"Well," said Laverne, sizing me up, "if you like whisky, I could send you down to my husband. Maybe he'll take you out on his barge." This was cryptic, but promising on two fronts. She gave me his telephone number along with other contacts and sundry information, and I went out.

I was staying at the Inverary, a very fine, low-key hotel right on the lakeshore. The room telephone was ringing when I opened the door. A Dutch-accented voice on the other end of a bad cellular connection introduced himself with a name that sounded like "Snout." He was the skipper of the *Atlantis*, and he had heard from the librarian I was interested in boats. Librarians really are the most helpful people. About twenty minutes later in the Inverary lounge, I made the acquaintance of two Dutch sailors who grinned at me like teenagers out on a lark.

"We have sailed here from Holland," said the man, whose name was actually Nout, short for Aarnout. "I hope we are not being too, too . . ."

"Forward?! Yes, absolutely, and I'm glad you are. I looked at the *Atlantis* today. She is a beautiful cutter." This made Nout beam with pride. He was every inch a sailor, fit, tanned, a Rolex watch bearing the scars of a life on deck. Jolanda, fair-haired and bright-eyed, had beautiful high cheekbones and a slight overbite that, with her Dutch accent, reminded me of a femme fatale from a Paul Verhoeven thriller. They had been anchored in Baddeck for weeks.

Nout had worked twenty-seven years afloat, first in the Dutch navy, then the merchant marine, and finally as a river pilot. Jolanda was working for a shipping company when the two hatched the plan to sell everything they owned and leave the crowded Netherlands for the open seas. They had been voyaging for five years. They took the traditional explorer's route south past the Mediterranean, picking up the trades across, poking around the Caribbean, retreating to the American east coast each hurricane season. Some cruisers make a lap around the entire planet in less time, but these two were more interested in people and life ashore than in lonely, epic crossings.

Netherlanders are the great internationalists, and it was fun to hear their views about this coast. In many ways it was more their backyard than mine; also, as would become apparent in the coming days, this corner of the country was increasingly being colonized by Europeans. Prior to coming into Bras d'Or, they had spent the summer cruising the Newfoundland west coast—just in the direction I was heading.

The pub began to fill up mostly with locals come to prop up the bar. A fellow with a guitar climbed a riser and began to play the inexhaustible regional repertoire—sea shanties, Scottish Highland dances, murder ballads, and, of course, "Farewell to Nova Scotia," reprised every set all night long. Many a tune became a sing-along, with whole drunken families belting out epic-long lyrics in reliably good harmony to boot. At one point we were the only three people in the room, including the bartender, *not* bellowing the words to Stan Rogers' "Barrett's Privateers" at paint-peeling volume.

From their Old World perspective, Nout and Jolanda found Cape Bretoners' devotion to a Scots-Gaelic tradition long past in Scotland itself just slightly amusing. The couple had lived in Scotland for a time, so you could say they knew shite from haggis. One day while touring around Baddeck, they had met a Scottish tourist who shared their amazement at the utter Scottishness of it all. Jolanda recalled the old fellow's exact words.

"It's ridiculous," quoth she in a Dutch-accented Highlands-brogue. "They're more Scottish than we are!"

Cape Bretoners may well ask, flintily, "And what's wrong with that?" Nothing, really. By the start of the twentieth century, there were some 100,000 Gaelic speakers in Nova Scotia, most of them on Cape Breton. Living around the lake, you could speak this poet's tongue all day and make a subsistence living from fishing, hunting, gardening. Neil MacNeil's classic memoir of his youth on the lake, *The Highland Heart in Nova Scotia*, captures this period before roads and the cash economy began to haul Cape Breton aboard the modern era. Assimilation and out-migration had winnowed Gaelic down to almost nothing before a revival movement began that continues today. Quaint though it may be, the Scottish tradition *is* Cape Breton. And it brings in the tourists.

As the singer and the crowd once more found themselves upon "the briny ocean tossed," we got ready to leave, but not before making plans for me to come aboard the *Atlantis* the next evening for dinner.

IN THE morning, I ate porridge in a fussy pastel dining room full of perfumed older ladies, mostly American tourists. There is a long and deep connection here with the New England part of America, or what Nova Scotians still familiarly refer to as the Boston States. There are many families with members on both sides of the border, creating fluid and friendly relationships up and down the east coast and a shared fishing and seafaring culture that predates both the United States and Canada. Following the great Halifax explosion in 1917, it was Boston that led the medical relief effort, the same day of the blast dispatching a supply train, which fought its way north to the flattened city through a blizzard.

Hoping to learn more about this cross-border neighbourliness, I was going to meet the librarian's husband. Gordon MacRae was a builder currently working on the summer home of an American customer, an industrialist of some prominence. Gordon was going out to the property that morning, and I was welcome to ride along. On the way down to meet him, Laverne's proviso about Gordon liking whisky played in my mind. I like whisky as much as the next man. A little more, probably. But the sun was hardly over the yardarm yet, and in any case the Nova Scotia government liquor store was still closed, and so I went empty-handed.

I met Gordon in a newly built boat shed by the government dock. He pulled up in a truck with a tag hanging from the mirror that read "Old Fart" and bid a quietly friendly good morning. He wore a suit of blue denim work clothes with his name printed on the pocket, and a pair of vintage eighties eyeglasses clouded by a skim of sawdust. This codger appearance was something of a guise, for Gordon was younger than he looked and possessed of that admirable kind of cleverness that does not flaunt itself. He traced his ancestry to all four of the original families who had settled the Baddeck River area about 1830. One of his great uncles had been a builder and put up a number of the local churches.

The lake lapped at the shop door in the morning sun, the light reaching into the loft where hardwood was stacked. Having recently built a sailboat in a dank garage, I envied him his elegant workshop. We jumped aboard Gordon's aluminum workboat docked nearby, backed off, and steered out through the moored vessels including the *Atlantis*, which lay all quiet. By way of conversation, I told Gordon that I was myself a boat builder.

"Mine's a twenty-four-foot sharpie, a double-ender. I put a cat-ketch sprit rig on her . . ." Being here upon the east coast, I made free with the shippy jargon, adding a few more details.

"Sounds like a good one," said Gordon politely. "I needed something to get around to work, so I welded up this one 'ere." He referred to the very boat that carried us so capably into the chop of Bras d'Or. I looked around at the complex framing, the perfect welds in the tricky aluminum, all of which he had designed and built while in the midst of many other tasks. Then we passed one of the most beautiful small vessels I had ever seen, the custom-built launch Gordon's wealthy patron used to access his secluded estate up the lake. It was done in authentic 1930s style, a carvel-planked white hull with just enough brightwork, the Stars and Stripes flying from its little stern mast—the kind of floating perfection that graces the cover of *Wooden Boat* magazine. I said no more about my little plywood boat.

There was a brisk southeast wind and there was salt in the air, but the waves over which we pounded were familiar lake chop, not ocean swells. These were protected waters. The shores were still mostly green, the breeze warm. We were bound to a private island that had been in the family of Gordon's American patron for generations, bought from the Canadian government, along with a handful of others, for six dollars. The current patriarch—Gordon did not volunteer his name, and I did not ask—had spent happy summers here as a boy and now wanted to recreate the Baddeck experience of his grandfather's 1930s era. He had commissioned the lovely wooden launch. And then there was the cottage.

Approached from the water, it was unremarkable at first blink. But as you touched shore, the fine details emerged. There were two magnificent piers—one for the family and guests, the other for workboats—built by Gordon to last a generation, with lead-capped pilings. The understated house was no bigger than it needed to be to hold a small family, set on a cut-stone foundation with a slate roof and copper gutters. Under an eyebrow window, the name of the island was written. Power came from an underwater cable run from the main shore at fabulous expense. The gardener was the sole occupant of the island at present, a young woman in overalls who smiled at us as she pushed a wheelbarrow across the lawn.

Inside, the main floor was one large room—living, dining, and kitchen areas all together—as a cabin, be it refined or rough, ought to be. The wood for the trim and wainscoting was milled from poplar trees taken from the island. The double-hung mahogany windows more than any other detail bespoke the era of skilled handwork that the owner wished to summon. A row of black-and-white photographs on a knee wall of the upstairs loft showed just how ghostly authentic it all was, contemporary shots seamlessly mixed with archival ones.

As I sat at the unnamed millionaire's kitchen table, it was impossible not to admire his muted good taste and the builder's skill in bringing them to fruition, and I could imagine the bond of tradition between the two—Gordon and the American—that transcended money-wealth or nationality.

Although excess capital can be a scourge upon the Canadian lakeshore, this elegant isle was so peaceful, of such traditional elegance, that I hated to leave it. We returned to the boat and started back for town, running down with the breeze and looking up at the great promontory across Baddeck Bay.

Certainly the most famous American associated with Bras d'Or is none other than Alexander Graham Bell, whose estate, called Beinn Bhreagh (Scots Gaelic for "beautiful mountain"), occupies the high promontory opposite town. The inventor of the telephone was born and educated in Scotland, spent much of his working time in Canada, and became a United States citizen—so he is claimed by three countries. But there was nowhere he would rather reside than this hillside above Baddeck. "I have seen . . . the Rockies, the Andes, the Alps, and the Highlands of Scotland, but for simple beauty, Cape Breton outrivals them all," he declared.

Bell's inventions had already earned him wealth and a place in history before he and his wife Mabel discovered Bras d'Or Lake on holiday in 1885. The couple built Beinn Bhreagh, which soon became more than a summer home. The lake property served as Bell's primary research park and outdoor laboratory in the latter years of his life. Among his many projects, he oversaw the flight of the Silver Dart, the first aircraft to log flight in the British Commonwealth. It took off from the lake ice before an audience of dubious Baddeckers who had brought their skates to make a day of it.

For the seventy-fifth anniversary of the 1909 flight, Gordon built an exact Silver Dart replica from Bell's original drawings. It now resides in the Reynolds-Alberta Museum. He built a second machine that was actually flown by a stuntman for the Bell television biography, *The Sound and the Silence*. It crashed during the shoot, though not catastrophically.

"The original didn't fly any too well, and mine flew just like it," said Gordon.

Beinn Bhreagh is still owned by Bell's descendants. Dr. Mabel Grosvenor, Bell's granddaughter, born in Baddeck in 1905 and an early female graduate of Johns Hopkins' medical school, was the reigning matriarch. "She's up there right now," said Gordon with some affection as we gazed up at Beinn Bhreagh. "She's getting pretty bent over with arthritis, but she's sharp as ever." Dr. Grosvenor had just turned 101, the last surviving family member to have spent time in the company of her famous grandfather. She would pass away not long after my boat ride with Gordon, on the day before Halloween.

From the water we could see the Alexander Graham Bell National Historic Site on the hill above Baddeck, a fine museum showing the life and work of the inventor. Bell was a pioneer not only in telephony and aviation, but also in hydrofoils and airfoils as well as speech pathology, being at the forefront of

communication for the hearing-impaired. He never turned away
a family with a deaf child.

Tucked among the technical exhibits are the Bell family photographs. I had viewed them on an earlier visit to Cape Breton,
and they stuck in my memory. Reproduced poster-size, they are a
captivating record, not of science, but of a very modern family at
play on a Canadian lake.

The pictures were of unposed, happy people: Bell, potbellied
in a scratchy-looking bathing suit and full white beard, swimming
with his daughter at Ingonish Beach; women building boats; kids
climbing the viewing tower; a gleeful Melville Grosvenor, four,
pulled off his feet by one of his grandfather's tetrahedral kites;
Bell running with open arms to embrace his little granddaughter
Gertrude, who has just arrived on holiday in a neat sailor suit and
shoes. In a picture taken a few minutes later, her neatly plaited
hair is coming undone, her shoes have vanished, and she is going
off in the company of a pet goat.

We came to Gordon MacRae's dock again and stepped ashore
in Baddeck. The sun was hot and it felt like a full summer, and
we leaned on the hood of Gordon's truck enjoying it. Gordon said
that the summer arrival of Americans from the Boston States was
a happy fact of life on Bras d'Or. Northern Europeans had been
buying a lot of property in recent years, and they were given the
same welcome. Gordon pointed around the hills above the silver
lake, where many a hundred-year-old farmhouse was standing
empty, the adjacent fields that once fed families now growing over
with brambles. Europeans had kept Mediterranean resorts for two
centuries. If an era of cheap air travel had widened the Old World
sphere of influence to touch Nova Scotia, Gordon was all for it.
Anything to keep Cape Breton from emptying out.

"All the young people are gone from our road now. All gone
out to Alberta, Fort McMurray, places like that."

I SPENT the rest of the day following the shores of the lake by car, a guilty pleasure for me. Cape Breton's little roads are inviting: winding, picturesque, almost traffic free. In quieter stretches you pass more people who are on foot than are driving. For these reasons, the island is a destination prized by cycling tourists, though most take the loop around the highlands with its stunning sea views. It was even quieter down here by the lake. I stopped often, at neat graveyards and tumbledown farms, to walk down through Acadian forests of sugar maple, beech, yellow birch, apple, and ash, always the silver half-salty water waiting at the hill bottom.

The afternoon grew late, and I was due for dinner aboard the *Atlantis*. I gathered a bunch of the small purple asters that were still blooming in ditches, returned to Baddeck, and bought a bottle of wine. I went down to the pier, and before I had even reached its end, Nout was at the oars of his dinghy, coming ashore to fetch me.

The *Atlantis* was the first real offshore sailboat I had ever set foot aboard. Jolanda came up the companionway to greet me with European double kisses, and Nout gave me the tour of the cutter's gear and rigging. She was a serious boat for open-ocean work, all business from chainplates to masthead. We went below into the warm belly of the little ship, where smells of a chicken dinner mingled with the salt of the air and the glowing lights of Baddeck were pretty in the gathering dusk. The boat had a pilothouse that served as a nice saloon in port. Jolanda put the wildflowers on the table, pleased by them.

Over dinner we talked of Newfoundland, where I was bound soon and from where these sailors had just returned. They had spent all summer cruising the west coast of that island. Jolanda produced a well-known photo book, *This Marvellous Terrible Place*, one of many portraits Newfoundland has inspired. It captures the innocence, the separateness, and the poverty of coastal Newfoundlanders, a fishing society now all but gone.

Every time the wake of a passing boat rolled under the *Atlantis*, I imagined a real cruise in her, the feel of her workaday motion in a real seaway. Nout and Jolanda had crossed the Cabot Strait between Newfoundland and Nova Scotia in fourteen hours. Nout revelled in piloting these historic waters. He drew out a modern chart of a section of the Labrador coast and showed me where it still bore soundings taken by a survey ship in the seventeenth century. I admit I dropped many less-than-subtle hints about hitching a ride, but my hosts merely smiled upon these entreaties. Even for two lovers, it was a tiny home.

Eventually, I needed to visit the head. This required instruction in how to manipulate the levers that opened the seacock and pumped the waste overboard. I asked my hosts if they had any qualms about this sewage arrangement. Nout uttered a Dutch version of *pshaw*; Jolanda said brightly that they did not flush any paper and that ducks and fish dealt with the rest very eagerly. But the topic made them uncomfortable.

Visible from where we sat was Baddeck's imposing former post office, the tall stone building now housing the Bras d'Or Lakes Preservation Society. The group operates an ecological museum detailing the many threats to the lake. Chief among these was sewage, both from ashore and afloat. Some seventeen thousand people live in the Bras d'Or catchment area, many of them using poorly maintained septic fields that allow excess nutrients to reach the lake. Large numbers of pleasure boats are drawn to the lake's excellent cruising: plenty of wind, no swell, and good anchorage. Sewage holding tanks were not mandated and are difficult to police anyway. Bras d'Or has a residence time—the period it takes for water to complete the journey from inflow to outflow—of forty years. Oysters, which can only be harvested from clean water because they serve as filters for pollutants, were under a fishing ban already.

We shifted to other topics and talked long into the evening. When it was time for me to climb up out of the *Atlantis* and go ashore, we traded addresses, future itineraries. They intended to haul the boat out on Cape Breton and spend the winter in a rented house. All of us planned to visit the Saguenay fjord the following summer, so there was hope we might meet again. I thought Jolanda seemed sad at our parting. The price of the freedom she enjoyed was that friendships made were soon ended.

I WAS going to catch the Newfoundland ferry out of Sydney in a couple of days, and used the time to complete a circuit around the entire shore perimeter. Everyone I met seemed to echo the perennial riddle of the Maritimes: hard to make a living here, sad to leave. Every half-hour an advertisement played on the car radio, selling the Alberta tar sands to the local work force. "Make good money this winter and be *home* for the summer!" said the voice.

At the Highland Village Museum just south of Iona, I bought some homemade jam preserves from a couple working the concession there. Jim and Donna MacNeil had done their time away in Alberta and had come home for good. They were busy putting up the fruits of the season. Jim was peeling wild apples he'd gathered, and Donna was making them into pies and jars of spread.

Donna and Jim had lived in Edmonton for many years and—following standard Cape Breton procedure—spent all holidays "back home." Twice a year they came all the way by car, driving around the clock. "We always made the trip in three and a half days one way," said Jim with pride. "Fourteen days a year we spent in the car." In semiretirement, they were part of a small but discernible influx of returning natives.

I followed the Baddeck River to a parking lot and hiked up to Uisge Ban Falls, over which pours the clear runoff from the Cape Breton Highlands, the pure water that fills Bras d'Or. This rich and diverse kind of hardwood forest is not found out west, and is much threatened here in the east. Many of the trees were unfamiliar to me, and the ones I knew were enormous. Rings of ripe wild apples lay under the boughs of their trees, waiting to be eaten by deer and filling the forest with their fruity scent. A kind of liverwort that Scottish pioneers used to make dye for cloth colonized the lower tree trunks.

At the northern end of the lake some modest cottage subdivisions had grown within reach of urban Sydney. The cabins were some of the tiniest little houses I had seen outside of Waskesiu, and I admired them greatly. Gentrification and overbuilding seemed not to have taken root here, though perhaps it might soon. I passed hundreds of realtors' signs; it seemed the whole lakeshore was on the market, and at prices that were attractive even by a writer's standards. The properties were mostly small pioneer farms that had always provided sustenance but could never raise much cash. The weather was too cold, the soil too rocky and thin, the northerly light too little, markets too far off. It all seemed incredibly ripe for the taking by the *Architectural Digest* crowd. But this was Cape Breton, not Cape Cod. Boston was twelve hours away by car—too far for a weekend retreat.

I spent my final Bras d'Or night in St. Peter's—one of North America's oldest habitations, founded as Saint Pierre in 1630 by New France, when Cape Breton was still called Ile Royale and Louisbourg was the seat of power on the Atlantic seaboard. Bras d'Or was then separated from the Atlantic by an eight-hundred-metre granite isthmus. Beginning in 1854, it took fifteen years to cut a canal. During Cape Breton's coal-mining-and-steel heyday it carried heavy commercial traffic. But, like Louisbourg, it too is now a national historic site and used almost exclusively by pleasure boats.

In the little house by the canal, I found the lockmaster, who seemed surprised to have any company now that the summer was over.

"We got 995 through so far this season, mostly in July and August," he said, showing me his canal log. He had snapshots of the more opulent vessels. "These folks here like to spend a lot o' money." One cruiser had a helicopter on its afterdeck. I wondered if it had a sewage tank.

Bras d'Or had staked its future on being a playground, drawing discretionary wealth from afar. By contrast, the people who actually lived here did not travel much. A soft-spoken woman who served me dinner in a restaurant not far from the locks told me she was born in Newfoundland. She whispered this dreamily, as if this were a place as remote as a fairy tale.

"I was pregnant with my first. It was a hot July day, one of the hottest ever. The capelin were running, we stood in the sea up to our knees, and when you looked out the icebergs were floating by. It was so beautiful." She last saw it twenty-four years before.

Well, I was going to see it in twenty-four hours. I had a ferry to catch.

FINDING LAKELAND

THE LAKES OF GROS MORNE NATIONAL PARK,

Newfoundland

We found great store of paunds [on] every side as
we passed, and in every paund great store of beavers nestes.
FROM THE Willoughby Papers, 1612, cited in *The Dictionary of Newfoundland English*

THE BIG DIPPER stood on its handle as the MV *Caribou* eased into the windy desolation of Channel–Port aux Basques. It was wintry on deck, but bracing and fresh. I had slept badly in a sea bunk surrounded by richly snoring moose hunters. The ancient, worn rock looked cold, black, and unforgiving in the predawn.

Newfoundland is a surprisingly far ride out to sea, as visitors to Nova Scotia discover when they try to hop over there for a look around. The ferry between North Sydney and Port aux Basques takes seven hours in fair summer weather, whereupon there is a ten-hour drive to reach St. John's—if that is where you have a mind to go—which is a full ten degrees of longitude farther east than Halifax. I was not continuing all the way across the island but instead up the west coast, to look in upon some seaside lakes that were cousins to Bras d'Or.

It was moose season, and many a Newfoundlander aboard ship was combining a visit home with the fall hunt. This was no mere sport but a survival tradition, a filling of the larder in a land without significant agriculture beyond backyard gardens. There had to be plenty of moose to entice so many hunters, and I vowed not to drive at night. A bumper sticker showing a moose on the highway read, "Newfoundland speed bump."

Escaping the metal haw of the ferry, buying a cup of drinkable coffee from Canada's national caffeine purveyor, the rising sun striking the boreal forest—all these things brightened my mood after pitching and yawing over the cold indifferent sea. A short distance in from the coast, the bush became familiar boreal forest.

"You're comin' to look at our *pahnds?*" said the flummoxed clerk at the provincial tourism office just outside Port aux Basques. She was in a hurry, for the ferry had filled her workplace with tourists who all wanted to know, "How far to St. John's?" She said that lakes—ponds, locally—had little role to play in the life of Newfoundlanders, though she admitted there were people who fished for sport inland, who used canoes or kept cabins of one kind or another. "Almost everyone lives *ahn* the coast. The whole middle of the island is basically *ahninhabited*. In this province, we face the sea!"

Her hostility was fascinating, and it took me a while going down the road to reconcile it with the landscape. We imprint our worldview on our home place, and perhaps lakes were just too *Canadian* for the clerk to countenance warmly. Newfoundland's shotgun marriage into Canada only took place in 1949, and the foggy isle still wears stubborn solitude like a badge. There were plenty of Newfoundlanders still who looked upon the Maple Leaf as a flag of convenience, convinced that the island was in many ways better off as a separate dominion. Newfoundland refuses to be grouped with the so-called Maritime provinces, and is almost as large as the rest thrown together. You could say the island is a collection of solitudes, a lobed leaf of peninsulas separated from each other by treacherous waters and only recently strung together by tedious roads that arc far inland. Even the clock that chimes the half-hour seems to play on the backbeat.

In any case, Newfoundland is as densely lake-strewn as the rest of the country. At the head of St. George's Bay I stopped to stretch at Barachois Pond Provincial Park and found all the touchstones of lake life in their proper places: the beach, the campsites along shore, the outhouses, the docks, the upturned canoes dusted with fallen leaves. A school group was there on a field trip, the kids' ringing voices carried by the rippling water.

Then there were the moose, who knew lake country when they saw it. These great animals, standing as high as a horse, were introduced to the island in 1904, and there are perhaps 100,000 now. Like the beaver, the moose is extensively adapted to lakes. They happily wade all day and can submerge five metres to lake bottoms to reach the aquatic plants that are their favourite. They travel on lakeshores and can comfortably swim a ten-kilometre crossing.

The central dome of Newfoundland is indeed mostly uninhabited—which may equally be said of most of mainland Canada. The equal-opportunity glacial ice has scoured many lakes into the island and mainland alike. Even on the very fringe of coastal Newfoundland there are lakes, some of the most dramatic in the country, and it was these I was going to see. The Northern Peninsula follows the Long Range Mountains until they drop off into the sea. Tucked into their steep folds lie the unique fjord lakes of Gros Morne National Park.

At Corner Brook the Trans-Canada enters the Humber Valley and Deer Lake comes into view. As in Cape Breton, Europeans were becoming a presence in western Newfoundland, too. They were colonizing resorts in this valley in sufficient numbers to support regular weekly charter flights into the town of Deer Lake from London, England. In the hills above the lake were fine houses that belonged to these mobile migrants. There was golf, boating, and an extensive all-terrain-vehicle infrastructure. In winter, skiing was good at Marble Mountain, and snowmobiles took over the ATV trails.

Jet travel plays tricks with scale. London lay four thousand kilometres from this valley, about the same distance as Calgary. Is that near or far? Time in transit and price were the only pertinent factors. The charters were being subsidized by a property development called the Humber Valley Resort, a vacation destination that specialized in selling land to Europeans. Not long after I passed through, the resort was under creditor protection and the flights faced an uncertain future.

Newfoundlanders themselves were building cottages on lakes off the highway, though this seemed a more recent phenomenon than on the mainland. On Big Bonne Bay Pond were rows of cottages in a chain of subdivisions, but no second-generation infill places, no mansions. It looked like Carwin Park circa 1970.

The Northern Peninsula and Gros Morne National Park, established in 1973, lay just ahead on the Gulf of St. Lawrence. The archaeological record is scant on the western coast, but Paleo-Indian hunters likely crossed from Labrador five thousand years ago. The first people to winter on this shore in the modern era were migrants from the Avalon Peninsula who came to poach on territory that was called the French Shore. In the late 1700s, France had exclusive fishing rights to these once-rich waters, and settlers were not allowed. They came anyway, and France continued to lose its grip on North America. The settlers fished for salmon and cod, and took to the winter ice for seals. They hunted and trapped inland. Even by the dawn of the twentieth century, stocks of fish and game were in decline, and a logging economy took over. It was only after the establishment of Newfoundland and Labrador as a Canadian province in 1949 that roads began to reach many former fishing outports.

Today the park villages spill into one another, the colourful, eaveless houses sitting all at angles. I followed a road down to Norris Point on Bonne Bay and pulled in at a small sign: "Terry's B&B." Another sign on the office window said, "I'm in the shop."

In a little windowed building practically touching the salt waters of Bonne Bay, sitting in the warmth of a wood fire, I found Terry Parsons reading the newspaper.

Terry was an affable innkeeper with a salty beard, a pink nose, and a kind smile. He had been running his place for eighteen years. He liked company. He had a lovely, strong accent, but one I could understand without difficulty. The fall was much further advanced here than in Cape Breton, and the tourist season all but over. I took a little housekeeping cottage next to a graveyard. Standing at the kitchen stove, I could read the names of departed souls that slept just a few feet from my back door, many honoured with bunches of plastic flowers.

Terry said that I could find him in the shop each night and was welcome to visit, to share news of the day and a little vodka. He rode a big motorcycle, which was parked there in the shop with him. He said that his wife was away in St. John's visiting. He had the air of a man with the homestead all to himself.

With the dawn arrival of the ferry, the day was still fresh, and I set out immediately for Western Brook Pond, Gros Morne's most famous lake. It was true that lakes were mostly called ponds hereabouts, and rivers were brooks. But you never knew. I had seen both Pond Lake and River Brook on maps. Two of the biggest inland "ponds" were Grand Lake and Red Indian Lake. This time of year, Western Brook Pond was the only place where I could get a boat ride, just a tourist boat sanctioned by the park.

Western Brook Pond, Trout River Pond, and other lakes like them along this coast are freshwater "fjords" that have lost their connection to the sea. This untypical circumstance is just one of the geological marvels of Gros Morne. Cut, like many a fjord, by glaciers, these great fissures have been sprung above sea level by the process of isostatic rebound. The tremendous burden of ice that once lay kilometres deep over most of Canada actually sank the earth's crust into the fluid mantle below like an overloaded raft. It has been rebounding ever since, a few centimetres per decade. Here, a coastal lowland or sill has risen above the sea, stranding the fjord inland.

Even so, this doorstep is low and narrow, a soupy strip called Gull Marsh. I made the three-kilometre hike in over the bog with fellow tourists mustering for the voyage. This would be an unhappy place to be caught if a tsunami came ashore. Freak waves and storm surges have killed many coastal Newfoundlanders. The lake itself is a threat. A century ago, an enormous rockslide tumbled into the water, shooting a tsunami thirty metres high out of the valley. It would not take much in the way of global warming and glacial melting for the Gulf of St. Lawrence to pour inward among these mountains again. The watery shrublands had a barren, northerly aspect about them, and the cold air off the sea had an Arctic feel. A half-dozen caribou grazed near the trail, and the bent, stunted balsam fir—called "tuckamore" locally—told of harsh, dark winters. Moss and lichen lay thickly.

The boat mostly carried foreigners, especially Germans. The voyage inland was improbable as a Disneyland ride, down a corridor of near-vertical faces across a ribbon of icy water. I doubt the foreigners took in a word of the guide's rapid-fire, heavily accented *parole*, and the scenery made it hard to concentrate on words. It did catch my ear when he noted that there were as many as six moose per square kilometre in some areas of the province— which I took as a hunter's wishful thinking—but this proved true when I checked later.

After the first bend eclipsed the sea view, Western Brook Pond became a claustrophobic canyon in a crossfire of cold montane winds tumbling down its slopes. Sets of aquamarine waves marched past each other in opposite directions, like enemy legions staging for battle. For all its narrowness, the lake is profoundly deep at 165 metres, much of its bottom well below sea level. Even aboard our large boat we could cruise within a pebble's toss of the shore and still find plenty of water under our keel.

Waters near sea level are usually muddy and rich. Western Brook Pond is extremely low in nutrients, as is typical of the highest mountain lakes. It is considered ultra-oligotrophic, able to support only the most meagre food web. Here Mother Nature tosses her purest water virtually straight from sky to sea. Five hundred metres overhead, the aptly named Pissing Mare Falls could be seen as a wispy veil of water spraying straight off the mountaintop plateau.

At the head of the lake, we stopped at a tiny dock and put a solo hiker ashore. He would climb out of this valley, getting one of Newfoundland's most famous postcard views in the process— of Western Brook Pond from the top of the fjord. The tourists applauded his intrepidness as we backed off and the young fellow grinned and waved. I wished I was going with him. But the country was too big to see on foot all I wanted to see. Tomorrow I would get out under human power.

It was late afternoon after the boat cruise and the hike out from Western Brook Pond, and I went north to Cow Head in search of food. I got a wondrously big bowl of chowder in a hotel restaurant decorated in a seventies Canuck-hinterland style, which is to say, an austere grey box of a room. Its windows were so exposed to the bleak Gulf of St. Lawrence it seemed the grey water might pour in at any moment. I found it menacing in an agoraphobic way that outsiders must experience sometimes on the prairie.

"Oh, that's Shallow Bay," said the kindly matron unhurriedly waiting tables, waving her pot of undrinkably weak coffee at the impending sea. "The waves usually break out on the bar, but when it gets loppy they can run in a good way." Near the front desk, copies of the 850-page *Dictionary of Newfoundland English,* second edition, foreword by Rex Murphy, were on sale. I opened it and learned that *loppy* referred to rough seas. I also looked up *pond*, which sure enough meant "lake," as it did elsewhere on the east coast. As for the word *lake* itself, I was amused to find that it had been commandeered for maritime use: it referred to an area of open water amid sea ice, or water pooled on the surface of same.

That book was a marvel to explore. I doubted if a collection of western Canadian English would be enough to require stapling. It was indeed a world apart, rich and strange, this Newfoundland.

Though old by North American standards, it is a human experiment still unfolding. The population reached its peak a generation ago and has dropped precipitously since. Newfoundland has lost much of its youth along with the cod fishery. Though nets are still cast in these waters, fishing is no longer the overriding culture. From the Lobster Cove Lighthouse just above Rocky Harbour, I noticed a half-dozen commercial boats trawling picturesquely around the little bay. When I pulled in for gas, I asked a twenty-year-old woman at the counter what kind of boats these were, these little trawlers. She mumbled something incomprehensible, then asked me about the weather. I got the feeling she did not know anything about fishing.

Safely back at my little graveside cabin, I threw some gear in the door, then wandered down to the waterside shed with a box of local ale I had bought, to see if my innkeeper was about.

Terry Parsons was just where I'd left him, reading the same newspaper. It transpired that he had just bid adieu to an earlier guest, who had arrived not much past noon and recently gone wobbling off home three sheets to the wind, as one may say in Newfoundland. I suggested to Terry that perhaps that was enough visiting for one day.

"Not a bit, set down here!" he said warmly and pulled a chair up to his workbench with a flourish. He was still in fine fettle himself, if a little overdeliberate of speech and peppering it with more Newfoundlandisms than earlier. When the locals really let fly the peninsular patois, a mainlander cannot follow. The waves of Terry's speech were not so heavy you foundered in them. A bed was a *bunk*. His son in St. John's was *the young feller*. He used the word *altogether* for emphasis, the way I would use *really*, or *very*. When I told Terry about seeing the big dictionary with Rex Murphy on the cover, he said with real affection, "Ah, Rex, he's a good old son."

I thought I could listen to Terry all night, which is about what happened. He could well remember the time before the national park came, before UNESCO named Gros Morne a World Heritage Site. All of this has brought more tourists every year. Like the Cape Bretoners, Terry welcomed the tourists at a time when the future of fishing was clearly getting short and the population of the coastal towns was dropping away.

"They livens things up a bit," he said cheerfully.

As to lakes, or ponds, Terry had no particular opinion. He lived most of his life within sight of Bonne Bay, could point across to a light on the far shore that marked the house where he was born. He said that cottage building was a recent phenomenon that he personally had no need for, living as he did within a few steps of water. But if the English wished to fly over an ocean to enjoy Newfoundland's fresh water, there was plenty to go around.

Terry only once tried to move away from Newfoundland. The RCMP were recruiting, and he'd gotten accepted to the training program in Regina. "My father was never so proud." Yet with every mile he travelled west, the sheer expanse of the country seemed to argue against him ever getting home. At a hotel in Winnipeg, a mining company was hiring, and Terry impulsively signed on as a way of dodging fate. He found himself in the lake country north of Thompson, thrown into training for high-top hydroelectric work.

One day, while helping string a new power line, Terry was almost killed when a loop of cable fell across a charged wire. He had had enough of the mainland. "I stuck my spurs into the pole and down I went. When I got to the bottom, I took off my whole rig and dropped it on the ground and started off home."

Upon his return Terry became a ferryman, running a four-car vessel across Bonne Bay between Norris Point and Woody Point. His father had run his own small coastal freighter, carrying things like appliances and store-bought supplies to ports down the line, so Terry was, more or less, following in the family tradition. He once calculated he had travelled 100,000 kilometres back and forth over the span of less than three kilometres that filled the view of his shop windows in the gathering dusk.

Terry confirmed my suspicion that the young woman I had met at the gas station had no idea who was fishing in her bay, or for what. Fishing culture was fading fast and young people knew little about it. The little boats were purse seiners fishing for mackerel by steaming around in a circle trailing a net with a dory at the end and pulling the purse closed at its bottom. The catch was pumped aboard via hoses. If the fish were not of marketable size, they were put back to grow.

"Them that survives, anyway," said Terry.

Terry eulogized the fishery, told many a funny story about tourists; the hours passed, and the beer disappeared. In degree of inebriation, I had long since surpassed Terry, who could stand up to drink formidably. Having hardly slept the previous night aboard the ferry, I was all in. But Terry insisted on a nightcap up at his house, mixing up sickly sweet glasses of vodka, Kahlúa, and milk to pour down over the beer. I would rue this bitterly upon the morrow.

Amid this debauchery, the topic of Vikings came up. Leif Erikson—whom I like to think of as an Icelandic relative on my mother's side—probably stepped ashore on this very peninsula over one thousand years ago. For a certainty, some of his contemporaries did, for they left archaeological evidence at L'Anse aux Meadows (pronounced Lance O'Meadows) about four hours north of us at the bitter end of the peninsula. Discovered in 1960, the site marks the first known arrival of Europeans into the New World. Very likely the Norse populated many other spots. Erikson established a New World colony in a place he called Vinland—or Vineland—as recounted in the Icelandic sagas, though the exact site could be any of a dozen locations on the coast between here and Martha's Vineyard.

"Vineland. They called it that alright," said Terry. L'Anse aux Meadows attracts some tourists, and a recreated Norse settlement has been built for their edification. In his entire life, Terry had made the trip to the end of the peninsula only once.

"'Tis a far ways to go, and when you get there it looks like pretty much what it does right 'ere."

With an uneasy belly I slalomed my way up the hill to my graveside cottage, bid the dead a peaceful night, and fell into bed. I had but one lucid thought left that day: *What the hell kind of name was Vineland?*

MORNING DAWNED fair, a peerless sky over the old grey mountains. I was driven out of bed by a punishing thirst and a headache as though Thor himself was drumming my skull with his hammer. I had ambitious plans for hiking up the Tablelands, but now wanted just to lie back down for good and all. With a battle of will, I got myself out into the car and made an hour-long, queasy drive around to the south side of Bonne Bay. Perhaps fresh air would help.

As outliers of the Appalachians, the mountains of this peninsula are a worn, ancient grey, familiar to any inhabitant of the eastern seaboard. The Tablelands are a different world altogether, one cast atop another in a great fluke of geology. You don't need to be a scientist to see the oddity at once. Coming up from the South Arm of the bay, you round a bend and there is a yellow-orange massif of fractured rock that clearly does not belong. It looks like a mesa of the Arizona desert has tumbled out of the blue.

The Tablelands' origins are almost as unlikely. They are theorized to have been formed from pieces of the earth's upper mantle, a lower epidermis under the planet's crust that begins several tens of kilometres down. This particular mantle section was formed under an ocean bottom. The deep-born slab was ejected like shrapnel during one of the many plate tectonic collisions that built this island piecemeal over billions of years. Not only fragments of sea bottom but crustal chunks of primordial Scotland, Morocco, and China were added to Newfoundland at one time or another.

Mantle rock at the surface is called peridotite and is rare. An iron-magnesium makeup gives the rock its distinctive orange-yellow hue, though it is green when fractured. It contains few of the elements to support plant growth, and many heavy metals that are hostile to it.

Despite their desertlike appearance, the Tablelands are cut with flowing rivulets of water. Some areas are too wet to find good footing, and along these I was delighted to discover numerous pitcher plants, Newfoundland's floral emblem, growing to impressive sizes. Looking like small purple-red wind instruments from the pages of Dr. Seuss, the pitchers trap insects for the nutrients that cannot be taken from the ground. The Tablelands looked easily climbable, though the plateau at the top is seven hundred metres above the sea, not much lower than the peak of Gros Morne itself. The map showed a flat at the summit, many streams flowing off the top, and an area of wetland, and I wondered if I might find shallow ponds up top.

I started up, but the distances were deceiving, my head pounded on, and I was going through my water very quickly. What looked like an easy walk from below was really an extended boulder-hopping session that demanded unbroken concentration. The great blocks that made up the mountainside seemed ready to shift at every step. Suspicious of the ocean's ways, I fretted that a fog might develop, making the descent difficult. Just when I decided to turn back, I came into a hanging valley and found a large family.

They were the Robin Family Singers. The troupe consisted mostly of teenage girls—sisters and cousins—and two adults, Glen and Brenda. They were inexplicably happy. Brenda was somewhat overweight, looking very flushed and clambering much higher up the mountain than I thought prudent. But the girls were patiently helping her along, and not a discordant note issued from this blissful gang. Glen was a small fellow with a hockey player's missing teeth and a terry-cloth headband. He latched onto me in a friendly way, and we walked along the valley. His group travelled in a rusty van from church to church all over Canada, sang the faith, and led a financially precarious life.

"Do you have a relationship with Jesus?" Glen asked briskly, the way a banker might ask, "Have you considered a fixed-rate mortgage?" I said I thought he was a great fellow, Jesus, but I knew that was not to deter Glen. From his back pocket he drew out a Bible tract. He said I could read it later for myself, but basically it explained that evolution was a devilish lie. The earth was four thousand years old. The dinosaurs were as fake as professional wrestling.

Hearing Glen toss Darwin upon the hell fires of damnation as we climbed a slab of 460-million-year-old sea bottom, I was hard pressed not to laugh. But I cannot help feel for people who burden themselves with the care of others' souls—Glen said that his mission was to bring anyone he could with him to heaven—and so I listened quietly. I might have converted on the spot if he had had a bottle of water to share, for I was in a hell of thirst.

While he preached from boulder to boulder, I thought about the land under our feet and our need to perceive it a certain way, whether or not it matched the physical truth that nature had laid down slab by slab, ice age by ice age. We clung to these ideas as if to a shell of ego. The lady at the tourism desk thought Newfoundland was empty in the middle. Glen seemed not to see this earth at all.

When he finally paused for breath, I stopped and turned to him. In the sweetest tones I could muster I told Glen that my god (I left it to his imagination as to whether that was a capital G) had indeed found me. By grace, a sinner like me had been granted the ability to see divinity in nature. I hoped that my caring for it would be enough for me to squeak by on Judgment Day. As he listened, Glen was crushing no fewer than six of the lovely pitcher plants under his dirty sneakers. He wore an expression of resigned defeat and wished me well, saying with sincerity that he hoped he would see me "up there." He meant heaven, not the mountaintop, for Glen and the Robin Family Singers had decided to turn back.

The curve of the hill flattened so gradually it seemed you could never reach the top, and the boulders were growing huge. If there were pools of water up here I would have to climb much farther to find them. My thirst was dizzying, and I decided to give up. Then I turned about and took in the spanning view.

Around the valley, glinting like mica flecks in mountain rock, were dozens of small lakes, glittering on the lower plateaus of the Long Range Mountains, shining on the green coastal flats. A shallow pool lay blue far below on the lower margin of the Tablelands.

It was not far from the trail, but I had been unable to see it before. There were lakes I could not see, yet knew were there. Some-where under the south bluffs of the mountain wound the arm of Trout River Pond. The small ponds I was looking for were out there too, a mere two kilometres farther. I would later see them in an aerial photograph. The true essence of things depends on the right vantage point, the strength in your legs to get there.

Vineland. The word came back to me, like an unsolved riddle. Why did the first Europeans to lay eyes on this continent use that word?

The name suggested little. *Vineland* was the title of an impen-etrable Thomas Pynchon novel. In the Norse language, *vinland* could have meant either "vineland" or "meadowland," etymolo-gists say. The sagas also refer to Markland, thought to refer to the forested coast of Labrador; and Helluland, which might be Baf-fin Island. But those stalwart and intrepid Norse travellers were a sea people. They never came far enough inland, climbed high enough into the interior, to understand the true nature of the place they had discovered.

This place was not a land of vines or meadows.

The season was ending. It was time to make my way down the primordial yellow hill. Time to return along the peninsula and across the Cabot Strait, down the Nova Scotia highway past Bras d'Or, to the airport at Halifax. Time to go home for winter.

The last thing I saw in Nova Scotia before the clouds swal-lowed it up was a small lake. When we flew out of the weather somewhere in Quebec or Ontario, there it was, still under my metal wings—the country rolling by one lake at a time. Lake Nip-igon passed by to the north and I got oriented. Lake Winnipeg came up and I looked into its narrows, imagining I might spot the vee of the *Namao*'s wake. Riding Mountain marked the ancient shore of Lake Agassiz, and the zigzag of Lake of the Prairies announced the Manitoba-Saskatchewan border. On the long glide into Saskatoon, I looked down and saw we were passing just south of Little Quill Lake, where my mother was born. Tracing the grid roads by eye, I found the way right to her farm, could see the very foundation of the old barn.

This country, its story, was written in the shapes of these million shorelines. This was not Vineland or Markland. This was not a Land of Lost Souls. This was a land of lakes.

This was Lakeland.

THE ICE ROAD

LAKE ATHABASCA, *Alberta-Saskatchewan*

*The caribou spend the summers out on the plains, but in the fall
they migrate by the tens of thousands into the forests, where they spend
the winter. The Chipeweyans eat almost nothing but deermeat and
bannocks. The only trapping they do is to kill enough white foxes
to trade for ammunition and a little flour and tea.*

FARLEY MOWAT, *Lost in the Barrens*

I T WAS −16°C and falling on a Sunday night by the time I
reached the town of La Ronge. My headlights spotted two
small boys in thin jackets trapping all the drunks inside The Zoo.
Years ago, The Zoo had been the roughest hotel bar in northern
Saskatchewan. Maybe it still was. The boys, wearing neither mitts
nor toques against the bitter cold, had found an old broomstick
and wedged it through the door handles, cleverly locking up the
town's drinking problem, if only until the next thirsty customer
arrived.

Along with a consortium of white, middle-class sharehold-
ers from the south, my family once owned The Zoo and the La
Ronge Motor Hotel of which it is a part. As a boy, I used to travel
often to the hotel with my father, racing the carpeted hallways
with the manager's son. Though we sold our hotel interest and
retreated south when I was still a kid, years later I felt guilty that
we had profited by selling firewater to the natives.

Fortunately, the Aboriginal renaissance that spread across Canada in the late twentieth century reached La Ronge not long after we left. Indians were beginning to rally themselves under the new banner of First Nations. Today, the La Ronge Indian Band, one of the largest and most economically successful in Canada, owns much of the local business—including the La Ronge Hotel.

Perhaps I could leave the old guilt behind, for they seemed to run the place pretty much like we southern honkies used to, Zoo and all. Climbing up to my room, I thought even the carpet looked oddly familiar. Of course there is a political righteousness to Aboriginal profiteering. The café was decorated with wood-carved images of Cree industry: a skiff harvesting wild rice on a lake, a Northern Resources Trucking rig hauling fuel up a hill. They resembled the socialist realism of Maoist China.

I headed for the hotel lounge—not the Zoo—to have dinner and a beer and to map the journey to Lake Athabasca. The eighth-largest lake in Canada at 7,850 square kilometres, Athabasca straddles the Alberta-Saskatchewan border and is the largest and deepest in both provinces. It passes its waters down to Great Slave Lake, thence to the Arctic Ocean via the Mackenzie River. Its north shore is only about fifty kilometres from the Northwest Territories.

Lake Athabasca is usually impossible to reach by vehicle. But for a few weeks each year, a rough winter road, across muskeg, forest, and frozen streams, opens a temporary portal into the heart of the Athabasca country. The trip ends with a crossing over the ice of the mighty lake itself, to a radioactive ghost town called Uranium City. It is one of the weirdest automobile journeys you can take in North America.

Though southern money still fuelled most northern enterprises, Aboriginal people were increasingly in charge of their own future. I wanted to see what these new captains of industry had planned for the North. The trip was a homecoming of sorts. At eighteen, I took my first real job in one of the tiny villages on the lake, a place called Stony Rapids at the mouth of the Fond du Lac River. My job as an agent for the provincial airline, Norcanair, left free many magical days for tramping in the bush. I was hungry to see that land again, the more rugged and lonely part of Lakeland that lies beyond the belt of weekend cottages. And seeing the great sweep of Athabasca in winter plumage was a rare opportunity.

A tipsy young woman plunked herself at my table. "You come into a bar alone and bring fucking *books?*" she said cheerfully. "That's sad! You need company!" Irene was a Cree from Stanley Mission (she called it Stab-Me-Mission), a village on the Churchill River about eighty kilometres north. Irene was a carpentry apprentice, or at least the government was paying her to attempt this career. The state strives to shape northern Aboriginal people for the modern labour force. She went to school with a lot of big brutes and did not much take to her trade. She had pretty fingers and cared-for nails and was afraid of the table saw: "I hate that fucking saw."

We were soon joined by Irene's look-alike cousin, Sherri, steered by a computer instructor named Dwayne. Sherri seemed to be teetering on the edge of an angry drunk, glaring at me as she sat down. Alcoholism remains the scourge of the North, and these might have been just three more addicts. The women were under twenty-five but looked much older. Cousin Sherri had a newborn at home and no husband, and the jailhouse tattoos on her thin forearms read like hard-luck tales.

And yet there were positive signs you would not have seen in a bar in La Ronge even a few years earlier. The party at my table kept filling with students from Northlands College, where you can get everything from grade ten to a bachelor of arts. This new type of northern citizen had responsibilities in the morning, cared about a world beyond the horizon of a beer glass. Except for Sherri, everyone pitched in to a lively conversation. We discussed the role of computers in society, the appalling cost of fruit in the North. Everyone was impressed that I planned to drive all the way to Lake Athabasca in the dead of winter. We all headed for home before midnight, with money still in our pockets. Even Sherri's mood softened. Though we had exchanged hardly a word, she surprised me with a kiss on the cheek. I read it as a kind of Cree blessing at the start of a journey.

In the morning, a heavy storm was forecast. The road ahead would be long and rough: there were about 700 kilometres to the shore of the big lake, plus the 150-kilometre ice-crossing itself to Uranium City. The first part of the route is an all-season gravel highway, and a sign warned of heavy trucks for the next 400 kilometres. That the road exists at all is owing to the presence of uranium in the sandy ground of the Athabasca basin.

While Alberta is boastfully oil rich, Saskatchewan quietly produces about one-third of the global supply of uranium, used mostly to fuel nuclear reactors, and from which the fissile material in nuclear weapons is derived. Semitrailers ply the road hauling yellowcake, as the lightly refined uranium ore is called. The trucks neither slow nor veer, and cast a hail of stones at passing windshields. Each time one approached, I came nearly to a stop, yielding to their might. Three of these yellowcake roads lead north, branching to a half-dozen mines, mostly named after lakes: Cluff Lake, Key Lake, Cigar Lake, McLean Lake, Rabbit Lake.

Each of those lake-named mines has been a battleground between the uranium industry and the antinuclear protest movement. In their heyday a generation ago, protesters in Saskatoon led the national war of conscience against nuclear power. They could not stop mining altogether, but they helped bring regulatory control to a dangerous industry. The public relations battle was easier then. Much of the mining development capital actually came from France, a country aggressively expanding its nuclear program. The effete snobs sent out from Paris to wring radioactivity from the Canadian wilderness were easy to dislike. Three Mile Island was still a fresh wound. The world still lived under the daily threat of all-out nuclear war between Americans and Soviets.

The original protesters are now senior citizens, the Cold War is over, and even Chernobyl is a fading memory. The industry has grown in power and wealth. Commodity prices have soared, and the uranium business has the ear of political leaders and media owners and the blessing of the working class. Much of the public-image turnaround can be credited to the efforts of one uranium company, Cameco, which funds scores of worthy local charities and is popularly seen as a sterling corporate citizen. There are proposals to use northern Saskatchewan to store nuclear waste. There is even talk of building a reactor, and global warming has helped that cause. The environmental problem of carbon dioxide emissions excuses the environmental problem of nuclear waste, I guess. Plus, it promises northern jobs.

This is the great dilemma of making a living in the boreal north, for the beauty of the land is tempered by its fundamental scarcity. The only way to profit richly from it is by brute force: by inundating the land for hydroelectricity, by digging dangerous heavy metals out of the earth. Soils are poor, the sun is dim, the temperature cold. The coniferous canopy grows slowly; the animal populations are spread thin. Likewise, historically, Aboriginal inhabitants of the boreal forest were few and scattered, surviving by cooperation.

Not so many years ago, along the canoe routes of the Churchill and its tributaries, you could still often see the large white cabin tents Cree families would occupy all summer, hunting moose, fishing, picking berries. It was a vestige of the old life on the land before money arrived, and a way to keep young people out of city trouble during the long summer. Like cottagers to the south, they came to enjoy the outdoors and each other. Yet this recreational style was more purposeful than wakeboarding and suntanning. The fish and meat would be smoked, the berries dried. These nutritious wild foods helped sustain a family over the winter.

Lilly Wilson is a Cree grandmother of my acquaintance who as a girl spent summers in this way. She was born on the Sucker River Indian Reserve near La Ronge. Each spring upon her return from residential school, she went out to camp with her grandparents. Her grandmother dyed spruce roots in bright colours and used them to stitch up birchbark baskets for berry picking. Lilly was never happier than during those summers, weaving together lifestyle and livelihood, letting nature feed the spirit along with the belly.

In the last decade or so, the tents have mostly disappeared from the lakeshores. Lilly says it is simply because the elders who grasped this hunter-gatherer thread have passed on or have been too long in the city. Roads continue to creep further north, and the young people ride them away. Lilly herself drifted all the way to Toronto. Now she struggles to raise her grandchildren out of urban poverty on Saskatoon's west side. Nearly seventy, Lilly still dreams of going back to the North.

The Stars and Stripes, bleached translucent, fluttered at the turn into one of the fishing lodges that cater mostly to Americans. The semitraditional work as fishing and hunting guides is the only reasonably well-paid northern job perennially available to Aboriginal men. But the work season is short, and the clients demand a certain folksy servility from their Indian helpmates.

This quaint industry remains closed to women, except as camp cooks and cleaners.

Governments actively encourage any employment scheme for northern Aboriginal people that links to a "traditional" past. These are few. About eighty thousand people nationwide still work in the three-hundred-year-old business of trapping. These days it is the Chinese who buy wild fur. Even so, it is at best a supplementary income for the average trapper.

Wild rice, *Zizania palustris,* is a native annual grass that grows in the shallows of Canadian lakes west of the Great Lakes. The Ojibway harvested its brittle, protein-rich kernels into the bilges of their canoes by bending the stalks over the gunwales and flailing the seed heads gently. Wild rice was introduced to Saskatchewan, the modern variety considered the best in the world. A modest million pounds per year of the nut-flavoured grain, harvested from specialized airboats, is sold to health food and gourmet markets.

As for commercial fishing, even on highly productive waters like Lake Winnipeg it did not provide a year-round living. Lake Athabasca was far too cold and remote.

The clouds split, and sunshine poured forth for an hour. The stark aspens flickered by, white and black. Signs of increasing latitude were unmistakable. The AM radio reception faded. Perched low in a willow thicket was the white arctic grouse called ptarmigan. Somewhere on this stretch, though imperceptibly, the road crossed from the Churchill watershed into the Athabasca, from the territory of the Woodland Cree into the land of the Dene.

The transitional land between the Cree and Dene is one of the great cultural frontiers of Canada. A line angling from northern Manitoba across to Lake Athabasca divides the Aboriginal inhabitants of Canada's northern forest belt into two broad language groups. East of the line, running all the way to Labrador, are Algonquian speakers: the Cree, Ojibway, and Montagnais-Naskapi. Running west into Alaska are the many tribes whose languages are Athapascan (Athabaskan) and who collectively call themselves Dene.

Dene is a confusing word. Like *inuit, dene* simply translates as "people." Capitalized, it denotes the shared Athapascan language and the collective tribes who speak it. To further confound, the easternmost tribe, into whose domain I was now driving, is called the Denesuline—but this is usually shortened to Dene.

The Denesuline are still sometimes referred to as Chipewyans, an uncomplimentary Cree word meaning "enemy," and rivalries among Aboriginal groups exist, as they exist along every cultural border. Farley Mowat used this term in his widely read children's books *Lost in the Barrens* and *Curse of the Viking Grave*, set in northern Manitoba. However, his Cree and Dene characters are portrayed as close allies, as they are in reality.

Absurdly, a pay phone appeared by itself in the ditch, like a last chance. A sign declared, "Highway 912 Ends," and the road curved into a tangle of metal buildings that resembled a set from a postnuclear sci-fi film. This could only be Points North Landing. Basically a low-budget transport hub in the forest that supplies northern uranium mines with workers and equipment, the evasively named town is typical of transient southern investment in the North. It had a long gravel aircraft runway, tanks of fuel, and maintenance yards. There were no permanent residents, no nearby community, and no sign of a woman's touch anywhere. The only pretty thing was a half-tame fox that came out to sniff around my boots in the −30°C evening. Somewhere in this metallic maze I had a room booked.

Rooms are reserved for overnighting pilots, truckers, geologists, phone company men—and there was a cheerful bustle inside. At a prairie-motel price, I got a private room, acceptably warm despite the half inch of ice on the inside of the window. A trip to the only buffet in the Athabasca watershed was included— chicken, lasagna, plenty of vegetables, and a real salad bar.

That night a plane touched down in the blizzard and taxied past my window, a large turboprop carrying commuting mine workers. Most miners are non-Aboriginal city people from the south, flown in for weeklong shifts, living in bunkhouses and see-ing little of the North beyond the mine pit. For political reasons, mining companies make herculean efforts to train and employ northern-born Aboriginal workers, and have pushed the number close to 40 percent. Ironically, many of these no sooner get jobs than they move their families to southern cities.

IN THE morning, I filled my truck with diesel and prepared to journey beyond the pale. I did not know if the night's blizzard would have drifted over the winter road, but it was good to leave Points North. One day, when the price of uranium dipped or the road got extended, this temporary trailer town would become a pile of rusting metal.

An enormous sign announced the start of the Athabasca Sea-sonal Road, though the road itself would have no signage at all. Unlike normal highways, which are elevated and crowned in the middle to shed snow or rain, winter roads are cut flat, like a giant footpath in the forest. They are best used frozen, since they cross muskeg, sand dunes, ponds, and creeks. They can be deceivingly smooth and straight for a time, then turn to sharply rutted and hollowed—or just turn sharply—without warning.

At first I could manage only about thirty kilometres an hour, traversing dense fields of shoulder-high spruce growing out of a burn. Farther south the aspens would mature first, but the sub-arctic weather was too cold for them here, the actual tundra lying only 150 kilometres farther north. I stopped on a rise and got out in −38°C air. The wind gusted to perhaps eighty kilometres an hour. The stunted trees neither afforded shelter nor blocked the view, which was the same in all directions. I was cold with all my gear on. My fingers and toes, if not sweet life itself, depended on the continued smooth running of one Cummins diesel engine. The power locks on my rented pickup seemed to have a mind of their own, so I kept the axe in the truck box in case the beast shut me out in the cold. I carried food and water and enough warm clothing to survive many hours in −40°C temperatures. My faithful backcountry skis rode in the box of the pickup, and with them I could cover perhaps fifty kilometres at need.

I should say that local people took a far more casual view of the dangers. Not long after this break, I passed a car, the only traffic of the day. It was a late-eighties Camaro that, for the moment, was in running condition, packed with people and blasting southward over the hollows at spring-bottoming speeds. Its trunk was likely to contain just enough clothes for the occupants to survive a weekend of shopping in Prince Albert's Northgate Mall.

The first European to enter the Athabasca lakehead from this direction, a route little travelled even by the Dene, almost died on the journey. In 1796, the intrepid Welshman David Thompson had just been appointed mapmaker for the Hudson's Bay Company, and his first assignment was to explore the Athabasca, both as a new trapping ground and as a shortcut into the Mackenzie country. With two Dene companions he came northwest from Reindeer Lake, over the height of land into the Athabasca, then descended the deep sandstone gorges of the Black and Fond du Lac rivers. It is a dangerous trip even for modern canoeists with every advantage. The party arrived without incident at the east shore of Lake Athabasca.

It was on the return journey when Thompson—an extremely capable hand who travelled eighty thousand kilometres through the Canadian bush in his career—was swept over a three-metre falls. The party lost most of their gear, powder, shot, and fishing nets, though Thompson did save his trusty brass sextant. The trio proceeded to starve while making slow progress back to Reindeer Lake, saved only by a chance meeting with a Dene family who gave them enough smoked fish to get them home.

Thompson deemed the whitewater route he had surveyed too difficult for heavy fur canoes, and the winter ice that lingered into late spring on Reindeer and Athabasca cut the travel season short. The fur route to the Mackenzie was established further west, through Fort McMurray. Lake Athabasca remained a vast backwater until the flowering of the nuclear era. My era. I came to work in the Athabasca basin straight out of high school in 1979, joining a uranium boom that was about to bust.

After five hours of heavy pounding, the road swung around due north and followed the shore of Black Lake, the last lake in the watershed above Athabasca. High-pressure weather had followed behind the storm, the sky blazed blue, and the sun shone upon the deep new snow. The road turned back to real gravel, and just ahead, civilization reasserted itself in the form of a stop sign at a T-junction. To the east was the Black Lake First Nation reserve. I turned west up a familiar road into the little hilltop town of Stony Rapids.

Stony, as we called it, had changed little in twenty-three years: a few sand streets, a few hundred people, same RCMP detachment. I went to the airstrip, where I had held the grand title of Base Manager, lord of a one-room shack sixteen feet on a side, and where Norcanair's forty-passenger turboprop sked would linger as briefly as was possible three times per week, often with one engine left running. I sold air tickets, loaded freight, drove the company comptroller down in Prince Albert toward early retirement with my shoddy bookkeeping. Still, I never questioned the idea that an inept eighteen-year-old should be imported to a town full of unemployed Dene people.

Norcanair was one of the largest and oldest Canadian bush airlines. We operated all the classic bush planes made by de Havilland—Beavers, Otters, DC-3s—and were immersed in that uniquely Canadian form of aviation that used lakes as runways. Whether Stony Rapids was on Lake Athabasca or the Fond du Lac River was a matter of context. As the town name suggests, there was appreciable river current. Nonetheless, Stony was on the route of the lake sked, a thundering Single Otter on floats that leapfrogged along Athabasca's north shore. Into it I would stuff drums of fuel, toothless grandmothers wearing toe rubbers over their mocassins, snowmobile parts.

After a quick lap of town, I drove to the White Water Inn, a simple gabled box with all its windows shrouded in plastic against the icy drafts. The hotel café was busy with a familiar mix of itinerant southerners: a teacher, a camp man, a driving examiner. There was a touring husband-wife musical act called Dan & T.K., come to perform for the school kids. Fellow outlanders, we all began talking with one another about the place in anthropological terms. The teacher said that the standard curriculum did not work here, not on *these kids*. T.K., a lithe blond woman in tall moosehide moccasins, nodded sagely. She said she and Dan's stage repertoire had to be *different up here*.

The manager of the hotel, a woman who had been in Stony Rapids for fourteen years, said, "You can live here a long time, and no one really cares what your last name is. I like the people, the land, the pace, the not-keeping-up-with-the-Joneses. If they ever get a shoe store or traffic lights, I'm gone."

These, of course, were purely southern ideas. Though they typically enjoy uninterrupted, well-paid work and housing that is posh by northern standards, southerners can always go back to where they came from, and eventually most do.

The camp man had come to town to pick up his mail and have dinner, a weekly ritual. His name was Lionel Conant.

"As in Conant the Barbariant," he said by way of introduction. I had not seen the old Arnold Schwarznegger caveman movie he used for a calling card, but his delivery made us all laugh. Another import, he was hired simply to guard an empty fishing resort nearby from thieves and vandals. He had a wild reddish beard and the slightly scruffy mien people take on where hot running water is not plentiful. He wore stylish eyeglasses and had a pile of quality newspapers, including a Sunday *New York Times*, among his mail, and a hefty cardboard box. It transpired that we had some friends in common, and he invited me to visit him at his camp the following day.

Night had fallen and I went out on foot. My old Norcanair trailer sat with its bay window looking down the wooded path to the water. On Halloween night just after I had moved to town, the kids wrote "Tincanair" on the metal siding with a crayon. It seemed a friendly tag of endearment, and I left it there. An added porch covered the spot now.

There is little for kids to do in northern villages—no sports teams, music lessons, movie theatres, or malls. So I was surprised to learn that a kind of youth drop-in centre had just opened. It was run by Therese and Edwin Mercredi, an estimable family name in the Athabasca basin.

Outside, the place was unmarked and unlit, and looked like any other house. I opened the door a crack, half expecting to startle a family in their living room. Instead, a dozen kids were gathered around pool tables, and the smell of new latex paint hit my nose. And there was Edwin, looking much as I remembered him, though he had had children and grandchildren since. He called the place a pool hall, but it was really a homemade social agency.

"The kids, if they don't come here, they have nothing to do, except watch TV," said Edwin. "Or worse." Bored youth are easy prey for drug dealers, and Edwin figured there were a half-dozen serving the town of four hundred.

While overseeing pool games with hands on hips, Therese Mercredi said the lack of constructive activities in town for kids was not due to lack of money, but leadership. Parent volunteerism was not a local tradition—though she herself had learned it somehow. She was stern but eminently respectful to the kids. She racked every game, whistled down swearing and jumped cue balls, and charged the loser a loonie.

A young boy named Winston challenged me to a game. Like nearly all the kids, he was dressed like an East Los Angeles gang-banger, in baggy pants and a DayGlo orange hooded sweatshirt. He ran around the table, shot without aiming.

"He's hyper," said a girl. "He's on drugs for it." Everyone nodded, including Winston, who was actually sinking a few. He lost, but looked slightly hurt when I offered to pay.

Therese admitted that there were now more opportunities for Aboriginal youth—if you went south. Her youngest was twenty and in university in Saskatoon, but that was bittersweet. "Not so long ago, nobody went to university," she said wistfully. "Now lots of them do, but they don't come back."

Edwin had been on the town council for nineteen years and the area's first nonwhite RCMP officer for nine years. He saw too many hard things during his stint and eventually had enough. He referred to them only vaguely, darkly, and said he was writing a book about it all. I hoped fervently that he could finish his book, for the hard truth of northern towns and reserves—beaten women, toddlers freezing to death in search of their parents, fetal alcohol syndrome, suicide—must be told from an Aboriginal perspective. Alcohol and drugs were desperate problems when I lived here, and the road had only made things worse. Besides the drug dealers, there were many bootleggers, and Edwin had given up on the RCMP doing much about it.

Thus far resigned in tone, Edwin turned vitriolic when I asked him about his neighbours over in Black Lake. "Everything they have is paid for. They don't do nothin'. They play cards all night and sleep all day. Sugar diabetes is out of control." He said that someone should write a book about corruption among chiefs. "But they'd wind up dead."

Mercredi was, in fact, Metis. And whereas Stony Rapids is a Metis town, the village of Black Lake is on a reserve whose registered Indian inhabitants enjoy treaty rights and other benefits that Metis in Stony do not. When it comes to playing politics with well-meaning liberals from southern cities, the Aboriginal "community" maintains a remarkably united front. In fact, there are many rivalries among the people who think of themelves as Aboriginal: between status and non-status people; between those on reserves and those off; between Christians and traditionalists; between Cree and Dene, Dene and Inuit, male and female; between the chief's wealthy friends and the chief's poor critics. In all, it is a minefield that even Aboriginal people struggle to understand. Anyone who oversimplifies it is selling something.

When I drove onto the reserve the next morning, the village seemed utterly the same, except for having changed its name from the humble Chicken Indian Reserve (*chicken* signifying ptarmigan) to the Black Lake First Nation. A collection of unpainted shacks on the denuded western shore of Black Lake, the village displayed few visible hints as to the century we were in except ExpressVu satellite dishes and snowmobiles, a handful of cars, and a glittering new school built with southern money. Government largesse was still the only significant source of income. The yards were formidably stockaded behind tall, wrist-thick alder or willow branches driven into ground, perhaps to defend against feral dogs, maybe just to fill time. Some reserves are more welcoming to outsiders than others. Undented, clean pickup trucks like mine are an interloper's flag, and no one so much as glanced my way in Black Lake.

Modest though it was, stubbornly unchanging and insular perhaps, Black Lake had a permanence about it. The town's ties to the land that still sustained it were visibly painted on the lake ice as a thousand snowmobile tracks—subsistence hunting expeditions heading to all points of the compass. It would never thrive, but it would be here long after the uranium ran out and Points North Landing had faded.

The fishing camp where Lionel Conant stood guard was back along the road, and I went to find him, as arranged the night before. The sun came out in full February brilliance, though it was −29°C, and Lionel emerged squinting when I pulled into his yard. He had skis leaning near the door, and I suggested we explore together, but he demurred. In the box that came with his mail the previous day he had gotten a shipment of rum. He'd already had a start on it and planned to plug away all afternoon while reading the news by the fire. Men alone in northern cabins have their priorities.

"Hunter would enjoy going with you," Lionel offered. Hunter was a gorgeous pale-eyed husky cross with a bit of some leggy breed in her ancestry. She was thick-maned and completely at her ease in the cold air. It was agreed that I would ski until fatigue or darkness arrived, and Lionel would have moose steak for us that evening. I suited up and filled a pack with extra clothes, water, some energy bars, and we set off, Hunter in the lead. By the swagger in her tail I could tell she felt as good as I did about our unexpected partnership. In a way, this was better than travelling with Lionel, for two people must fill the day with talk that can spoil the quiet truth of natural places.

The caribou used to be plentiful here in fall when they came off the barrens and into the trees to their winter ground, squeezing between Lake Athabasca and Black Lake. The local people hunted them aggressively in the bottleneck. One late fall day I had gone fishing for arctic grayling with a fellow from the phone company who always brought his rod and tackle when he worked in town. It was a warm Sunday afternoon in mid-November, and we knew this perfect eddy where the hard-fighting little fish would hit our tiny brass spinners. With twilight falling, we had caught a small mess and decided to cook on the spot. Grayling are easily scaled with the back of a knife and, once gutted, can be roasted whole over coals with a forked stick. We ate with our fingers, the meat steaming in our mouths, and they tasted better than they ever did in town. Large snowflakes began to drift slowly down—the first of winter. Yet we were warm by the fire. Then we saw the caribou.

The animals were filing along the rim of the gorge just above us, silent and close. Perhaps because we lay so still, our scent masked by the smoke, they showed no concern. We continued eating the fish without speaking, watching their flanks go by in the snow that fell thicker each minute. More than a hundred caribou passed. For me, it was an exquisite, transformative moment of attachment to the earth, a simultaneous sense of belonging and of witnessing something divine. In some ineffable and good way, my life was never the same after that hanging instant.

Sadly, the skittish caribou have no longer passed this way since the seasonal road was built.

Hunter and I searched for the grayling eddy for hours, but the bush was altered by many seasons of growth and the mantle of snow. Dense, verdant spruce mats had filled in old burns, as inscrutable as a corn maze. Nothing moved, except a ptarmigan that Hunter scared up. My water ran out, and the long hours in the dry cold left me thirsty, lightheaded. I had no sense of the hunger I should have felt. These are warning signs that must be obeyed when travelling alone in such temperatures. I let Hunter lead the way home.

By the time I got back to Lionel Conant's cabin, I was deeply dehydrated and therefore feeling the chill. The heat of the fire was stupefying, and I drank a pitcher of water in one go before I could say much. Lionel was in no rush. He had marinated the moose steak all day, and his chair was surrounded by newsprint. The rum appeared gone, but he had a second bottle standing by for my arrival. I was soon revived by a succession of liquids sweet and strong, by warmth and conviviality.

Lionel and I sprawled all evening at the top of the food chain, filling our bellies on moose meat cooked to a delicacy. My host was a fine and roving conversationalist. We talked about the meditative life in the North, fallen priests, driving trucks, going back to the land and coming out again. And women. Entanglements in this latter category were partly the reason for him taking this hibernal, escapist job. The North is a perennial line of retreat from the oppression of normalcy, though Lionel would head south in spring. Sometime late that night, I left Lionel to his lonely guard over the interests of southern capital and made my way back into Stony Rapids.

THE HIGH-PRESSURE weather still held this part of the world in its bright, cold hand. After the exertions of the previous day, the long hours of driving ahead would not be such a hardship. Uranium City, that modern-day ghost town, waited at the end of the road, and I relished the thought of crossing the ice of Lake Athabasca. First, though, I had to endure yet another two hours of bumpy winter road following the south shore of the lake.

Just before the road went down the bank onto the ice, there was a final creek to cross. The road had already crossed many, but this one looked mushy, with water running generously over the top. I dropped into four-wheel drive and eased across. With a bang, the driver's side rear wheel broke through. The truck kept moving forward, but the lurch knocked my head into the door frame rather painfully. I very nearly got stuck within a truck length of the lake.

After 1,257 kilometres, I was at last upon the ice of Lake Athabasca. I got out and paced around on the strange new pavement. Before the road can be officially opened to heavy truck traffic each season, there needs to be at least seventy-six centimetres of clear ice. Officially there was twice that already, though just fifteen centimetres would hold up my little truck. The ice was beautifully clear, enough to gaze through in places, though there was nothing to see in the inky deep.

Immediately, the road crossed to the north shore and the white vista of the great lake opened to the west. Halfway across, I met a front-end loader being used as a road scraper and stopped to take a picture as it approached. The operator pulled up to a halt as he came abreast, and opened his cab door. A social call. I climbed up the ladder and met Ab McDonald, another well-known family name in the valley. He was six hours out from the town of Fond du Lac and would turn back when he touched shore. It had to be a long day in the iced-up glass box of the big loader, with just the clattering diesel for company.

The road was as wide as a major airport runway. Ab explained that with the insulating snow pushed aside, the ice underneath thickens, and it is desirable to create as wide a bulge as possible. The ice is tremendously thick but ever moving, like plate tectonics on a small scale, and fault lines or pressure ridges are created where vast plates grind against each other. Workers grind down the high spots or pump water from the lake onto the ice surface to fill the low ones. It's a good system, but equipment has gone through the ice before, with loss of life. Neither of us could stand the cold very long, so our visit lasted perhaps three minutes in all.

Modern ice roads are found across northern Canada, Siberia, and other high-latitude places. Mining companies maintain extensive private ice roads. Public highways like the Athabasca are less common. On the smooth surface I could average eighty kilometres an hour, weaving among rocky islets along the shore much as a boat would. The ice is too cold to be very slippery, but there is never a reason to hit the brakes. After an hour, the spire of the Catholic church in the north-shore village of Fond du Lac appeared.

After the Church, the single biggest colonial institution in the north was, until recently, the Hudson's Bay Company, which for 166 years had a retail and fur trade monopoly over almost the entire Canadian North. The HBC sold off its backwoods retail chain in 1987. The same outlets continue business under the utilitarian moniker of Northern Stores, selling everything from brassieres to shotgun shells at monopoly prices. A small mixed bag of oranges and apples costs as much as a good restaurant meal down south. Fresh produce is a luxury few local northerners can afford. People rely on processed nonperishables and the dietary Unholy Trinity—salt, sugar, and fat—at great cost to their health. Diabetes is rampant.

Like Black Lake, Fond du Lac is a reserve town where outlanders are studiously ignored. Thus I was surprised to be waylaid by a store employee who seemed eager to visit. There was a prescience about Doug Bruno, as if he knew I needed the information he possessed. When I told him I had come north to see how Aboriginal life and the political economy had changed in the last quarter century, he held forth for a full half-hour.

Doug, thirty-eight years old, was fierce in a quiet-spoken way. He told a story of systematic corruption by the local band, favouritism played by the chief and council, squandered money, lack of accountability, and runaway addiction problems among the young people who had begun roving in gangs by night. He said that the chief and council had gone two years without a local meeting. Its members travelled south at band expense but failed to report on their business. They drove new trucks and snow machines. Meanwhile, the village was virtually without a civil service.

In First Nations across Canada, the chief and council control every aspect of reserve life, from housing allotments to health care. There are no checks and balances, no formal opposition. This has led to abuses of power, fraud, election rigging, nepotism, economic development projects that line only a few pockets. A few reserves are shining beacons of good management; too many are nightmares. These realities are too widespread to be disputed by top Aboriginal leaders. Rather, they blame the colonial reserve system itself and the Indian Act that governs it.

Doug insisted I make a tour before leaving and see with my own eyes. The recreation centre and hockey rink, opened two years before, already sat empty, a load of sand dumped against the doors, its operating funds vanished. He told me to compare two buildings in particular. One, the health centre, was run by the province and looked well-kept and busy. Across the street sat the band office, its long-unpainted siding coming down, a large section boarded shut. "Walk around those two places," Doug said bitterly. "One is a real office. The other is a coffee shop."

When I asked him if he feared reprisal for speaking out, Doug said he cared too much about what was happening to the village, and risked losing no favours from the band in any case. Of Inuit ancestry and originally from the Arctic, Doug came to Fond du Lac in 1978. He still felt like an outsider. He and his wife paid many thousands a year so his two boys could go to high school down in Prince Albert, and the couple was considering moving south themselves.

With relief, I drove down off the village shore and back onto the ice. The problems faced by northern Aboriginal people are in many ways more desperate than ever, but the solutions must originate from within the community.

Ahead was some of the most beautiful and rugged country in the Athabasca. The trees grew large and the rocky hills climbed to hundreds of feet. It could be a stand-in for the B.C. interior plain. After I had followed this northern shore for ninety minutes, the ice road left Lake Athabasca and climbed into the bush. Ahead lay the mines of Uranium City, quiet as tombs. It was almost the end of the road.

When I last saw it in 1980, Uranium City had a population of 4,500. I travelled through there on my flights south from Stony, and the pavement, lights, and traffic were always a shock. There were schools, a hospital, a choice of hotels and restaurants. It had a movie house, and regular Pacific Western Boeing 737s landed from Edmonton. It was a pretty place, not a flat spot anywhere, the warm-toned bedrock visible. No one knew that the Eldorado uranium mine upon which the town depended was about to close.

I came into the ghost town over a rise on the east road, and the first sight I took in was the Norcanair logo, sadly faded and old-fashioned, on the staff rooming house by the water base. The view from downtown Fission Avenue was a grid of empty lots, a few boarded buildings. It was hard to believe a hundred people still resided in the area. A group of children appeared from somewhere and trudged off down one of the derelict side streets.

Fuel for the return trip was a priority, so I followed some directions I had to a set of rusty pumps and called the number that was posted there. A young man's voice said he would be along shortly. While waiting, I looked into the dusty windows of the gas station, the service counter inside stacked with faded cardboard boxes. I could not shake the impression it was all a movie set.

An old fuel truck came around the corner and pulled up right beside mine. A striking young man with shoulder-length blond hair climbed down and began to pump diesel straight from the tanker to my truck. Perhaps eighteen, he was dressed fashionably in snowboarding wear and seemed to have someplace else to go. I wondered who his friends might be, in this place.

The sun was beginning to run down, filling an already eerie place with shadows. The Candu High School had trees growing out of its smashed windows, and the gutted apartments on the hillside were a vision from Sarajevo, missing sections of their walls revealing interiors. Some of the older houses, many of which were fallen apart completely, were still inhabited. Now and then a vehicle moved down a street. The hospital was still open, the only enterprise that remained in town because the long paved runway accommodated medevac flights.

Eventually I came to what must have been the last houses to be built in Uranium City. The year 1980 was perfectly preserved in these cul-de-sacs that were still ploughed by some agency, though home to no one. I had imagined exploring the abandoned houses of Uranium City, seeing my breath in cold empty rooms. Now that the chance was at hand, it seemed prurient and morbid to do so. Ganged together in the dead of winter, in this remote place, these modern houses looked like the End of Days.

Gold was discovered here in the 1930s, then uranium, and these heavy metals were prospected and dug all over the surrounding hills through the years. During World War II, mining was shut down for lack of manpower. The advent of nuclear reactors renewed interest in the area. There were twenty mine sites over the years, but Eldorado was the biggest and deepest at Uranium City. It had thirty-seven levels, each thirty metres in depth.

In contrast to the rotting carcass of the town, the Eldorado mine site was swept clean as a crime scene when I found it atop a hill overlooking the place where the ice road came ashore. The

Sierra Club of Canada, MiningWatch Canada, and the World-watch Institute all assert that Uranium City is among Canada's most polluted sites. Watching my big Sorel boots disappear into the hip-deep snow as I waded across to the mine shaft, now wrapped in barbed wire and warning signs, I wished I had a Geiger counter.

Some in the mining industry assert that the Canadian Shield surface geology that has created Lakeland also makes an ideal environment for waste storage. After the metals are separated from their ores, the waste products, or tailings, must somehow be contained. Typically, they are enclosed within a berm, and the containment is allowed to fill with water to keep toxic dust from blowing. Cement might be added to solidify the tailings and keep them from leaching from their ponds.

Later I was saddened to learn that through a loophole in fisheries law, natural lakes were being reclassified as tailings ponds across Lakeland. In an investigative report for CBC's national television news, Terry Milewski showed how pristine Canadian lakes—lakes full of trout and otter, lakes at the headwaters of salmon rivers—are being turned into mining waste dumps. Dozens of lakes from British Columbia to Newfoundland had already been reclassified without public consultation. At this writing, debate over the legality of this practice seems bound for the Supreme Court.

I left the mine site and descended to Fish Hook Bay Lodge, a fishing camp that operates a few kilometres out of town and rents rooms to occasional winter visitors. There was no answer to my knock, so I walked in. A commercial kitchen served as the foyer. Beyond, in a carpeted living room with a large, dark television on the wall, sat one Harold Grasley. He was a bear of a man, with untamed hair, absorbed in a hand of internet poker. Turning about unhurriedly from the screen in a blue aura of cigarette smoke, he grinned at me gap-toothed and said: "The writer is here."

Harold was a friendly, blustering fellow who would have been a cornered badger in a real city. As for Uranium City, he arrived in 1960, age ten, and was now one of its longest-standing citizens. "I can count the people who have been here longer 'n me on one fucking hand," he beamed. "Want some moose ribs?" For the second time in twenty-four hours, a half-wild man was offering to cook me an all-wild dinner.

Harold knew his way around the kitchen, and in no time laid foil-wrapped potatoes alongside a preposterous quantity of ribs in the oven. While the smell of roasting meat filled the room, we simply sat and talked over beers—one each—from his private stock. I forced myself to sip slowly, knowing how costly it must have been to bring them this far north.

Harold did most of the talking and seemed to find my occasional observations amusingly naive. "Tell me the name of one fucking person who got left high and dry when the mine closed," he roared at me in a friendly but intimidating way across the kitchen table when I remarked how sad it all must have been when the shutdown came. "Name one!"

"All the houses in town were owned by the mine, except for just a few," he said in a slightly moderated tone. "Nobody was surprised when they shut down. That's how it works in mining towns." Uranium ore was quarried out of hard rock, the ore flown out on DC-4 aircraft. As new surface mines opened near roads farther south, Uranium City was no longer profitable.

The great feed of moose emerged, and I somehow ate my way through two finely spiced racks, keeping pace with Harold. He had even stir-fried some vegetables from the freezer. In all, it was an incredibly fine meal, and entirely unexpected from this uncouth creature, whom I began to like a lot. I continued to play

Barney Rubble to his Fred Flintstone. Grasley had not had an audience in a while, perhaps, and held forth on fish and game policy, tourism, and the need to keep the Athabasca watershed separate from the south.

After dinner, we took a drive through the dark streets that no longer seemed sinister in company. Perhaps I had passed some sort of compatibility test, for Harold's manner softened a great deal. He confided that he liked it here in the ghost town by the big lake, as locals call Athabasca to distinguish it from the many smaller ones around. He hoped a paved road would never reach this far.

"There's lots of uranium and gold left. It didn't run out. It just depends on prices. If the price goes high enough, people will come back for it."

Even if uranium's price did turn a happy corner on a piece of Bay Street graph paper out in Toronto, Uranium City was unlikely to rise again. Mining companies have learned their public relations lesson about building towns then knocking them down. Bunkhouses are far easier to get rid of than hospitals and schools.

Besides, mining interests have new public relations strategies in the North. Exploration companies are signing highly publicized cooperation agreements with northern chiefs. In these vague memoranda of understanding, the companies promise an unspecified share in any wealth they dig from the "traditional lands" of the chiefs and their bands. In truth, "traditional lands" do not exist except in a loose sense. Except for reserves, Aboriginal people legally own no northern land to sell or rent to claim stakers. Rather, it is all Crown land, and thus belongs equally to every citizen, Aboriginal or otherwise.

Such lopsided deals are entirely political: mining interests seek only the moral authority that Aboriginal partnership brings. They play upon southern ignorance of the North, upon southern sympathies toward a struggling community. They cast northern chiefs as rightful stewards of forests and lakes, as benevolent kings to their communities. They ignore the shady fiscal management record of the dysfunctional, discredited reserve system. Above all, they ignore dissenting voices in northern towns.

Eventually, southerners and their money go back whence they came, and so must I. At 6 AM the next morning, Harold cheerfully bellowed the time of day through the door of my room. I would not see him again, but my hibernating bear of a host had left coffee for my Thermos in the kitchen. Moonlight shone in the windows when I turned off the lights and stepped into the bitter cold. In ten minutes, I was bumping down onto the ice road, back to the land of cheap produce.

Out upon the Athabasca ice, the full moon was setting in the rear-view mirror, the sun rising in the windshield next to it—a lovely juxtaposition. The moon bowed away from the battle, and the orange sun stood over the lake, conqueror of the sky for a time. Looking southward far over the ice, I saw a fox moving at a steady, travelling pace. Where was she going? Shifting camp with the season? The sun would set and the moon would rise again before I was back on the prairie, sixteen hours from now. The days were brightening, would soon bring an end to this final cold snap of winter. In two weeks, the ice road would be abandoned to the spring melt. It would not be built again until the trees of the basin had grown a new ring.

EAT THE PEACH

LAKE OKANAGAN, *British Columbia*

Water, water, water... There is no shortage of water in the desert
but exactly the right amount, a perfect ratio of water to rock, of water
to sand, insuring that wide, free, open, generous spacing among
plants and animals, homes and towns... There is no lack of
water here, unless you try to establish a city where no city should be.
EDWARD ABBEY, *Desert Solitaire*

IN THE cruel month of April, desperate to see growing things again, fed up with gritty streets and dirty windows, losing my faith in the resurrection of crocuses, I abandoned the Wasteland of the prairies and struck out for Paradise. It lies in a precious valley in the western mountains. In that warm, dry vale, magnolias would be already blooming above lawns. Great cottonwoods would have spread their full canopy of leaves, and patio cafés would have their umbrellas out. And lapping at the end of every street, spreading warm blue under every lookout, would be the lake, not skimmed in ice but shimmering alive.

By grace and jet fuel, I was delivered unto the promised land. When I stepped out of the Kelowna airport, the sun hitting my chest felt like the warm embrace of an old friend. Make that an old girlfriend.

There is nowhere in Canada more inviting to the five senses than the Okanagan Valley in spring. It is a warm, dry place. And

yet, by some stratagem, verdant. The scent of its millions of blossoming fruit trees is fanned by gentle winds. The valley turns
to true desert in its southern extremity near the border town of
Osoyoos, where people go in shirtsleeves under the sun while
rains still strafe Vancouver. People are drawn to deserts for leisure
just as they are to lakes. Here, by some miracle of nature, they
have both.

Lake Okanagan makes possible one of Canada's richest agricul-
tures. The lake may be called riverine, which is merely to say long
and narrow like a river, a type common in mountain corridors. It
is only the largest of six connected lakes along the valley, all remnants of a single glacial lake. Yet Okanagan's 130-kilometre length
straddles the interface between the boreal forest and the great
American deserts that run all the way south to the Sea of Cortez. It
is a narrow hourglass, a portal between two very different natural
worlds, a reflection of both.

The Okanagan Valley and its watershed neighbour, the
Similkameen Valley next door to the west, compose a great biodiversity hot spot. Most of North America's birds can be seen
here. The range of the grizzly overlaps with those of the scorpion
and the California bighorn. Given so many ingredients, the area
tends to mimic other locales: California, Tunisia, Lebanon. Here
you could film a Bible epic or a Western, take your pick.

The Okanagan is a study in altitude, lying in a deep trough
cut by the glacial tides into the highlands between two mountain ranges, the valley bottom not much above sea level, the
rim reaching toward 2,500 metres. A vigorous senior citizen can
climb from desert up through subalpine in a day. Climatologi-
cally, it is a wonder. The Cascade Range to the west casts a rain
shadow over the valley, which thus enjoys warm Pacific temperatures, but without the downpours. Toward the Monashees on
the eastern flank, the precipitation shadow ends and twenty-five

metres of snow fall every year on ski resorts like Big White and Silver Star. Okanagan tourist brochures do not lie: ski in the morning, golf in the afternoon, view the city lights by boat in the evening.

Given such amenities, people have been pouring into this perfect lake valley for decades, gradually transforming a sleepy, agrarian backwater into . . . what? The highway from the airport, which I remembered from family car trips as a winding byway through orchards punctuated by mom-and-pop fruit stands, was now a six-lane freeway. Greater Kelowna had cracked the top five fastest-growing urban areas in Canada in the last census. New California-style housing developments filled every side valley, crowned every bluff, were offered for sale on billboards painted in heritage colours. One slogan boiled down the psychology of such vacuous places to six words: "Your life. Your way. Your town."

Downtown was still a collection of wide, quiet streets, like in any western town, the perennially generous magnolias for all to enjoy. Yet in the angle parking under their inclusive boughs were Ferraris, Rolls Royces. The spring boat show was on, and a fashionable crowd idly shopped the marina piers for thirty-foot cigar racers. There were a lot of new ways to spend money in sunny Kelowna.

I followed Pandosy, the road that used to take you more or less out of town along the lake, though town now followed right along. Gyro and Rotary parks, the family swimming stops that once exemplified the beaches-and-peaches Okanagan experience for 1970s station-wagon tourists, were still there. But they looked tiny and hemmed in by palatial houses, condominiums, and high-rise hotels going up.

I encamped just across the road at the elegant Hotel Eldorado, a low-key Kelowna landmark. The "El" is a European-styled lakeside inn overlooking the marina and public boat launch. It is a faithful copy of the Eldorado Arms, built in 1926 by an Austrian countess who catered to the ranching capitalists in the days before the Okanagan became a fruit-growing region. It retains the small-scale charm of a bygone era.

Spring is the best time for peering into lake water, which has yet to be colonized by plankton and can be amazingly clear. I took a stroll on the hotel marina docks. Carp worked the sandy bottom around the footings like hotel groundskeepers. I thought to rent a kayak, but the idea lacked adventure. The action was all ashore, among this throng of people.

Despite Lake Okanagan's fairly large size, its narrow breadth at any one spot gives it the feeling of a cultured pond. It has a warm top layer—having frozen completely just a few times in the last century—and is inviting to swimmers. It rarely blows up a gale. Compared to island-strewn lakes typical of the rocky Canadian Shield, which can appear labyrinthine and forbidding, Okanagan never cloaks its landmarks, more like a well-travelled canal.

As if to compensate for the lake's overdomesticated surface—like a debutante with a tattooed bum—the depths of Lake Okanagan contain a monster. Ogopogo's origins are folklorically deep. Both the Salish and Chinook people had names for the snake or beast of the lake. The English name Ogopogo originated in Vernon much more recently, a palindrome borrowed from a novelty tune of the 1920s. There are other lake monsters around the country, but none touches Ogopogo for brand recognition. More of an Ogologo, it appears up and down the lake on signage as a friendly dragon-headed serpent, sometimes feminized with mascara and lipstick. Ogopogo is easy to explain away. Rattlesnakes occasionally take a swim, loons have sinuous necks, and scale-distance illusions are common on the water.

Anyway, I was sure the real monster had already crawled ashore and taken the guise of a property developer.

Retreating to the inn's lovely lake-view restaurant veranda, I took a seat at a white-linen table among the Eldorado guests. A family of three sat nearby.

"I think we should pick up that condo this afternoon," said the man, looking out across the lake. The woman across from him did not look up from the *Globe and Mail*. Meanwhile, a girl of about thirteen was working on some kind of school assignment. The subject was "The Sixties," presumably, and the mother was dictating the words the girl wrote. "It was a time of great upheaval in society. Since the war ended, new political ideas were reshaping the world . . ." That kid would get a good mark.

"Two-fifty-nine—that's just seventy down," said the husband, idly scheming, "and our boat will be right across from us." The woman shrugged, nodded, not looking up from the paper. She continued her dictation " . . . a period of great wealth and prosperity was beginning."

That burgeoning era had filled this paradise to brimming, with people and expectations. Everyone wanted something from it: a condo, a boat, a glass of wine. The Okanagan was a blue-ribbon peach, and bites were being taken on all sides. The valley was filled with competing visions. It rang with many voices.

THE SNAKE MAN met me at a highway gas station, and we drove together up through a recently built suburb until the road dead-ended in a ponderosa forest. Mike Sarell was one of those people whose age is hard to guess. He had a greying mustache, but was slight and agile and wore an army surplus sweater like a Boy Scout. He reminded me a bit of Levon Helm, the drummer of The Band, and that dirge about Dixie's last night played in my mind as we set off along cattle trails under the rock face of the valley.

Mike's business was wildlife inventories. Like social work, it was a heartbreaking job some days. His surveys often became part of what are known as environmental impact assessments. Damned latinate jargon! An EIA is usually step one in paving paradise. Another new Okanagan neighbourhood was planned for the valley below. The houses and fractional condos would be bought up by migrants from Alberta or Australia. They would come towing wake boats, snowmobiles, quads. "Man must recreate," said Mike resignedly. Their blossoming yards, en suite bathrooms, and love of golf would demand more water from this semiarid country.

"I am intensely busy because development is happening here at an unprecedented pace," said Mike. For a conservationist, it was a tough position.

"Why do you keep doing it?" I asked.

Mike felt he could do more good from within the machinery of progress than from without. If he did not perform the wildlife surveys, someone less able would be imported, from Calgary or Vancouver. Wildlife habits and distributions, and their variations from year to year, are astoundingly complex and subtle, Mike said. Diplomas mean little without the kind of sensitivity to wild space—to *home place*—that can only come from a lifetime of experience. Unlike most of the people you meet in the valley, Mike actually grew up in the Okanagan.

"Newcomers think it's beautiful here. They don't know how beautiful it used to be."

We walked in the company of Mike's assistant, Wade, and two fellows on a work furlough from the local First Nations band office—Rob and L.J.—who seemed to want to be elsewhere. L.J. walked along sullenly, smoking.

"Nobody told me we were going to be looking for snakes," he said, petulantly but with real fear in his voice. "I wouldn't have come." After a brief, awkward moment, we all laughed together. The western rattlesnake was indeed our quarry, and I was not sure I wanted to find him either.

Mike called his business Ophiuchus Consulting, after the snake handler of Greek myth. I was fascinated and amused to see how a professional herpetologist knocked on doors. Scrambling across the jagged red-black talus, he tilted up every large flat rock he found. If no serpent was home, he carefully laid the stone back in place. The task was made difficult by a dirty plastic cast he had been wearing since receiving a nasty cut the week before. He found a small frog. This sun-blasted hillside felt dry as bleached bone, but the amphibian was coolly moist to touch and knew where water ran from the rock even if we did not. So did the numerous poison ivy shrubs that grew thick in the hollows. Leaves of three, leave it be.

Mike kept tilting rocks. He said that without expertise, this technique was dangerous. Red-tailed hawks routinely dine on rattlers, he added, as if this explained things. Presumably he, too, knew what he was doing, though at each rock his face was perilously close to the steep slope and the danger that might be coiled. Then he tilted a plate-sized slab and struck. "Nightsnake!" said Mike in a triumphant whisper, cradling something small and alive in his good hand.

The desert nightsnake was a startling find. Considered the rarest vertebrate in Canada, fewer than fifty have been positively identified here, most by Mike himself, mostly from shed skins or skeletons. Small and exquisite, this juvenile might rest comfortably on a two-dollar coin. Slightly venomous, she showed no interest in biting as she explored the warmth of Mike's palm, plotting her escape. Her body was slender as a cocktail straw, her head a tiny diamond shape. Over the radio, Mike summoned his crew for a look at this living wonder, pulled out notebook and measuring tape, and somehow lit a cigarette to celebrate the discovery.

With all of us gathered around the tiny creature, there was a party mood. Even L.J. seemed to awaken to his surroundings.

Duly photographed and measured, the nightsnake was restored to her lair, whereupon Mike immediately found another, this one nearly the length of a forearm. By dumb luck and excellent company I had been able to see in half an hour what few ardent Okanagan naturalists glimpsed in a lifetime.

We continued over the talus, Mike resuming his rock-flipping. He said he did not think the presence of nightsnakes here would be a "show-stopper," consultancy parlance for flora and fauna that can halt development. If an exceedingly rare desert nightsnake cannot do it, I asked him, what would? He thought for a while before responding.

"Recession."

The third snake I found on my own. Leaving Mike to his work, I decided to climb the bluffs for the lake view before hiking out to the road. The way grew gradually steeper until I came to a short scramble up a defile. Reaching for handholds, I heard a small noise ahead that sharpened my attention like a Buddhist's bell. It was a western rattlesnake. I had never seen one in the wild. Her warning was not the shaking-congas rattlesnake sound from a Western movie. To human ears, inured to roaring noises, it was almost an insect buzz, easy enough to miss if you were gabbing down the trail in company. But a more-than-fair warning from a being that itself cannot hear at all. I yielded. No need for venomous bites or six-shooter blasts. Tacking around her, I admired how the dusty grey-and-white flanks seemed the perfect crowning adornment to this rock world, the unperturbed water of Okanagan a ribbon below. She was stunning. Even Solomon in all his glory was not arrayed like one of these.

"IN HALF a generation, between 1900 and 1914, this valley turned from brown to green," said Wayne Wilson, historical geographer and executive director of the Kelowna Museum. He had worked for a time as a cowboy and had the kind of thin, rugged face that would look good under a Stetson. We were having breakfast at a table that was, like every good restaurant table in the Okanagan, in view of the water. Like in that Roman Polanski film *Chinatown*, the whole plot of the Okanagan Valley story is about fresh water in a dry place. Water, specifically for irrigation, was the switch that turned on the valley, let the desert sprout wealth.

"People see the Okanagan as this orchardist, bucolic setting. But what was the source of this landscape we drive though today?" Melting glacial ice wrote the first chapter. When Glacial Lake Penticton roared away to sea down the Columbia River, this valley was left with a chain of interconnected riverine lakes from Vernon to Osoyoos—Okanagan, Skaha, Vaseaux, Osoyoos— separated by alluvial fans that would make perfect building sites eventually.

The Okanagan-Salish people fished kokanee, hunted deer, picked saskatoons and wild onion. Their trails were used by the fur brigades of John Jacob Astor's era coming upriver from Fort Astoria on the Pacific Coast. Settlement began with Fr. Charles Pandosy, who built his Oblate mission in 1859 on what would become Mission Creek in Kelowna, when British Columbia was a year old. Pandosy noted that upon the fertile benches of the valley, anything would grow, if given a little water. Anticipating the future, he even found time to plant some grapes.

For decades after Pandosy, ranching was the only way to squeeze profit from a dry valley. Prime lakefront was occupied mainly by cows and a few starstruck cowboys with harmonicas in the fin-de-siècle west. Then dams brought the future.

Small upland lakes strung along the valley began to be used as agricultural reservoirs. The streams feeding Lake Okanagan were diverted in an extensive system of ditches, flumes, siphons, and furrows. The smart money began to subdivide the old ranches into small lots, and the orchardist culture that would define the Okanagan was born.

What shaped the future once will do so again. "Water is going to be a problem," said Wilson, a sentiment you hear everywhere in the valley. "Already there just is not enough to go around comfortably." The water flowing to the lake is virtually 100 percent "managed." About 70 percent is used for agriculture, which contributes almost one quarter of the B.C. harvest. Homeowners compete with wild plants and animals for the rest.

Newcomers mostly fail to understand how a valley blessed with many lakes could ever be short of water. Lake Okanagan alone is over 100 kilometres long and 230 metres deep. Yet it has an extremely long residence time of fifty-two years; only the top one metre is replenished annually. A study completed in 1989 suggested that existing water in the valley could support a maximum population of 400,000—provided agriculture was scaled back significantly. The valley was already full.

Yet regional governments continue to promote the valley to new settlers. The growth "industry" is retirement. The Okanagan Valley today is certainly worth more than ever in dollars, but it is producing less intrinsic value all the time. Today, the city fathers are intent on producing leisure where once they produced food. They have demoted labour from a place of honour and on its pedestal put indolence. The producers are also the consumers—the snake eating his own tail.

"There are two major urban regions in British Columbia now: the Georgia Strait and the Okanagan Valley," said Wilson. Despite the water crunch and bromine-coloured air pollution often visible in the windless, cloistered valley, he accepted the inevitability of more population growth: "You can't stop people at the bridge and keep them from coming in."

"HAVE YOU seen that movie *My American Cousin?*" said the voice on the telephone. "The Coke was the end of that era." Ken Ashley was a limnologist from Vancouver, where he studied lakes, fish, and the threats thereto for the provincial government. He had worked extensively on Lake Okanagan, heard I was in town, and called. The film he referred to was the autobiographical coming-of-age story by Penticton filmmaker Sandy Wilson. It was set in the summer of 1959, when Lake Okanagan was a sleepy rural backwater where nothing exciting ever came down the road to relieve the tedium of apple picking.

In many ways it managed to remain that way until 1986. Just in time for the Vancouver Expo, Premier Bill Bennett's administration pushed through construction of the Coquihalla Highway. A billion-dollar toll freeway across the Cascades, "the Coke" effectively reeled the Okanagan into Vancouver's backyard, reducing the trip to under four hours.

Ken had been part of the effort to save the kokanee, as the lake-locked form of the sockeye salmon is called. It was already in steep decline before the Coquihalla. Like its big brother, the kokanee goes upstream to spawn and die, dressed in ceremonial red. The Okanagan's extensive waterworks—channelization and straightening of creeks, flood controls, dams—had extensively damaged kokanee spawning habitat north of Penticton even by 1950. But the Coquihalla drove recreational lakefront development to new heights. A study in the midnineties found that 65 percent of the boat docks in British Columbia are found in Lake Okanagan alone.

In the sixties, hoping to prop up the kokanee, the province introduced mysid shrimp into the lake as a food source. Instead of feeding the kokanee, the mysid competed with them for other plankton. That was not all. Eurasian water milfoil, another invasive species, loosed from somebody's aquarium tank, now threatens to choke the entire lakeshore. Peak water use by people coincides with the spawn, leaving eggs high and dry.

Extensive stocking of the lake with hatchery fish is just PR, said Ken. "The public has been brainwashed to think hatcheries are good. They're a blinking neon sign that says, 'We fucked up the habitat.'"

Once numbering several million, the Okanagan kokanee population is down to 100,000. A keystone species like the beaver, salmon define the lakes where they swim. In spawning and dying, they transport nutrients from deep water to shore, kindly turning bright red in the process so that other species will not overlook a free meal.

Ken said that so much money and effort have been spent to help kokanee, so far to little avail, that there were those who felt it was time to give up. The kokanee was still doing well in other B.C. lakes. But Lake Okanagan will not be the same without the red fish. "There will still be a nice view, sunny days, and blue water. The winery tours will go on. But under the water, that self-sustaining ecosystem will be gone."

"AS A nation we have to start caring about where our food is coming from," said Nicole Bullock, the third-generation proprietor of the Kelowna Land & Orchard Company, est. 1904. KLO runs one of Canada's most productive orchards, turning Okanagan lake water and sunshine into apples. Once, Okanagan fruit was a specialty product prized all over the world. Plenty of good fruit is still shipped from here—25 percent of British Columbia's total farm output. But Fujis, Ambrosias, and Granny Smiths face cut-rate competition from Chile to New Zealand. Nicole had just come from a Kelowna supermarket: a kilo of B.C. apples was $2.10; imports from nearby Washington cost $1.65.

"I'll say it over and over: buy locally. It's up to us growers to educate people."

To that end, Nicole had taken the family farm into the new market of agricultural tourism. Visitors could now take tractor rides and learn the workings of a modern orchard, see the new tree varieties that use half the water of the old ones, and taste their fruit. KLO had also started a cidery and a restaurant. As a visitor draw, the business was a great success, giving seventy thousand people a year—many of them schoolkids—a chance to rethink the vital role producers play in a small valley and in a modern democracy.

"I don't know what else to do, short of sticking a roller coaster in here," said Nicole. She had the direct manner of farmers every-where, for producers' margins are too thin to waste time mincing words. She had a shiner over one eye—it is a fact of agricultural life that you may not always get paid, but you will certainly get bruised. Hers was the familiar story of the family farm in the glo-balized world: the work is hard, a great deal of operating capital is needed, the returns are marginal, the risks to life and limb are real. Young people find easier ways to make a living in town. One-third of B.C. farmers are age 55 and over. With no heir-apparent in her own family, Nicole was likely the last in her line. "That's why farms are now becoming lakefront property, with McMan-sions instead of fruit trees," she said as we looked down into the spreading city of Kelowna.

In theory, the Okanagan Valley is one place where urban sprawl should never happen. The Agricultural Land Reserve was legislated in 1973 to protect British Columbia's relatively tiny slice of arable land—about 5 percent of the province—from urbaniza-tion. The zoning law means you cannot simply turn a farm into a Cineplex or a drive-through. In practice, the ALR is an admin-istrative grey area that allows applications to be made, on such shifting grounds as "community need," to remove land from the ALR. And once removed, it will never go back.

Some friends of mine moved to this valley to take jobs a decade ago. New houses were going up in a neighbourhood near the lakeshore, off Sarsons Road, and they decided to buy. They could barely scrape together the down payment, but prices were climbing so fast it was now or never. Not long after they moved in, the doorbell rang. It was Mr. Sarson himself, the orchardist, with some fruit as a gift. It was the last he would grow, for his farm was turning into streets.

"KELOWNA ITSELF is not beautiful. The surroundings are," said Ingo Grady mischievously as we spilled from our minivan. Framed by the dramatic pelican-motif entrance arch, gesturing to the priceless view down to the lake behind him, Ingo welcomed us onto the grounds of Mission Hill Family Estate winery, an umbrella on his arm.

The director of wine education for Mission Hill, Ingo plays a very priestly role in the contemporary Okanagan, where wine is liquid gold and deep-pocketed crusaders quest along the valley for a case of the grail. I had joined a tour of wine aficionados for a tasting. Mission Hill is not the only good wine maker here. But as an arbiter of style, it is the ne plus ultra. "The pelican is a symbol of altruistic behaviour. We feel like we are the guardians of aesthetics in the valley."

The "we" referred to Mission Hill's owner, Anthony von Mandl. Like Ingo a British Columbian refined by time in Europe, von Mandl actually made his bulk fortune selling a very North American beverage called Mike's Hard Lemonade, a candied vodka concoction drunk to emesis at frat parties. Wine is a more boutique wing of capitalism. Von Mandl bought property here in 1981, intent on boosting the cachet of the Okanagan appellation just as his mentor, Robert Mondavi, had done for the Napa Valley. "I find it is easier to be altruistic when you have a healthy bank account," said Ingo, leading us down the promenade.

Recently re-visioned—*renovated* would be an inadequate term—Mission Hill is an architectural triumph, from its grassy amphitheatre to its twelve-storey bell tower chiming the quarter hour. "Dining is *al fresco*..." said a brisk-striding Ingo, gesturing at a single row of tables silhouetted against the blue lake, "...at a very high *niveau*."

He swept us into a great hall where a Marc Chagall tapestry hung, modernly. We sat like schoolchildren while he told us the short, happy story of Okanagan wine, casting it as the saviour in a flagging agrarian region. A video played, culminating in the image of a single grape, a sweet microcosm of Lake Okanagan itself, waiting to be swallowed. Then the screen magically hoisted itself away to reveal a kitchen behind it where a smiling chef, his face familiar to us from television, was standing over a rack of fresh loaves. Maybe this was the promised land; it sure as hell was Disneyland.

We rolled away from there an hour later, drunk at 10:30 AM. You are supposed to spit at wine tastings, but I was too shy and the juice was too good. It is impossible not to be charmed by the winery experience. It is an elegant form of landscaping, this viti-culture, each property appealing to the senses in its own way. It seemed, through the rose-coloured windows of our boozy mini-van, a part of the natural order.

Yet a vineyard is at best an homage to nature, not the thing itself. And the burgeoning business demands ever more from a slender valley—especially water. The Okanagan is still a micro-appellation on the global scale, but demand for more vineyards is extreme. Fruit growers can easily sell out their orchards for a price per acre that assures comfortable retirement. There were already over one hundred wineries—one per kilometre of Lake Okanagan—and the scant remaining virgin wild lands on the valley bottom were being converted to vines.

Wine culture was just one more force driving the tsunami of settlement. As we caromed around a freeway bend somewhere near Westbank, through a strip of cardboard-cutout retail, fast-food, and auto dealer franchises, a woman from Calgary sitting beside me in the van piped up. "I think my parents live up there," she said, peering uncertainly up a side valley.

"Can't you tell? How long has it been since you were last here?"

"About a year," she said. "All of this is new."

THE WILD Okanagan begins south of Penticton. Fifteen years ago, Doreen Olson came here to escape development. At sixty, her life had coincided with the age of urban sprawl. Having watched the once-humble Toronto of her youth spread around Lake Ontario, its wild spaces cut and filled, Doreen migrated to Vancouver—and the pattern repeated itself. Moving to these hills above Okanagan Falls just in time for the wine boom, she realized it was time to stand and fight.

She started by putting a legal covenant on her own land where we stood—a gorgeous vertical slice of Okanagan bio-diversity, from riparian to subalpine, where saw-whet owls were nesting—that will in perpetuity prevent it from being developed. Then she became an activist. She was instrumental in founding the Meadowlark Festival, a spring ecology fair that now enjoys international reach and for which the lieutenant governor gave Olson a Queen's Jubilee award. But she struggled to give her own work a label. "I try to bring people together, so they can learn from each other."

Olson is one of many Okanagans—the vast majority, according to surveys—who believe that a new national park is the only sensible response to the pell-mell rush of building. "Working towards that goal is basically all I do. It is important to me that this park go through, and that it is done properly."

To win one more convert, Doreen was taking me on a tour of the uplands west of Lake Okanagan that were being considered for inclusion in the park. For persuasive power, she had invited her friend Dennis St. John from the neighbourhood, who also happened to be one of the province's foremost butterfly experts. We wound through the back roads of the watershed past many acreages until we came to a field. We got out of the car, and stepped through a gate onto a trail.

"You are standing at the centre of biodiversity in Canada," declared Dennis. He had a grey beard and very long legs that I guessed had covered a lot of ground over the course of a lepidopterist's career. Despite some shortness of breath, he possessed a stentorian voice: "Amphibians, butterflies, nightsnakes, Brewer's sparrow, spadefoot toad. It's all right here." The shallow valley did not appear to contain much besides last year's tan-coloured grass. But the richest places in nature often cloak their wealth.

The new park would protect lands in the sos, or South Okanagan and Similkameen valleys, an area often described as one of Canada's four most threatened ecosystems. Six of the fourteen major ecosystem types in British Columbia—the most biodiverse province—are found in the sos. In all, there are 250 species at risk.

Parks Canada officially wants to establish a presence in the sos, but in the modern era new parks require years of negotiations. Indian bands with hunting rights and fouth-generation ranchers—especially around Keremeos—tended to oppose the park as a threat to traditional access. Others worried that a new jewel in the national park crown would draw hundreds of thousands of visitors into still trackless areas now visited only by California bighorns and hunters. Much of the land that a new national park would encompass already enjoys degrees of protection, including provincial park status.

"The land that is protected now is very subdivided," said Dennis as we stumped along the trail. "And the province has more parks than Ramses has children. Those are not Class-A parks, and the province is constantly pushing their boundaries to make room for things like power lines. They spend zero on research." It was true that British Columbia had over eight hundred parks, many of them tiny parcels devoted to recreation surrounding a boat launch or picnic tables.

"A national park is the highest form of protection we have," said Doreen, who chipped in whenever Dennis paused. "And they are good educators."

"Yes, yes!" Dennis said. He stopped, turned to me. "A national park is, above all, a repository of knowledge," he said. After a long career of studying butterflies, he realized that science had so far gathered only a little about individual species and almost nothing about complex interspecies relationships. Mike Sarell, the Snake Man, said the same thing. "How can we protect what we don't understand?"

On balance, I like national parks. But they are far from perfect solutions, do not address the fundamental human acquisitiveness that necessitates their creation. And by setting aside lands in one place, we only give development a freer hand next door. As plans stood, the new SOS park would do nothing to protect the scant remaining pockets of Basin Desert on the valley bottoms that are so attractive to human development. In fact, it would add to the pressure upon these by enticing even more people to the Okanagan. National parks are, after all, just one more perk for migrants.

On the other hand, the valley would not cease to fill with people if the park did not come. A third of the country's endangered species are here; one-half of the threatened species. The SOS was on a trajectory toward oblivion like the other three ecosystems on the list. Who, after all, knows where to find the garry oaks of Vancouver Island or the tallgrass prairie or the Carolinian life zone?

I signed the petition, for there was nothing to lose.

OSOYOOS, PRONOUNCED locally to rhyme with "a screw loose," is the end of the road, the U.S. border within walking distance of downtown. The Okanagan Valley marches blithely into the next country without a passport, but it is spelled "Okanogan" on the other side of the medicine line. The valley bottom here is baked all year. Osoyoos Lake is warmer than a heated swimming pool in summer, and the town regularly appears on TV weather maps as Canada's hot spot. People sometimes inaccurately refer to this dry country as Sonoran Desert, and Osoyoos is reminiscent of little dry-wash towns near the Mexican border. No saguaros, but the hills have that sun-blasted look. But the Sonora is the southern fringe of the North American desert. North of it lies the Mojave, and beyond, the Great Basin Desert. It is this northern form of the desert biome that reaches up through Idaho and Washington to touch the dusty hem of the Okanagan. It is also sometimes called antelope-brush desert for its signature plant species.

The pockets that are left are hard to find, having been mostly converted to orchards and vineyards. I passed the small refuge called the Osoyoos Desert Centre three times before seeing it. When I finally reached it, the last real desert in Canada looked not much different from the gravel parking lot. That's the thing about deserts: it takes imagination to see them at all.

"It's a tough sell," said Joanne Muirhead, wildlife biologist and director of this outdoor classroom for dryland ecology. "People think it's just weeds." We set off along the laboriously made 1.2-kilometre boardwalk that allows eight thousand people a year to scrutinize this fragile plot of antelope-brush desert without trampling it. We stopped often, getting on hands and knees to peer over the boardwalk at small mysteries: needle-and-thread grass, mouse scat, a coyote paw print. The ground was so dry, the plant stalks so brittle, it felt more like archaeology than biology. In the heat of day, in the long dry season, a desert guards its secrets.

Joanne's voice held a strain. She was suffering from burnout, common in wildlife advocacy where the stakes are high, money scarce, the problems plentiful. The Desert Centre lease was about to expire, and a winery was eyeing the land. Few residents showed an interest in conserving a site that is locally considered wasteland, bordered by vines, the highway, a landfill, and a sewage lagoon.

Virtually every animal you see at the centre is *listed*, biology jargon meaning "more or less endangered." Buttercup was the American badger living on the site. Badgers need about five kilometres of range, so Buttercup regularly foraged as far as the golf course, a perilous route that took her across the highway.

The valley bottom is a tenuous place for wild things, and their advocates. Kelowna takes its name from an Okanagan-Salish word for "female grizzly," though you will not find the great bear fishing in the valley bottom anymore. The kokanee is increasingly known as a beer brand. Because the badger cannot compete in the overheated real estate market, business is untenable for the burrowing owl, which depends on the badger to dig its holes. And so on.

The year-round human population was climbing fast. New migrants from Quebec came for the blasting summer heat; Albertans came in their RVs to dodge the prairie winter.

"People move here because of the desert climate," said Joanne. "What will happen when the desert itself is gone? Will they notice?"

THE LARGEST single remaining piece of the antelope-brush desert belongs to the Osoyoos Indian Band, also known as Nk'Mip. Nk'Mip (pronounced IN-ka-meep) is an Okanagan word meaning "bottomlands"; the skyrocketing market price of their namesake turf had made the Nk'Mip band among the wealthiest in Canada. They were razing their desert holdings to make room for their many business ventures: an adobe-style resort hotel, a golf course, an RV park, a large winery. The band was courting manufacturers to relocate there and trying to start a new ski resort up-mountain.

The centrepiece of Nk'Mip was a ten-million-dollar cultural centre, built with government money. It tells the story of a people's connection to the land and how the spirit animals made sacrifices in order to create a place in their perfect world for man. The grizzly had given his very life.

The band's business mastermind was Chief Clarence Louie. But when I went to meet him, his assistant said that he was "giving a speech to Aborigines in Australia on how to make money." She admitted that the pace of business on the reserve was fast. "We get a lot of flak even from our own people that we are over-developing." But, she reminded me, it was not fair to single out Nk'Mip on the development score while the valley was being exploited by people from all over the world. No, I agreed.

I descended onto the bench at Nk'Mip near a sign that said "Rattlesnake Crossing," threading my way carefully through the brush, mindful of where my feet trod. A desert chill came into the air as evening approached. Osoyoos Lake was turning pink in the last light. At that very moment, it was drinking upstream water than had been aged fifty years in the cask of Lake Okanagan. That was good vintage. The fauna that had been so demure in the heat earlier now began to assert a presence. Meadowlarks broadcast their electronic twitters from proud branches. Two deer came atop a knoll ahead. I followed an aimless arc until it was nearly dark, not sure if the land belonged to the reserve or to somebody else, only that it was sweet-smelling and cool.

Back on the road, a fellow in a truck stopped and offered me a ride back to town. Gary Dhaliwal was a fruit grower of Punjabi descent, like many others in the South Okanagan. Although Gary had come here thirty years before as a kid, and this was home, he said that many Punjabi orchardists also had farms back in India.

They stayed for the summer heat and the summer profits, then went back to the subcontinent.

When I remarked on how beautiful the section of desert bench I had just walked was, Gary said, "Good thing you saw it when you did, then. That will all be under vines soon. Within the summer for sure." He said the land had been rented to a multi-national wine company that owned many Okanagan brands and many others around the world. He seemed to know what he was talking about. He had rejected similar offers to sell off his own orchards. "Then what would I do? Take my kids to Vancouver to grow up?"

Gary dropped me at a pub, where I ate pizza and watched the Vancouver Canucks breathe their last of the season. *Requiescat in pace.* I thought of all the voices I'd heard in the valley, hoped they were more than a eulogy. I toasted the desert, with beer, not wine. It was still dark in the valley when I left, so I did not see it again.

RIDING IN BOATS WITH WOMEN

LAKE OF THE WOODS, *Ontario*

Even when the benefits are obvious—and what can be more obvious than the economy created by tourism—there is still an undeniable, abiding emotion that sticks in the craw of those whose livelihood depends on outsiders. Especially so if those outsiders tend to view the locals as support staff.

ROY MACGREGOR, *The Weekender: A Cottage Journal*

WHEN I first saw it as a kid, I thought Kenora, Ontario, was the luckiest town in the world. Not that there was much remarkable about its streets that wound over the northern bedrock, its red-brick houses, the old hotel. What made Kenora more magical than anywhere else, more than even Banff or Jasper, was the great island-studded lake stretching away south. The sprawl of islands was speckled with cabins, boats went busily to and fro, floatplanes landed—all these Lakeland marvels were available right downtown.

The view of Lake of the Woods from Kenora is still my favourite sight along the Trans-Canada Highway, a blue, rock-studded brooch pinning Lakeland together in the middle. Located close to Canada's longitudinal centre, Lake of the Woods marks the boundary between east and west. Whereas the lake belongs to Ontario, it is heavily colonized by Manitobans, who print it on their official highway map every year like an occupied territory. It straddles the edge of the Canadian Shield, its south shore touching the prairie—and another country—in Minnesota. Like so much of Canada, it is part of Lake Winnipeg's watershed, connected thereto by the Winnipeg River.

For me it was the western gateway to 1,500 kilometres of northern Ontario, a double slice of Lakeland I planned to cross during the summer days ahead. Upon reaching Ottawa, I would fly into Quebec for a week, then return for the drive back home. I would be on the road for a month and had filled my truck with camping gear, two bicycles, and an Alden rowing canoe strapped onto a hastily built headache rack. It was an absurd-looking conveyance that contained everything but my clothes, which I had forgotten at home.

Kenora's thousand-islands lake view stirs the desire to explore, and I wanted to get on the water. I set off by bike to find a boat, stopping briefly in Kenora's Lake of the Woods Museum, the town's top tourist attraction. The collection included priceless Aboriginal costumes preserved by Frank Edwards, an Indian agent from 1920–45 who worked among Sioux, Cree, and Ojibway whose territories each included the lake. There was also a rack of very old outboard motors that drew a crowd of very old men.

From the museum, I pedalled around the shoreline west toward Keewatin, one of the many once-independent towns of the north shore amalgamated to form Kenora. *Keewatin* is an Algonquian word that strikes my ear in a pretty way and means "north." But there have been less sonorous names for the end of the lake where it flows into the Winnipeg River. For 150 years it was called Rat Portage, a European translation of the Algonquian for "portage to the land of the muskrat." There is a persistent story in town that Maple Leaf Flour once balked at building a mill here because they did not wish to have the word *rat* appear on their flour bags. In 1905, Kenora was coined from the first two letters of the villages of Keewatin and Norman, and of Rat Portage.

Today, most journeys on Lake of the Woods begin in the town of Keewatin, which serves as a harbour for the sturdy crafts that are a practical necessity for cottagers whose island properties are accessible only by water. I followed Keewatin's mapled streets down to the Two Bears Marina.

Joanne Hill had been the proprietor of the marina for eighteen years, along with her husband John. They sold fuel, groceries, bags of ice, and navigation charts, and tried to keep greenhorns from mishaps at the boat launch. They bailed and tended 225 boats at their marina, charging about six hundred dollars a season. "People from Toronto think the price is per month," said Joanne without a hint of humour, hands on hips and sizing me up. She was an un-made-up woman of grandmotherly mien and stern manner. She had not made up her mind about me and my vague errand. She looked suspiciously at my notebook and my bicycle.

"So, you want to rent a boat with a guide," she said. Not quite. I said I wanted to learn about Lake of the Woods through the eyes of the people who worked upon it, the ones supplying the labour that made cottage life happen for vacationers. One eyebrow went up.

I spotted a picture of a lovely wooden launch not unlike the one I had seen moored in Baddeck Bay on Bras d'Or Lake the year before, and asked Joanne about it. This instantly won her over, for wooden boats turned out to be common ground between us. She had made a specialty of saving classics from storied Canadian boatworks like Cadillac or Peterborough. In fact, Two Bears Marina itself was once a boatworks. When she found a vessel languishing, Joanne would broker a deal between a suitable builder-restorer and someone with money and taste. Each summer, Joanne led a wooden boat parade along the shore of Kenora, everything from wooden kayaks to the *Grace Anne II*, a palatial mahogany yacht, built by Ditchburn Boatworks of Gravenhurst, that still goes about on Lake of the Woods. Launched in 1931, it belonged to Grace

Anne and John Furlong, whose family had spent summers on Lake of the Woods since 1893. The *Grace Anne II* can be hired for a few thousand dollars a day if you are interested.

Historically, though, typical vessels on the lake were not luxury ones, but simple and seaworthy boats. And, at least five days out of seven, the fleet was piloted by women while their husbands worked in the city. Joanne had been skippering boats since she was a girl. "There was no steering wheel, just a tiller, and you had to wind the string around the flywheel and pull-start them." She, her grandmother, and her mother used to boat into Keewatin every Friday and meet the lake train, the Camper's Special, which brought fathers out for the weekend. A station then stood on the shore opposite the marina. "All the moms and kids would be there, the rich ones with their boat boys." The ice house was there too, and trips into town both Friday and Sunday meant they could open the icebox all they wanted on the weekend.

Joanne said that, while cottages have always been a luxury, increasing prosperity had changed the social dynamic on the lake: "You have to be rich to come here. It is sad that long-time residents who have been enjoying the lake for years are being forced off by prices that almost reach Muskoka levels."

Meanwhile, the workaday economy of Kenora was facing hard times. The local paper mill had recently closed, throwing hundreds out of work and the whole community into an identity crisis. Hitherto a resource town on the frontier, Kenora was now servicing vacationers—forestry seemed to have followed fishing into the museum.

Joanne said this would be her last season running the marina. She had heart trouble and needed to slow down. She hoped whoever took over the place would have a care for its long history. Upon this somber note, she said the person I needed to meet in order to really understand the lake from the working man's perspective was a barge operator by the name of Tim Thorburn. He and his wife Paula were the only people who still actually lived out on the great lake year-round. Indeed, they might be the last people in all of Lakeland who did so.

Saying goodbye, I took the long way back to Kenora, crossing the bridge to Government Road and climbing the hill across from the marina, stopping to take a look down at the Two Bears Marina as it would have appeared to a fellow stepping from the Camper's Special—a sprawling boathouse hovering over the water on pilings that belonged to a wooden era. A few months later I would see it from just this angle in a real estate ad online. I shouted to Marlene from the computer: "Do you want to move to Ontario and run a marina?" "No," she shouted back. And thus a boyhood dream of living on Lake of the Woods slipped away.

Back downtown, the afternoon heat radiating up from the urban pavement mingled strangely with the cool of the lake. I surveyed the once-grand Kenricia Hotel, built in 1910 during the great western boom when farmers were making enough to send their children to university and commodity speculators down in Winnipeg were building mansions. Down at the water, troops of school-age kids were climbing into large aluminum skiffs with their luggage, bound for one of the many large summer camps that operate on islands on the lake. I wondered if they knew that during World War II, some of the islands were used as German prisoner-of-war camps. Either way—as a kid's summer vacation or as soldier's place to sit out armed conflict—Lake of the Woods is an inviting labyrinth.

Crammed into the lake's 4,350 square kilometres are precisely 14,632 islands. This fantastical figure is widely boasted by local pamphleteers and appears in the *Canadian Encyclopedia*. Counting islands is, like counting lakes themselves, a slippery business that depends on definition. The lake is also reported to have more shoreline distance than even Lake Superior, but I think that may be a stretch. Remarkably, the islands are nearly all crammed into the northern half of the lake, the great southern basin being mostly open water. Lake of the Woods is, like Lake Winnipeg below it in the watershed, a remnant of Glacial Lake Agassiz.

Navigating lakes like this is a challenge even with a modern map. For the missionaries and early fur traders who steered it by memory from the Rainy River at the southeast to the Winnipeg River at Rat Portage, it was easy to lose the way. Or even more. The French built Fort St. Charles on the north shore in 1732, under Jean-Baptiste de La Vérendrye. Four years later, on June 6, 1736, he and a Jesuit priest, Jean-Pierre Aulneau, set out on the lake with a party of nineteen. Not far from the fort, all were killed by Sioux warriors. Their thoroughly eviscerated bodies were left as a grim calling card at a spot today known as Massacre Island. Aulneau's name now belongs to the huge peninsula that bisects the lake, attached by a tiny neck of land.

Like the Great Lakes, Lake of the Woods does not belong to Canada entirely. The border not only cuts across the water, it gives a queer little jump in the middle, like a spiking heart rate graph. The confused border jogs briefly northward, comes ashore and turns back south, and forms the geographical curiosity called the Northwest Angle.

With the Treaty of 1818, the 49th parallel became the agreed international boundary between the Pacific Coast and Lake of the Woods. By earlier agreement, the eastern section of the boundary was to terminate at the northwesternmost point of Lake of the Woods. Unfortunately, these two lines were found to not quite meet at their tails. The redoubtable surveyor David Thompson was dispatched with his trusty sextant to remedy matters. He stitched the border together with a short north–south line, but it orphaned a piece of Minnesota from the rest of the lower forty-eight states. There is a whole raft of detail to the story, which I am glossing over here. If you want to know all, take a seat on a waterfront bench in Kenora. An old timer, or several, will soon arrive to enlighten you.

The Angle can only be reached overland by going through Canada. I decided to follow the American example and stay away altogether. The Knights of Columbus of Minnesota have reconstructed Fort St. Charles, but there is little else to see. Americans who spend time and money in Lake of the Woods focus on the much more scenic Canadian side, and they own many of the camps—as cabin sites are called in much of Ontario—visible from Kenora. American novelist Tim O'Brien set his *In the Lake of the Woods* in the Angle, where the unlikable protagonist broods in a cottage. It is an unresolved moral fable and detective story on post-Vietnam themes. The Angle and the lake setting serve as a metaphor for moral limbo. And who needs to drive for two hours to another country to visit limbo?

It was past noon, the afternoon sprawled ahead, and I had as yet no fixed purpose. The feeling reminded me of being at the lake in summer as a kid, easy in the embrace of long summer days, yet never quite able to escape the thought that all this would end and school would resume its tortures. I enjoyed just sitting there on Kenora Bay watching boats. But Ontario was a big landscape to digest, and I was not going to do it sitting still.

I had the cellular number for the barge man that Joanne had given me, but it had so far been out of service. I formed a mental image of him at the helm somewhere out on the lake, maybe chewing a stogy like Humphrey Bogart in *The African Queen*, and dialled again. This time a voice answered.

"Is that Tom Thorburn?"

"Uh, *Tim* Thorburn," said the voice. Despite my gaffe, Tim was kind and immediately receptive to the idea of a complete stranger wanting to watch him at work. He was at that moment steering his barge to a gravel quarry to pick up a load. The problem was getting me out from town. His barge was too slow to be crossing half the lake to pick up guests. But he said that he would "talk to Paula" and that I should call back after work. For Tim this meant sunset, which in mid-July at this latitude was 9:30 PM. God bless the working man.

The moment I hung up, my phone rang. It was Gerry Wilson, a colleague from the publishing world who edits a magazine called *Lake of the Woods Area News*. We had never met in person, but I had left a message that I was in town.

"I just skipped out of a meeting. Can you meet me outside the museum in twenty minutes?" she asked breathlessly.

"I am two blocks away."

"Can you bring a bathing suit?"

"I think I'm wearing it already." In Winnipeg, having discovered most of my clothes were left at home in a forgotten dufflebag, I had spent a small fortune on quick-dry textiles at the Mountain Equipment Co-op. I told her I would be on a bicycle and dressed like the host of a television nature show.

I rode to the museum and waited. A beaming, fit, tanned woman came up the sidewalk from the direction of the lake. "You're easy to spot," Gerry said. She carried a bag of snack food and drinks hastily pulled from the shelves of the big drug store across the street, the makings of a picnic. She led the way down to her boat, a sturdy, unadorned runabout docked at the bottom of Main Street. She jumped in, I cast off, and the big Honda four-stroke pushed us away from shore. Out of nowhere, the day had shaped into something. The old excitement of boats and of going somewhere under the summer sun just for the pleasure of going came over me. As the Buddhists say, with a snap of fingers, just like that, your world can change.

Gerry moved us west only a short distance to buy fuel and ice, a double errand people run often around here. Her boat-handling skills were refined, landing us with effortless precision, as they would all day. The pumps were staffed, as they had been over at Two Bears Marina, by uniformed teenage girls, who crept aboard in clean bare feet and expertly avoided spilling fuel into the water or scuffing the brightwork of the customers' boats. I had arrived in a culture of adept female lake mariners.

Underway again, we began to get a close look at the cottages on the lake. Their density was highest close to Kenora, especially on Coney Island. Gerry referred to this busy section as "the city," assuring me it thinned out fast as you went south into the big lake. She knew most of the owners and the amount paid on recent sales, as people do in buoyant markets. She was pained that the lake was too crowded—there were roughly eight thousand cottages on the lake, or about two per square kilometre of water. She talked about maybe selling her place, retreating to some "pure trout lake" back in the bush, except that it would be like giving up, an act of disloyalty to the lake itself. I could not bring myself to admit to Gerry that back on Emma Lake, there were three thousand cabins sharing twenty-five square kilometres of water.

Lake of the Woods had its share of problems, including nutrient overload, which Gerry mostly blamed on runoff coming north out of Minnesota. She said that the water later in the summer would bloom up with plenty of algae, the bane of cottagers. I floated the idea that cottaging itself might be making things worse. Dealing with sewage was a challenge on these tiny islet camps, and I had heard from a local health official that a discreetly placed open pipe running directly into the lake was the easy, illegal answer for some cynical owners.

Gerry did not believe this. She said that cottagers were the solution, not the problem, and that there was evidence to back

her assertion. Her magazine was the official voice of the Lake of
the Woods District Property Owners Association, and her pages
covered the whole gamut of lake ecology issues, including responsible sewage management. As Mike Stainton had told me back on
Lake Winnipeg, the Lake of the Woods owners were not waiting
around for the government. They were funding science directly
with their own dollars, and Gerry was publishing the results in
her magazine.

I thought the island cabins themselves lay rather lightly on
the land. Many places lacked power, telephone, or much running water. Restrained in style, built *among* the Ontario pines,
not in place of them, they harmonized architecturally with their
rocky purchases. None of the properties suffered the ignominy of
urban-style landscaping. Gerry pointed to a couple of new places
she considered garish. They were nothing bad compared to some
of the vinyl-clad boxes on untreed lots taking over Emma. On
the islands, cars and roads played no role, nor ATVs. Two-storey
boat houses with accommodations up top were common, and in
lieu of sandy beaches there were extensively built covered docks
and floats. We passed some happy teenagers in a custom wakeboarding towboat worth more than the average Canadian house-
holder earns in a year. Gerry made a face. The huge wakes of
these vessels can devastate soft shorelines and silt up lakes, and
she has published stories on them in her magazine. Even so, her
own sons ride wakes with friends sometimes. As the late New York
adman Tibor Kalman said, "It's tough to be pure."

Gerry piloted us out beyond the last of the cabins toward a
tiny, flat rock islet, slowed, and coasted in. With the engine shut
down, the peace was complete. Gerry said the rest of the lake
going south was wild and empty. My host was already down to
a green bathing suit and wading in, and I followed. Though this
resembled a much more northerly lake, the water was warm and

inviting. By August, algae might make swimming unpleasant. But at the moment, the lake was a balm that washed away the heat of the town.

Over our shore lunch we talked about Al Gore's *An Inconvenient Truth*, about optimism and pessimism, about biodiversity and nutrient loading from Minnesota. It was hard to care about any of these things under the kindly afternoon sun as we were eating crackers and cheese, drinking the lagers Gerry had brought.

"This was a good idea you had," she smiled. Gerry said that often her association would have people fly in from Toronto or Ottawa to discuss lake issues. The out-of-towners stayed at the high-rise waterfront hotel in Kenora, had their meetings, then went back to the airport without ever truly experiencing the water. We swam again. Gerry suggested we circumnavigate our little islet, and so we paddled around, balancing at one point on the slimy submerged peak of a rock like two children. Back ashore, the warm stone was somnolent, and I could have lain back upon it and drifted off.

We eventually rose, gathered our things back in the boat, and pushed off the rock. On the way back to town, Gerry took a different route, stopping once to consult her chart. She used to own an island camp she wished to see again. We passed a flotilla of cormorants fishing the calm water, then reached Balancing Rock, a local landmark and natural diving platform from which Gerry used to plunge as a girl. It was now owned by a woman from France, who flew the Brittany flag from her high keep. Such is the nature of private property.

Gerry's former camp was on the next island. The owners were away, but we went ashore nonetheless. Gerry was palpably emotional to be back. The island was larger than it looked, and we walked the trail back to the old boathouse, looked at the swimming steps cut into the rock by owners two generations before, the tamaracks Gerry herself had planted. Places like this were no longer affordable, she said. She regretted selling it.

I said to Gerry that price notwithstanding, Lake of the Woods cottagers seemed to be keeping their developments reasonably small-scale. Yes, she said. Exactly. Because cottagers cared about such things, whereas local residents were more interested in economic development than conservation. Cottagers were the real hope for Lake of the Woods, she said. Maybe she was right. Still, why did both of us prefer the parts of the lake with fewer cottages? What would my barge man, Tim Thorburn, have to say about these things, if fate managed to bring us together?

I said nothing more to disquiet my kindly host as we motored back through the gap and on into town in the late afternoon sun. Gerry may not have had all the answers, but she was as keenly interested in finding a balanced, sustainable approach to the proximate wilderness as I was. It felt good to have met an ally. She dropped me back at the same dock downtown, wished me luck, and was gone.

AFTER MY tour with Gerry I sprawled on a hotel bed watching the Tour de France and fighting to stay awake until sundown, when I could call Tim Thorburn. The same kind voice answered. Tim said that Paula, his wife and business partner, had agreed to come into town early and ferry me out to meet him.

Morning came and I was back in Keewatin, just up-inlet from Two Bears Marina. Right on time a boat hove into view. The woman silhouetted under the canopy executed a perfect docking, grabbed the stern line, and stepped lightly ashore. Paula Thorburn wore a sun hat, jeans, and a yellow blouse. She had slightly wild shoulder-length hair and pretty eyeteeth that showed when she laughed. She greeted me like an invited guest, some cousin come to the lake for a visit. In fact, I was intruding on a busy workday, which was every day for the Thorburns during the long light of summer. Today would unfold with a bit of mystery, since I knew little about this couple, except that Gerry had called them "real pioneers." Moreover, it was not Tim I was going to be spending much time with, but Paula herself. That was fine by me. She was funny, articulate, and forthright.

"You can't make a living at freight even if you haul all day," she said brightly as we climbed aboard her boat. A capable runabout much like Gerry's, it had brought her to town from her island house that morning, about twenty straight-line kilometres to the south. "So we're trying to concentrate on installing septic fields. Tim's very good at it." We made the obligatory stop for fuel at Two Bears Marina, where Paula and Joanne Hill greeted each other with the unspoken warmth of long acquaintance.

Joanne appeared not to recognize me. Then she said to Paula, "Taking good care of my writer?" Flinty exterior; heart of gold.

Paula was an adept boat handler, like every woman I had met in town. Out into the incomprehensible maze of islands and shoals, she piloted her six-metre Harbercraft pushed by a massive 130-horsepower Honda four-stroke with the unconscious ease of an suburban soccer mom riding the freeway to IKEA.

Like Gerry, Paula knew the owners of every property we passed, but saw the shore through different sociopolitical lenses: "These are working-class people along here. Local people have all the cheap property." We went down through a rush-filled narrows that was the route of the ice road by which Paula drove to town in winter. I began to appreciate the practical difficulties of living on a lake island. Coming out to open water again, we passed some cormorants, which Paula called crow ducks as she cursed them. Cormorant populations were exploding and were popularly believed to be destructive of fish stocks.

We arrived in a pretty, perfectly snug cove on Paula and Tim's island. Something about it was so beautiful I got a lump in my throat that took me by surprise. Perhaps it was the contrast with the thousands of million-dollar cottages I had seen across the country in the past two years, most of them empty playhouses, fair-weather escapes facing the lake but rooted in the city, places of retirement, of senescence, of lying fallow. Here was a real home, an honest living in the middle of a lake. In its details was written a whole living family history.

"Everything you see, Tim built with his own hands, with his back," said Paula after we had tied off the boat. A wind turbine spun in the breeze, collecting power that went into batteries in the basement. An array of photovoltaic panels picked up more energy from the sun. Tim had built his first system using recycled batteries, surplus parts, and his own burgeoning ingenuity years before there were books on the subject. The motor that let the solar panels track the sun was not working, so Paula had to reposition them by hand every two hours until Tim could fix it. This was a temporary hardship that reminded Paula that everything we enjoyed upon this earth, every bite of food, ray of light, and watt of fossil fuel energy, originally came from sunlight.

A large garden lay under the windmill. It used to be even bigger when Paula and Tim's two children were here. Their daughter was a commercial airline pilot in Florida. Their son was an electrical engineer somewhere. The kids returned to visit often, and the daughter's airline pass helped the parents travel, a recent luxury for Paula and Tim. We passed alongside the garden from which Paula had harvested many tonnes of food over the years, food that would otherwise have come by truck from California or southern Ontario.

Paula led us past the island's original house, more of a cabin, built of square logs, in which she and Tim had lived for many years. The new house was much larger—though still small by suburban standards. Tim and his nephew were halfway through adding a room, which meant pulling up some of the natural flagstones of the walkway. "They never finish anything," said Paula, with a tone more of wonder than rancor.

Indeed, Tim had lot of wildly ambitious projects simmering for a man who worked long hours afloat. In a little vale just north of where we stood, he had hauled up an enormous pleasure boat—almost a ship—that he had picked up at salvage cost. Its purpose was uncertain. In the little swimming bay in front of the house was a small wooden lighthouse, another rescued orphan, that he had somehow managed to stand on metal stilts over the water. He planned to build a little footbridge to it from the point. He also built and flew his own floatplane, a tube-and-fabric machine with foldable wings that called to mind the bush planes of the Canadian frontier.

Inside, the house was open and modern, built into the sloping shore so the basement opened at water level and the main floor felt like upstairs, a wide veranda around it. It was a sensible house, economic of materials, generous of light and space, not designed but imagined into shape. The kitchen and the main bathroom had recently been done with great refinement and using store-bought cabinetry, an expediency for the sake of Paula. The black-ash flooring Tim had bucked out of a swamp by hand, living there for three days in a tent. Afterward, Paula had lived three years in the basement of the house while the ash was being milled into boards and dried upstairs.

Despite many irons in the fire, Tim was clearly a man of tremendous accomplishment, and Paula wore her love and admiration for her husband like a badge: "He is such a good man. He always does the right thing. And he doesn't even know he does it." I guessed that if husband sat where wife did now, Tim would talk mostly about Paula. A few days before, the pair of them had had a party for two. "We drank a case of beer. We had our music blaring."

Paula skipped lightly over her own contributions to this fulfilling island life, which lay all around us. On the kitchen counter were fresh-baked loaves and buns for the next few days. She had already brought out a coffeecake with a rich icing, laid in a bulk margarine container, the way women did more commonly when I was growing up. On the table, the account books of Fish Hawk Freight Ways were toted up in Paula's fine script. It was a close-to-the-bone operation, and she knew the whereabouts of every dollar.

"You couldn't love anyone enough to live out here on the lake if you didn't like it for its own sake. When we started out, I had two kids in diapers and I had to go down to the lake and chop a hole in the ice for water and put it on a propane stove to boil. It's one thing to come out for a few weeks and live in your bathing suit and eat store-bought food. It is another to raise kids, fight fevers, get them educated, make a living, and stay warm in the winter."

On the wall hung Tim and Paula's wedding portrait from 1975, Paula teasing up the hem of her wedding dress and laughing brightly, a slight, blond Tim on bent knee. There was an old car from the thirties with the bridesmaids, trees and water filling the scene. The groomsmen had slicked back their hair with lake water to resemble villainous gangsters. "The boys had so much fun at that wedding. There was no such thing as getting a hotel room in those days. We partied until 6 AM." The honeymoon was a three-month odyssey in an Econoline van. In California, they camped by the side of the road for three days to wait for the Rose Bowl Parade to pass. Tim bought her a rose from the Hare Krishnas.

"Looking back, we were hippies. We just didn't know it."

Or the last pioneers. Tim and Paula were only a half-generation older than me, but seemed to have been born in another century. Beginning their married days on the lake, they fished and trapped commercially to make a kind of living, work Tim had learned from his father. The lake that had once produced sturgeon like cordwood became fished out—Paula blamed sport anglers. They hunted for meat and trapped for money, stretching hides in the basement to sell to the Hudson's Bay Company. Paula showed me a picture of the log cabin where Tim was raised. And at first I assumed she had misspoken, that it was actually Tim's grandfather or great-grandfather who was born there, for it appeared to have been taken circa 1900.

"We come from very humble origins, Tim and I."

Paula was the daughter of Cape Bretoners who left that rock and came to the west in search of a better living. When Tim asked Paula's father for permission to marry, the patriarch politely said no. He explained that he had left the hardships of old Nova Scotia so that his sons would not be coal miners nor his daughters marry fishermen. The marriage went ahead on strength of character.

It was time to leave the island, to find Tim, and for Paula to get back to real work. She left the room, then reappeared, having exchanged the yellow blouse for a red tee shirt and work boots. The first outfit had been for my benefit, she admitted. This one was for the job site. She was going to help Tim finish installing a septic field, then fetch the inspector to sign off on it. We left the house, followed the path down to the docks, and went back aboard.

As she throttled the boat back onto a plane over the calm water, Paula pointed out an undeveloped island opposite their landing. She owned it, having bought it half an age ago when Crown land was still available for purchase and prices had not yet gone insane. She was recently offered $800,000 for it, but declined.

"What would I do with the money? Well, buy a Sea-Doo, I suppose." I was surprised to learn that Paula coveted a personal watercraft because several of her girlfriends had them and social-ized afloat. Spotting a sail up ahead, I mentioned my own boat to Paula, and that I had considered exploring these waters under sail. "It's a good thing you didn't. Nobody would have talked to you. Locals don't hold sailing people in high regard. They bring their little trays of poop to shore and dump them, they think they can land at any dock they see, they anchor right in front of your house." We flew past the sailboat, which had the words *Carpe Diem* printed in letters a metre high down the side of the hull. Paula gave the sloop not the slightest glance.

We found Tim's barge nosed into a point and bearing a load of sand and two Bobcats, those compact loaders and diggers that do a great deal of small-scale earthmoving. We docked alongside. And there, in the flesh, was the much-introduced Tim.

He was talking with a neighbour, maybe his next customer. Dealing with sewage is perhaps the single greatest challenge of the cottager's leisurely life. When one cottager does right by the lake by spending thousands on a proper septic field, the people next door feel some obligation. Whatever kind of hot air envi-ronmentalists blow, that's how real change happens at ground level—from door to door, neighbour to neighbour.

Tim came striding over the field and extended a hand. He was built like one of his Bobcats, short and powerful, big pipes com-ing out of a sleeveless work shirt. He had blazing blue eyes, white hair, and a profoundly tanned face that reminded me of a certain professional wrestler from television. Tim patiently exchanged pleasantries, but I could see there was work to be done on the septic field, and offered to pitch in. Physical work, like music and dancing, was a universal language that Tim and Paula under-stood. He thrust a rake in my hands and we all set to.

This septic field was typical and consisted of a central hold-ing tank where solids precipitate from liquids and an anaerobic bacterial culture consumes them. The clarified liquid portion of the effluent travels out through an octopus of perforated pipes buried in the ground—the leach field or septic field—and any remaining suspended material will be decomposed in the soil. The water itself is taken up by the plants that grow above the field. Without sufficient setback from the water, even the best septic system will load nutrients into lakes.

Tim had already half buried the pipework in coarse gravel, which we had to smooth by hand. Then a layer of untarred building paper had to be laid down to keep the gravel from becoming clogged with the sand layer to be placed on top. Before the sand could be laid, a health department official would have to inspect the whole works. In a short time, we readied the site, Paula left to pick up the inspector, and Tim and I went down to eat lunch in the pilot house of his barge.

After fishing got too poor to live on, Tim needed a new venture. His father had done some barging, so Tim borrowed $25,000 and built his own rig. It was a large metal raft that could carry several tonnes of building materials, fill, vehicles, etc. Tim built it with an integral engine, but then the federal government changed the shipping rules, preventing him from operating such a vessel without an expensive captain's licence that he had neither the time nor the money to acquire.

"If the government sees you working, they want to put a stop to it," Tim said with the philosophical chuckle with which he prefaced most of his gentle assertions. To comply with the rules, he built a separate tug that pushes the barge from the rear like an outboard motor. An ingenious attachment system provided firm control but allowed the barge and tug to move independently with the waves. He just thought it up and started welding.

Tim heated himself a little bit of homemade frozen soup on a propane camp stove in the cool refuge of the wheelhouse. Next to

it he had a copy of *The Economist* to read during long lake crossings. We talked about prosperity and inflation and how there got
to be so many people who could afford a million-dollar vacation
home to sleep in twenty nights a year.

"I don't know, because you can't get rich working," smiled Tim.
Those cottagers were the bread and butter for him and plenty of
others. They preferred to neither fix nor build, but to hire and buy.
But this blessing was mixed: commensurate with their economic
might, they liked to set political agendas, too. They came from
the city and immediately formed associations. They needed to be
in groups, Tim theorized, because they lacked the attitudes and
abilities to do for themselves, at least out in the wilds of Lakeland.
They struggled even to launch their own boats single-handed.
When I pointed out the good work some associations seemed to
be doing on the ecological front, Tim considered for a moment.
It was one thing to find problems with the lake, he said, but they
usually wanted other people to solve them. "Local people just
know that if you want something, you do it yourself."

Blue-collar versus white. Self-sufficient hippie versus The
Man in all his middle-aged flaccidity. We are fundamentally a
tribal species. Still, there was truth in what Tim said—the working class is bound to chafe here and there when rafting alongside
the leisure class from May to October.

It is true that physical work has fallen from grace in our new
economy of service and information, wine bars and back rubs. But
honest labour still defined Tim, the Omega Man of Lakeland. His
bit of soup did not seem nearly enough to propel him through his
travails, yet after a lunch of barely twenty minutes—mostly taken
standing up—he descended to the work deck of his ship, started
the Bobcat, and began bringing bucketloads of sand up the shore.

As for writers, they compose rhapsodies about the labour of
others, but they prefer to do it reclining in the shade. Especially

after lunch. From a comfortable spot, I watched Tim go back and forth for half an hour. Even sitting still, I felt the summer heat like a weight.

Paula returned with the septic inspector, who took nearly an hour to go over the installation. Normally, his visits lasted just a few minutes. Finally ready to depart, we returned to the float, and Tim walked down to see us off. I cajoled him into posing for a picture with Paula, the red barge in the background. I think he hated cameras, and he made a memorable sour face. Perhaps he just wanted to get back to work. Between the neighbour, the inspector, and me, he'd lost a significant part of the working day to unpaid jaw wagging. While the sun shines, one must make hay. In the few seconds it took Paula to skipper us into deep water and hit the throttle, I looked back and Tim was already back on his machine, working, working.

We dropped the inspector at a Keewatin float, then continued up the narrows, passed Two Bears, and nosed in to the dock by the parking lot where my truck sat waiting. It had been a day of overwhelming good fortune, to have seen the lake from the singular vantage point of Paula and Tim Thorburn and to have glimpsed a living connection to an old way of life. Paula had run her boat out of fuel with all her comings and goings and would have to buy more to get home. Deep in their debt though I was already, Paula said she and Tim wished I might have spent the night as a guest on their island, but the next day's schedule would not provide a chance to take me back. And so we said goodbye, and hoped to see each other again.

Lakeland is such a big country that the possibility was nowhere near certain. I went to the truck and opened it, releasing its infernal air, and climbed in. Back on the highway, following the lakeshore deeper into Ontario, I did not know where I would sleep that night, but knew I had to keep moving east.

THE WALLEYE FACTORY

LAKE NIPISSING, *Ontario*

William Benjamin Robinson...on behalf of Her Majesty and the
Government of this Province, hereby promises and agrees...
to allow the said Chiefs and their tribes the full and free privilege
to hunt over the territory now ceded by them, and to fish in the waters
thereof, as they have heretofore been in the habit of doing...
FROM THE Robinson Huron Treaty, 1850

O NTARIO IS only the fourth-largest Canadian province or territory by area, but it always feels like the biggest when you
ply overland on the highway. Unlike the other provinces, standing like books neat upon a shelf, Ontario is flopped on its long
axis, spreading two thousand highway kilometres east–west. The
Trans-Canada is treacherous and narrow-shouldered, a glorified
logging road marauded by heavy trucks, wandering motor homes,
and suicidal cross-country cyclists.

The pavement closely parallels that of the voyageur fur route
through the densest agglomeration of Precambrian ice-scour
lakes in the country. I had pretty much made up my mind where
the next lake stop would be, but around every corner I found reason to detour. Lakes and more lakes—it would take a lifetime to
explore just those visible from the Ontario highway.

Taking the southerly Trans-Canada route to Thunder Bay,
I passed through a country more water than land around the

border towns of Fort Frances, Ontario, and International Falls, Minnesota, the elevated highway skipping across Rainy Lake like a stone, then into the bush. Here were the boundary waters of Quetico Provincial Park. But I was hardly over the horizon from Manitoba.

In a punishing heat I reached the shore of the greatest of the great, Gichigami, and parked the truck behind an autobody shop to look out upon the never-warm water. *Lake Superior!* The largest freshwater lake on earth—all the other lakes I would visit put together could vanish into this one. Perhaps the spirit in charge of this vastness knew that I was going to snub her, for she blew a haughty cold breeze through my tee shirt that made me shiver. This collision of hot and cold air would create pounding rain all along the north shore for the next twenty-four hours, and it was beginning to spit.

Lake Nipigon was tempting, the largest lake wholly within Ontario, noted for massive shore cliffs and green-black pyroxene beaches—but I let the turnoff slip by. The wipers slapped ineffectively at the pounding rain, which occasionally eased enough to reveal that birch and aspen had given way to maple. I passed a yellow-and-black moose warning sign, and immediately next to it, an actual moose standing surreal in the downpour, with darkness falling. Like Janet Leigh in *Psycho*, I rubbed my tired eyes and looked for a motel.

I survived the night and continued in the still pounding rain. I almost followed my nose into the Algoma country, to paddle under the ancient rock paintings of Missinaibi Lake. But I kept going, and at Sault Ste. Marie the deluge ended. I was nearly snared by sirens at Sudbury, the rock city surrounded by hundreds of tiny kettle lakes, ground zero of a great meteor impact nearly two billion years ago. The sun and heat of summer returned. Near the highway south of town, two free-spirited women had stopped their car by one of these pools and were wading in for a dip in their underwear.

Lakeland is a big country. I kept going.

WHEN I finally reached my goal, it was so humble my doubts redoubled. North Bay was a gritty, red-brick town with confusing streets and a lot of places to make your own beer. Much of the lakeshore on which it spread was a half-reclaimed rail yard and industrial wasteland, the granite still pierced by iron drift bolts from last century's log booms, its shallow bays graveyards for boilerplate and sawmill detritus. The town's history was told in steamboat wrecks. North Bay straddled a swampy height of land above a yellow-tinged lake with an unmusical name.

I reminded myself that often the most desirable places from nature's point of view look unremarkable to human eyes. The name Nipissing probably rings fairer in the Algonquin language spoken by the local Aboriginal people, who trace their ancestry here back before time. It means "people of the little water," as distinct from the much larger waters named for the Hurons, who lived down the French River.

Like most of the tourists, I was drawn here by the good fishing—though less as a sport than as a subject, one in which I was overdue for casting a line. By turns shallow, warm, swampy, and rocky, Lake Nipissing was teeming, a fact revealed in its place names: Sturgeon Falls, Cache Bay, Blueberry Island.

As for the scars of logging and mining, those heal eventually, and the more permanent blight of gentrification had not taken hold here. In the misleading parlance of a sprawling province, Lake Nipissing is Ontario's Near North. Which means that from Mississauga or London it is an epic-long drive in weekend traffic, far enough away to remain rough at the edges. Pop divas, chief executives, and professional golfers do not build rows of mansions here as they do farther south in the geographically more accessible, economically remote Muskoka area.

My paternal grandfather and namesake, Allan Casey, was born here. A railway machinist and semiprofessional baseball player who vaguely resembled Buster Keaton, my grandad migrated west around 1920 to pursue both his vocations. Though Grandad never moved back east as he intended, he used his free railway pass to send my father to Lake Nipissing for summer holidays. Dad was only five years old when he made the first of many solo trips across the country. My grandmother would pack him enough food for the journey and triple-pin five dollars into his jacket along with a letter to her in-laws. Then Grandad would take him down to the train, hand him to the conductor, and say, "Pass him along to North Bay." And so Dad would be handed from crew to crew, from divisional point to divisional point, until his aunt retrieved him three days later on the platform alongside Lake Nipissing. For Dad, these were halcyon days of swimming in the sandy-bottomed lake, eating ice cream with cousins, and charming his Ontario elders with his impeccable manners.

I took a room at Nipissing University, which offers its residences in summer. It seemed like a good way to meet people, but the place was eerily empty. I had a five-storey building to myself. Grateful to leave the truck behind after two days of inactivity, I climbed on the bike and made for the lake, where Saturday crowds were enjoying perfect summer weather.

Long separated from its own waterfront by the railway that divides the downtown, North Bay had reclaimed its beach and was rehabilitating the adjacent industrial lands. There were two ornate merry-go-rounds, flower beds, and benches strung along a lakefront promenade. It was a jealously guarded urban investment. Police cruisers went along the beach at intervals of not more than six minutes. Capital for the project came from North Bay's leading citizens. Chief among them was Lynn Johnston, author of the well-known comic strip *For Better or For Worse*. Johnston bases a number of her cartoon characters on actual North Bay people; for their part, actual North Bay people kindly guard the artist's privacy.

I rode slowly to Callander, stopping at beaches where possible. Most of the urban lakefront was in private hands, the water often inaccessible except down garbage-strewn alleyways. But the beach itself appeared to be public commons, whether by convention or law, a tradition you find almost everywhere in Lakeland. Swimmers waded far from shore to reach deep water, and the sandy bottom was kind to feet. I imagined my father running along this strand as a boy.

Callander Bay itself, a round inlet in the northeast part of the lake, was heavily industrialized from the arrival of the railway in 1880 to the last log boom in 1962. It was here that the Ottawa lumber baron John Rudolphus Booth gathered his white-pine logs and jacked them up Wasi Falls to his railway. Steamers that once worked the lake were hauled out here, and the great drift bolts used to lash the log booms to the shore can still be found in the rock. The local historian Don Clysdale has documented the places of many of these. He told me that the bolts were hammered into the rock by two-man crews, the senior fellow wielding the sledge, the junior man holding the chisel bare-handed and hoping for the best. The last mill was taken down in 1967, and the bay has evolved into retirement country.

Extremely aged motels stood all along the water road, a vestige of the automobile tourism culture that struck North Bay like a tsunami seven decades ago. It began on a spring morning in 1934 when the city editor of the *North Bay Nugget* received word that a mother had just given birth to five babies in a farmhouse in nearby Corbeil. The soon-to-be-dubbed Dionne Quintuplets became the signature human-interest story of the Depression era, and overnight North Bay became *the* North American destination for a family driving holiday.

The babies were raised in a de facto zoo by the Ontario government. Offered for public viewing at a profit to all but themselves, in current dollars they brought roughly $250 million in tourism to Ontario per year. Three million people saw them during the eight-year period when they played to crowds all summer at the "hospital" where they lived. The curious came especially from neighbouring Pennsylvania, Ohio, and New York.

But North Bay visitors needed something more than a freak show to fill their summer holiday. Inevitably—no doubt relievedly—they came down to the warm sandy shore. The gentle charm of Lake Nipissing was planted like a seed among these early Dionne tourists. Mostly, they went fishing, and their descendants are still casting their lines here today.

I RARELY go fishing anymore. As sport, it is pretty slow. As a means to fill the belly, it is too much work. Still, I am glad to know how to catch a fish—almost a badge of citizenship in this country. It is a knowledge acquired without conscious effort, like language, by anyone who grows up in Lakeland. And I marvel at the power there is in angling to connect people to nature. There is a mythological ripeness to the act of plumbing the unconscious deeps for a meal, feeding the soul and the body at the same time.

A taste for fishing cuts through social strata. The poor student fishes below the weir in town. The wealthy industrialist charters a plane for the Far North. But they tie their lures on with the same knot, are hooked into the same primal anticipation. Fishing is an elemental form of sounding the matrix of life on earth, and touches a deep place in the collective unconscious. It is an act of passion. When a man of the Canadian hinterland says, "I love to fish," this may be the most heartfelt truth he can express about himself in casual company. Women, though emotionally more capable, also love to fish. My reserved and elegant neighbour, Ivy, goes out in her Lund skiff every summer, looking like Sophia Loren there in the bow. Kids can hardly be prevented from fishing if there are water, rod, and tackle to be had.

David Suzuki devotes much of his recent autobiography to the subject of fishing. He never travels without his rod, and he fundamentally defines himself as a consumer of fish. Most of the photographs in the book are of people holding up big fish they have caught, a thing impossible to do with artifice or pretension. What is left is always bliss and childlike wonder.

As a university student, I worked at a lake camp for mentally handicapped adults who languished fifty-one weeks a year in institutions. During their precious days in Lakeland, they enjoyed nothing more than to fish. To their line leaders I would clip Len Thompson red-and-white spoons—or five-of-diamonds if they preferred—and get the lures safely overboard before anyone hooked me. I would help them light their pipes and cigarettes so they could enjoy a double pleasure, and then watch them fall under the spell of fishing while I trolled the "reef" off our camp. Fishing calmed those troubled, forgotten souls in a way drugs could not.

THE SECRET to good fishing is local knowledge. And few people knew as much about the fish in Lake Nipissing as Richard Rowe. I found him just west of the city in a place called Garden Village, a grassy bank of a winding creek that seemed indeed like a good place for planting vegetables. A cool wind came across the lake and shook the small maple leaves like little flags. *O Canada.* The water bore a muddy yellow undertone that suggested fertility, and many fish.

Garden Village is the main settlement on the Nipissing First Nation reserve. Richard himself was not of Aboriginal descent. A fishery biologist, he had recently been hired by the band to manage its commercial fishery. But this job description hardly did justice to the political nature of his new post, or to the scale of the task before him. Or hinted at the possibilities if all went well. Much rested upon his shoulders. He was a slender fellow, his head shorn like a monk, and he spoke with Jesuitical passion about what seemed to him like destiny.

"This was always my dream job, to manage the fishery on Lake Nipissing," he said, sitting behind his desk in an office housed in one of those metal portables. Richard first saw Nipissing as a boy vacationing with his family. People who visit here once tend to return for many summers—the locals say the average is seventeen years—and Richard's family did likewise. A picture of him from those early days stood behind his desk like a window in time: he and his older brother on a dock wearing life jackets and holding a catch of fish between them.

Technically, Richard had already been managing the Lake Nipissing fishery for years before the band hired him. He worked for the Ontario Ministry of Natural Resources. But it was frustrating in the way of government bureaucracy. He spent 95 percent of his time in the office, writing reports to ministry headquarters in Peterborough, just another lake scientist who never got on the lake. When the ministry granted him leave to take up this new office, he jumped at the chance.

"I never want to go back. This is where the action is."

That was certainly true. Even in the context of Lakeland, a country defined by superlative fishing, Nipissing is outstandingly productive. Of the two hundred–odd freshwater fish species in Lakeland, forty-four are found here, including most of the important sport fish: muskellunge and northern pike, bass, perch, whitefish, bullhead, and ling. There are also ciscoes, stickleback, darters, shiners, and suckers. The antique, long-nosed gar preys aggressively near the surface, whereas the equally primitive lake sturgeon lives unobtrusively on the bottom.

The sturgeon is one of my favourite Lakeland creatures, though I have never seen a wild one. These resilient animals have come down to us almost unchanged in the fossil record in two hundred million years, still wearing their armour plating from the dinosaur age. They grow slowly, feeding almost exclusively on tiny invertebrates of the muddy bottom with their tooth-less mouths. They can live well beyond a century and grow to over one hundred kilograms, by far the largest freshwater fish we have. Occasionally, a large sturgeon is caught somewhere in the country and six or eight people are required to hold it up for the photograph.

Most Canadian lakes accessible to southern human popula-tions have been depleted of fish, and the sturgeon is the bellwether of an ill-fated flock. A hundred years ago, sturgeon were so com-mon in Canadian lakes and rivers that they were harvested and stacked on the shore like cordwood. They were thought of as coarse fish, though their eggs, or *roe*, became a pricey delicacy as caviar. Overharvesting, dams, and its own slow-growing ways have conspired against the lake sturgeon, which is now rare over much of its range. Still, I like to think its long tenure in the bio-sphere will tide the lake sturgeon over the blink of time it will take our species to either expire—or achieve sustainability.

Though Lake Nipissing, too, had all but lost its sturgeon (it was closed to sturgeon fishing two decades ago), it remained rich in walleye, probably the most prized angling fish of all in Cana-dian inland waters. Like Lake Winnipeg, Nipissing was shallow, warm, and turbid. Its shores were lined with numerous rocky shoals and good spawning grounds, perfect habitat for the emerald-and-gold fish.

"Lake Nipissing is a walleye factory," said Richard Rowe. "You could not design a better lake for it."

The walleye—called pickerel around Lake Nipissing and else-where in Lakeland—has large eyes for hunting in low light for smaller prey fish, especially yellow perch. It has two dorsal fins, the foremost of which has needle-sharp spines that every child is warned about when landing his or her very first catch. The northern pike ambushes a lure explosively and is more exciting to play. The lake trout is much bigger. But the walleye is somehow the all-around champion. And when it comes to taste, it is hard to better it from either lake or ocean. Its flesh is firm and sweet, especially when pan-fried over a fire in good company.

Many compete for the walleye factory output. Some 5 percent of all angling in Ontario is done on Lake Nipissing alone, an astounding one million angling hours per year. Nearly half this time is spent fishing through the winter ice. A survey in the nineties counted two thousand fishing huts on the frozen lake, or 12 percent of Ontario's total. Sport angling brings billions of tourism dollars to Canada every year, approaching $100 million on this one lake alone. There are 125 fishing lodges on Lake Nipissing. But tourists are not the only people fishing.

Net fishing remains a marginal livelihood for some. A large proportion of net fishers are Aboriginal people. Generally those under treaty may net fish for subsistence food. In many northern communities, netted fish are the only inexpensive source of quality protein available to families. Meanwhile, commercial fishing is done on lakes where fish stocks are deemed sufficient by Fisheries and Oceans Canada and other provincial agencies. A licence is required and, in theory, available to anyone. But in practice, commercial licences are often steered into the hands of Aboriginal people as a way of boosting northern employment. There is little money in lake fishing, perhaps $100 million a year nationwide before expenses, about a quarter of which comes out of Lake Winnipeg alone. Sport angling, in contrast, is worth billions.

Sport anglers and net fishers—divided by ethnicity, social class, geography, and purpose—do not coexist happily. Each group accuses the other of taking too many fish. The Nipissing Band is signatory to the Robinson Huron Treaty of 1850, along with many other First Nations in the north Superior watershed. Unlike the later numbered treaties, Robinson Huron appears to recognize the Nipissings' right to fish not just for subsistence but commercially, for they have always done so. Writing in *Nipissing from Brûlé to Booth*, Murray Leatherdale notes that it was the custom of the Nipissings to spend each winter with their Huron neighbours, taking great catches of Lake Nipissing fish to trade for corn.

Special commercial fishing rights for Aboriginal people are political dynamite in Canada. They have led to armed stand-offs between Aboriginal and non-Aboriginal groups, notably in the Donald Marshall case over lobster fishing by the Mi'kmaq of Burnt Church, Nova Scotia. For years Lake Nipissing seemed to be likewise heading toward a confrontation. The Nipissings were increasing their fishing pressure on the lake each year, but refused to supply catch reports. The government considered any walleye they sold illegal since the band lacked any kind of licensed fish-cleaning facility. The band accused the Ontario government of spying by placing a video monitoring system on utility poles in Garden Village. Meanwhile, the walleye catch was dropping year by year, and in 2004, the numbers dropped precipitously.

Treaties notwithstanding, governments may wrest back control of Aboriginal fishing if it is deemed to be harming the fish stocks, and so the stage seemed set for the kind of conflict that delights news editors: a police raid, or perhaps a Nipissing First Nation barricade on Highway 17 in protest. But such things did not come to pass.

Instead, the band voted to invoke new sustainable fishery laws to govern itself. The province reduced its angling limits and introduced a "slot size" for the lake, whereby fish caught in the prime spawning size of between forty and sixty centimetres must be thrown back. The band offered Richard Rowe his dream job, including carte blanche to manage the fishery any way he saw fit. And the government gave him leave to go.

No one was more surprised at this outbreak of common sense than Richard Rowe himself: "It is surreal that I am here now, because when I was with the government, I wanted to play hard-ball with the First Nation. They had a lot to answer for." Indeed, Richard had been an outspoken critic of Aboriginal fishers. The *North Bay Nugget* newspaper seemed to include a quotation from him in every fishery story it printed. Clearly, his co-optation by the band was strategic and political. Either they put in place a functioning and accountable fishery management plan, or the Ontario government was going to take over the whole show.

Richard's first priority was to get accurate counts of the lake-wide catch. Though there were angling records going back thirty years, 2005 was the first year in which the Aboriginal net catch was reported. As Richard's data stood when we met, anglers took twenty thousand kilograms of whole walleye a year, Aboriginal netting another forty thousand kilograms.

A key objective was to set up a proper fish-cleaning plant and bring all the native-caught fish into legitimate markets. By the following year, this would be achieved. Lake Nipissing pickerel, for so many years a black-market item, could at last be bought at waterfront fish markets.

Not everyone was happy with these developments. Commercial harvesting of fragile wild game stocks is still a threatening prospect to many Canadians, myself included. Nipissing is a fairly big lake at 875 square kilometres, but I found the tonnage of fish caught alarmingly high.

"Fishery management is risk management," Richard said. "You can deplete a fish population to the point where it will never recover, where it just drops off the edge of a cliff. The question is, how close to the cliff can you get?" It was a disturbing metaphor, though Richard assured me that, with the right mix of proper science and local knowledge, a fishery could be sustained permanently. Indeed, he would arrange for me to go out on the lake and see for myself how it was done. The next afternoon, I was to look for a Nipissing First Nation truck at the North Bay marina. It would be driven by a fellow named Hugh Grant—or so I thought Richard said—who would take me out on the water.

I imagined spending the day in small boat with a handsome, stuttering Englishman with a lot of fine white teeth.

HUGH GRANT turned out to be two guys. I found them the next afternoon schlepping jerricans of fuel down to the docks. Grant Stevens, burly, talkative, and smiling, set down his load to shake hands, explaining that the tax-free gas they were hauling in from his reserve would power the day afloat and avoid the high prices at the marina pump. He introduced me to his partner, Hugh Martel.

"No Hugh Grant jokes from me, I promise," said I, breaking one of my own rules against ever making light of a person's name. Grant blinked at me uncomprehendingly.

"You mean the hockey player?"

Hugh and Grant were cousins, extended and removed, and neither had ever lived anywhere but on the reserve, except to study for their fishery technician tickets down at Lindsay. They probably watched few British romantic comedies. Hugh was Grant's opposite, rail thin, serious, and spare of words. The pair led the way down the pier to the boat, a sturdy aluminum vessel of about five metres built by Stanley Machine of Parry Sound. Most of the hull was an open, flat workspace, and there was an enclosed pilothouse on the stern. I had come prepared for a day in the blazing sun, pounding over whitecaps in a small skiff. This was going to be easy riding. I helped pour the jerricans of fuel into the filler, wondering if it was enough to move such a big boat all day. It turned out that it was not.

Hugh took the wheel, Grant sat in the chair to port, and I took station between them on a piece of afterdeck. We trolled out beyond the breakwater and turned for the west to begin a day of creel surveying. Much can be inferred about fish populations and movements by looking into an angler's creel—the traditional wicker or osier basket used to hold caught fish. Though actual creels are seldom seen these days except among traditionalist fly-fishers, creel studies are a mainstay technique for fishery biologists worldwide. They involve interviewing anglers about their catch and about how hard they worked to get it, how many fish they caught and what kind, what kinds of tackle and baits they used, whether they used jigging, casting, or trolling, how long they fished, how far they travelled to find fish, and so on.

Richard Rowe had mapped Lake Nipissing into twenty sectors, and we were bound for the farthest southwest corner, some sixty kilometres off. Lucky for me, for without a fast, seaworthy boat and knowledge of the lake's innumerable rocky shoals, casual visitors on the North Bay shore didn't get to see this area. And the way these fellows drove made for pure excitement.

A long area along the north shore where the reserve is located is a treacherous rock maze. On the marine chart, the area is marked "unnavigable," yet Hugh was tear-assing straight through it at full cruising speed. He threaded a needle from point to point, ranging on landmarks I could not discern, repeatedly taking us within a metre or two of sharp, grey rock.

"Don't worry," said Hugh, calmly playing the wheel with fingertips as we bore down on a rocky islet. "I've been doing this since I was a kid. This is our place." In fact, I was not worried. Complete competence could be seen in his body language. Grant sprawled in his copilot's chair like a man about to fall asleep in front of a television. Through the windows, the long, wet rock rolled by like passing orcas, and those iconic, asymmetric white pines found a way to grow from stone. At the last moment, the islet ahead became two, and we cut our wake between the points. We passed Garden Village, and Hugh waved to his brother going by in a lovely old wooden skiff.

Our first creel customer was fishing alone from a custom bass boat. Hugh eased us out to him amid a hundred small rocks near the surface just waiting to shred our propellor. Somehow, he managed not to graze a single one. Our fisherman kept casting as he watched us approach, but he wore the expression of some-one being pulled over by a cop. Our boat carried the Ministry of Natural Resources logo, after all. Within hailing distance, Grant went forward to state his business, and our man relaxed. Survey response is entirely voluntary, but citizens rarely refuse to help the cause of science, once it is explained.

The angler, a francophone from Sudbury in his late twenties, was dead serious about fishing. He had been out for twelve hours. He had caught twenty-five bass, the species he was targeting, plus three walleye and many perch he had not bothered to count. He had released all of them. As we backed away, he tipped his hat, which carried the logo of his expensive outboard engine, and immediately resumed fishing. Hugh guessed he was practising for a big bass derby two weeks hence, and was scouting the lake for productive holes.

The next boat, manned by a father and son, was a tired old tri-hull jury-rigged as a poor man's bass boat with lawn chairs set on a plywood deck. They were anchored in a similar rock garden but had caught nothing in two hours. Their blaring radio may have been the problem. The father asked if we knew where the fish were. This, Grant told me, was the question you heard all day doing creel surveys.

Hugh and Grant always made a point of asking about blue pickerel, a variant of walleye with a pale blue-grey cast that used to be the dominant form in these waters. A century of genetic pollution from the introduction of hatchery yellow pickerel has all but absorbed the blue variant. Government hatcheries are operated all over the country and have wreaked genetic havoc on native fish. The sullying of wild stocks with hatchery ones has occurred in virtually every lake in Canada close to population centres.

Touted as a cure for dwindling stocks in overfished waters, many hatcheries were established during the Great Depression as work relief projects. Thus they have always been a form of political window-dressing. Hatching fish is a cheap, visible way for governments to be seen responding to the problem of fished-out lakes—a problem government fish managers allowed to occur in the first place.

Hatcheries do not solve the problem. Richard Rowe had assured me that a healthy lake will produce plenty of fish without human interference. One female walleye can lay a quarter million eggs in a season. In an unhealthy lake, where stocks have been pushed over the brink and the food chain has been permanently altered, hatchery fish won't survive any better than wild spawn.

"Hatcheries are just producing expensive fish food," Richard had said. "If fishery management was that easy, don't you think it would have worked by now?" Government-led genetic degradation of wild populations continues because the taxpaying, fish-catching public believes hatchery fish are the answer to every problem. At every public meeting Richard attended, demands for more stocked fish were always atop the agenda.

The long summer afternoon waned into evening, which we mostly spent cruising, finding few anglers to interview in our remote sectors. Hugh and Grant switched places after three hours, and we made the crossing to the south shore. We fell in behind another boat, which turned out to be Grant's father out for a ride with his nephew. We passed the log cabin where his father was born on Hays Point. Hugh's ancestors had also inhabited the cabin at various times, and it was actually built by his great-grandfather. It bore a striking resemblance to the one where Tim Thorburn was born back on Lake of the Woods. Lake Nipissing turned to rush-filled shallows and we came to the last bay in our sector.

Finding no more boats, Hugh declared the survey finished. We now had the long run back to North Bay. A shoal of dark rocks seemed to have appeared along the return route where before there had been none. This turned out to be a large flotilla of cormorants. Sometimes mistaken for the loon, the double-crested cormorant swims lower in the water and wears two nuptial crests on its head in breeding season. Unlike the loon, it is gregarious, living and working in a flock, and can perch comfortably in branches. It can be seen with its wings spread out to dry after swimming.

Just as on Lake of the Woods, the cormorants were generally hated by anglers on Lake Nipissing, who felt the black birds ate all the fish they themselves wanted to catch. This prejudice runs throughout Lakeland. Richard Rowe told me that cormorants do not directly prey upon walleye, but compete with them for food to varying extents. The walleye is naturally adapted to the cormorant's presence in large numbers. And, of course, many other species compete for the lake's food: merganser, kingfisher, gull, osprey, eagle, the beloved loon.

But none is despised by taxpayers like the cormorant. At meetings, they call with mob fervour for destruction of cormorant nesting colonies. The Ontario and New York State governments have, at times, given in to these demands, and recently conducted cormorant culls. Other times, people take matters into their own hands, though attacking cormorant nesting sites is a serious crime.

Woe betide a creature that is thought to compete directly with humanity. It cost the wolf his livelihood over most of the Northern Hemisphere. It wrought the end for the bison. Like many bird species, the cormorant nearly succumbed for good in the 1970s due to the egg-weakening effects of DDT. Its resurgence is not celebrated by anglers.

The wind had freshened considerably, and the big boat began to pound in the yellow-tinged whitecaps. Grant had to slow down to an inefficient half-plane, dragging a large wake behind us. He tapped the fuel gauge, which was dipping low. The only thing for it was to stop at Garden Village for more gas.

I did not mind the detour—it was just more time on the water. We docked at Hugh's father's house, which stood over a small rocky cove, with a veranda and three dormer windows reflecting the water. Hugh's brother and nephew were playing catch with a toy football in chest-deep water as we nosed in, the warm-hued sun glistening on their shoulders, their faces grinning up at us. The Nipissing First Nation and the big lake seemed an idyllic, complete world just then.

The detour also meant another race through the shoals of the north shore. Grant drove as expertly as Hugh. We passed the rest of the voyage with talk—of life in the city, the great economic lure of Alberta, of making a living versus making a life. We all agreed we were lucky to work outdoors, in the wild. Hugh, ever serious, said he would never live anywhere but with the Nipissing First Nation. Grant said he wouldn't either. And therefore, they said, protecting the fish stocks in the lake was the only way to ensure their future.

It is a comforting idea: that the hunter keeps fit the prey, that the farmer will never damage the fruitful soil, that the lumberjack guards the forest as the shepherd does the sheep. And that a fisherman will never harm the fishery—Paula Thorburn had uttered these exact words with sincere passion on Lake of the Woods only days before. Sadly, they have been proven false time and again in my own lifetime.

And yet the day afloat was evidence of progress along the road toward a sustainable use of nature. Grant and Hugh were not just voicing platitudes about conservation; they were gathering credible data to gauge their success at it. After years of antagonism between a government science bureaucracy and a suspicious First Nation, the two sides had risked sharing a boat. There it was again: citizen science, local people pledged to monitor their backyard corner of the biosphere, and a scientist to give their labours shape and usefulness. Come what may, Hugh Martel, Grant Stevens, and Richard Rowe would forever be associated with the data they netted this July day. It made them accountable to their children, tied them to future generations in the way planting a tree does. If something bad happens to the Lake Nipissing walleye, at least we know who to talk to.

It was deep dusk when we came abeam of the marina breakwater and nosed into our berth, the lights from town and voices of people strolling the shore reflecting from the water. Grant, Hugh, and I wished each other well, and they started back to Garden Village. I found my bicycle and rode away from the lake, through the warm North Bay streets to the university, suddenly feeling weary of the long day. Summer was nearly half done. It was time to leave Ontario, and time for a rest. My holidays started in the morning.

LA GRANDE TRAVERSÉE

LAC SAINT-JEAN, *Quebec*

We must abide in that Province where our fathers dwelt, living
as they have lived, so to obey the unwritten command that once
shaped itself in their hearts, that passed to ours, which we in
turn must hand on to descendants innumerable: In this land of
Quebec naught shall die and naught shall suffer change.

LOUIS HÉMON, *Maria Chapdelaine*, translated from the French by W.H. Blake

O F ALL the waters I had come upon in my travels, Lac Saint-
Jean took me most by surprise. The route up from the
Saguenay fjord climbed through a forest belt before emerging
onto farmland running dead flat seemingly forever and oddly
reminiscent of the prairie, right down to the yellow canola
fields. Suddenly the road dropped fifty metres of altitude over an
ancient glacial shore and the blue sprawl of the lake filled the
view. The Innu call this Piekouagami—Flat Lake—for the wide
plain that bounds the water. The humid air held to earth by the
muggy inversion weather seemed to have rubbed away the horizon line. The dull glint of silver-spired churches marked the little
towns that spread into the distance along the shore.

In a few days, the 53rd annual Traversée internationale du
lac Saint-Jean was to be run, and these lake towns were already
erupting in festivity. Open-water swimming races are part of the
Quebec culture, as are large civic parties, and the 32-kilometre
traverse of Lac Saint-Jean was the event of the season. The race

would go out on live television. Quebec has plenty of lakes but, across the province, Lac Saint-Jean is referred to as "the lake." Famous for its surrounding blueberry fields and cheddar cheese, the lake is the blue heart of Quebec nationalism, and I looked forward to seeing Lakeland from the other side of Canada's Anglo-French divide. Mainly I just wanted a busman's holiday by the lake at the pinnacle of summer, to take a break from blue-green algae, development, and stewardship, to relax, eat well, and enjoy sun and water.

Lac Saint-Jean takes its name from Jean de Quen, the Amiens-born Jesuit who was the first European to see these waters. Quebec's pervasive, lapsed Catholicism always feels homey to me. In Prince Albert, I went to Catholic schools run by nuns and priests with names like St. Pierre, Tremblay, Boutin, and Regnier. Many of my West Flat friends spoke French at home. They were altar boys and their mothers made tourtière.

It was to church that I was heading, a monastery in the hills above the lake. L'Ermitage Saint-Antoine was founded by one Abbé Elzéar DeLamarre in 1907. DeLamarre had fallen in love with the area on a vacation. He acquired property on nearby Lac Ouiatchouan, which drains down the river of the same name to Lac Saint-Jean, and built himself a cottage. On his new place, the clergyman noticed an indentation in some rocks that rather reminded him of the grotto at Lourdes. He put up a statue of the Virgin, and a pilgrimage was born.

With the hermitage being heavily visited now, there was room for tour buses, and covered picnic areas gave shade to the multitudes. Statues, shrines, and chapels, connected by paved pathways, had spread along the lakeshore among the birches. There was a museum and a shop where the trappings of Catholic devotion—crosses, candles, icons—could be bought.

I was supposed to find the innkeeper, but he found me. Guy Dufour was tall, dark but greying, striding up the hot pavement from his hotel with an outstretched hand, speaking English. "Welcome to Saint Anthony's Hermitage!" Guy reminded me of teachers from my old schools, of a priest who had removed his Roman collar to put the students at ease, that mixture of humble servitude and ministerial authority. He was dressed neatly but humbly in brown slacks circa 1978, a business shirt and tie, no jacket. He gave you his full attention. "Take an hour to relax in your room. We will meet at five o'clock, and you will have dinner at my table tonight in Roberval."

The room was hotel-like but monastic: a crucifix between the beds, no television, an ample desk for study. Pilgrimages were a growing specialty among seniors nostalgic for the days before Quebec's secularization. "Religious tourism," Guy had called it. "We are just beginning to exploit this." Down the dormitory hall, some local students were rehearsing a morality play in a kind of gymnasium. It was like spending the night back in St. Mary High School, *Alma Mater—Semper Veritas.*

That evening we were going to a street party down in Roberval, part of the carnival week preceding the swimming race. I passed the late afternoon walking through the hermitage grounds, past the Stations of the Cross, poking into chapels and niches. A row of confessionals resembled outhouses among the maples along the lakeshore. There was a miniature church just large enough to stand in, with little hand-written prayers—for sick children, for lost items—left by supplicants in piles on the altar. Below was the grotto itself. It had been enlarged with jackhammers since DeLamarre discovered it, and plumbed for running holy water, which poured into a copper sink with a hollow booming sound when I opened the tap. My dad, a Knight of Columbus, would have loved this place.

"Excellent!" Guy said upon our rendezvous at the hotel door. He still wore his 1978 slacks, but had traded shirt and tie for a

kind of gypsy blouse that only a French guy could pull off, a neck-
line open to the chest with brocade trim and bell-bottom sleeves.
"You will ride with me and tell me all about what you are doing,
Allan!" He preferred to speak in priestly declamations.

Guy was not a priest, but a travel agent, a hotelkeeper, and an
impresario. Like so many people I had met in Lakeland, he was
passionate about his home place, Lac Saint-Jean. He talked about
the rich agricultural soil that defined the region, about the *oua-
nanish* or landlocked freshwater salmon that drew anglers to this
area. He particularly urged me to visit the zoo, a source of great
civic pride. I have always hated zoos and vowed silently to avoid
this one. But Guy said, "I know the people there. Tomorrow, I am
calling them and you will have a free entrance."

"And now maybe we are speaking some French?" Guy said,
apropos of nothing. Though I have always felt an affinity to
French that I trace to my days in foster homes, I did not study
it until university, when I obeyed Pierre Trudeau's call for a new
society and went to live in Montreal to acquire the other official language. I dutifully rode a Peugeot bicycle to class each
day and was complimented on my good accent now and then by
my chain-smoking instructress. But I spent most of my time in
St. Denis clubs where the loud music precluded any language,
and I lived in Notre-Dame-de-Grâce, where you could evade
French completely. And that was long ago.

I drew breath and let fly a quasi-Gallic barrage—about my
Catholic school background, my francophone friends, even
a joke about Pierre Trudeau. All this was more than I had the
facility to say. Guy winced at my assault upon the language of
diplomacy and switched immediately back to English: "You like
Pierre Trudeau?" This was treacherous territory. The federalist
dog Trudeau had few friends among the separatists of the lake.

"Umm, not really, not anymore."

We found our way to the safer topic of boats. Guy used to captain a fifty-passenger tourist boat, which travelled down the river out of Saint-Félicien and onto the lake. He still had a small runabout and declared that we would voyage the next day.

Roberval was jumping for a party, the townspeople afoot, smartly dressed, all going in the same direction. For the women, short skirts, high heels, and piled-up hair were the default. The distance from neckline to hemline was breathtakingly short, whether they were twenty or sixty. The men wore trousers despite the heat, sandals, and billowy shirts. Parking seemed an impossibility, but Guy maneuvered into a back lot and found space. We walked a further two blocks and turned a corner to view a remarkable street scene.

Every year a few days before the Traversée, the citizens of the lakeshore gather in Roberval to dine communally in the street. The *Souper dans les rues* is eaten at two very long tables laid down the lakeshore street, one adjacent to each sidewalk. Some ten thousand people attend the feast, which stretches nearly two kilometres. All night a restless throng promenades down the middle of the road between them. Cafés open their doors and windows, and turn their sound systems up to fuse-popping volume, blanketing the streets in layers of music.

All the seats were organized into family blocs or office fiefdoms. Guy sat us among his travel industry pals. He knew everyone who passed by and introduced me to two dozen faces before he gave up the effort. These exchanges were quite formal, especially with the men, who all said *"enchanté"* as they shook my hand and offered some grand-sounding civic words of welcome along with an exhortation to visit the zoo. Then they ignored me completely. I did not mind. For them the evening was a family gathering to which they looked forward all year.

And I had Nancy Donnelly to talk to. Nancy was from the regional tourism office and had kindly paved my way with contacts and arrangements. She spoke both official languages like a diplomat, hailed from Ottawa, and had lived out west before her husband got a job in the Saguenay aluminum industry. She felt like an outsider here even after several years. The people were friendly enough, she was quick to add, but socializing in Quebec is mainly done within the bounds of the extended family around the backyard swimming pool. She and her husband had neither and mostly chummed with other importees.

We stood in line to pick up our meal, a French cover of "La Bamba" blasting through a café's open windows. A Lac Saint-Jean style of tourtière is known throughout Quebec, a deep-dish pan of sundry meats more like an outsized lasagne than the usual pie. Under the same name, something quite different was being served, mostly potatoes, and almost too salty to eat. It was the only bad meal I can recall having in Quebec.

There were many more diners than chairs, so Nancy and I relinquished ours and joined the flowing crowd. I remarked on the conformity of dress among the women in their skirts and heels, almost a uniform.

"It's more than that. After you've been here a while, you see how the people tend to look the same." It was true. The women's faces had a certain congruency that went deeper than tanned complexions and hair dyed with coppery highlights; the men, too, in their way. Most of these *pure laine* Quebecois could trace their ancestry directly to just 2,600 emigrés who founded La Nouvelle France in 1608, an insular population that has remained so into the modern era. And nowhere more pronouncedly than in the lake region. To scientists, the genomic homogeneity of the area—and the prevalence of several normally rare hereditary diseases that have dogged the Franco-American diaspora—is ripe for study.

Certainly the art of street partying was borne on some chromosome of these people, for they pursued it with both enjoyment and efficiency. Beer and wine, all brought from home, were openly consumed at every table. This would be unthinkable out west, where even regulated public drinking—like a Canada Day beer garden—soon devolves into felony. In Roberval, I spotted no drunks and only two bored-looking policemen at the far end of the street. When the supper ended, a large panel truck entered the street and rolled along the route, work teams loading folded-up tables and stacks of empties into its maw like the Cat in the Hat cleaning house.

The fullness of this communal street life has no counterpart in most of English Canada. Indeed, the *Souper* was just one of many communal celebrations around the calendar in Roberval. From January to March, the frozen lake at Roberval becomes the *village sur glace*. The townspeople build tiny, elaborate cottages and display them around a skating oval. They skate and socialize from these *maisonnettes*, gather by woodstoves, eat poutine, and drink hot chocolate.

However, there is something about French pop music that makes me want to want to go read a book. A band was striking up over toward the Jardin des Ursulines, and Nancy and I were ready to make a retreat. Guy was in his gypsy shirt, butterflying among many friends and having a great time. He gave me directions to find him the next day at his travel agency in Saint-Félicien, two towns up the lake from Roberval.

It had been a great evening. But then Nancy cast a shadow. She would *not*, as I had mistakenly assumed, be accompanying me in the days ahead.

"You do have the itinerary I sent . . . you did read it, right?"

"Uh . . ."

"You said you wanted to experience the authentic Quebec," she cooed encouragingly. "You can't do that with a translator hanging all over you."

The prospect of working in French for a week was suddenly daunting. The communities around the lake were staunchly francophone. Bilingual fellows like Guy were few. And I had not even brought a French-English dictionary.

AS I would come to realize over the next few days, my French was at its humble peak after a good night's sleep. Under press of caffeine, I felt almost fluent. In the morning, I navigated my way through an egg-and-toast breakfast at the hermitage cafeteria with a series of *ouis*, *nons*, and *mercis* on cue. I was surrounded by aged Quebecois pilgrims. There were fine views of the morning sun off the lake, and the light filled the dining hall. I wrote notes and drank coffee, letting time pass, enjoying the meditative surroundings.

Sifting through the religious pamphlets in my room, I read something about the spiritually restorative power of beautiful lakes and how Jesus would have understood this because he was "a lake man" himself. Odd images of the long-haired Christian saviour in a plaid flannel shirt—chopping wood, trying to prime the water pump—came to mind.

Looking into it later I confirmed that Jesus, a Galilean, was indeed a lake man. How had this escaped me before? The biblical use of the expression *Sea of Galilee* was certainly confusing, for that water body is assuredly a lake, and not a particularly large one at thirteen kilometres across. It is remarkable in being the lowest freshwater lake on earth, at two hundred metres below sea level. Only the saltwater Dead Sea is lower. In modern translations Matthew and Mark call it the Sea of Galilee on first reference. Luke first refers to it as the Lake of Gennesaret. John calls it the Sea of Galilee and the Sea of Tiberias. After that, all refer to it simply as "the lake."

The Son of Man was constantly getting in and out of boats,

crisscrossing the lake. He travelled along its shores, soul-fishing the apostles Peter, Andrew, John, and James as he went. Jesus conducted much of his so-called Galilean ministry by small craft, sailing and rowing. He preached from afloat when the crowds got too big, steered his disciples to miraculous fishing holes. The happiest stories about him, his greatest miracles and teachings, happened in the lake country. The Sermon on the Mount took place on a hill overlooking the lake. It was stormy lake waters he calmed. When he fed the multitudes with a few fish, it was a shore lunch. The lake was his means to escape those same multitudes—a situation familiar to us today. And of course it was the lake upon which he walked. Amen.

I descended again to Lac Saint-Jean, always surprised to come upon its rounded blue expanse. Almost exactly one thousand square kilometres in size, Lac Saint-Jean is surrounded by municipalities and farms, yet has so far been spared serious eutrophication. Amply fed by pure water from many streams, it has a residence time of only four months and capably flushes anthropogenic sins down to the Saguenay fjord.

It does, however, suffer serious siltation from water-level fluctuations caused by the hydroelectric dam at Isle-Maligne near Alma. Canada is so trussed up with dams that the word *hydro* means "electricity" in both French and English. On a watts-generated-per-capita basis, Quebec leads the world in making electricity from the kinetic energy of water. Hydro-Québec is the single largest dam company in the world and has aggressively dammed all Quebec's major waterways, though the other provinces are not far behind.

The paddler-conservationist Bill Mason decried the dam-building boom of the sixties that drowned so many of his favourite watersheds. American Edward Abbey was so incensed by the Glen Canyon Dam on the Colorado River that he often threatened to blow it up. Wisely, he wrote a novel along these lines instead and called it *The Monkey Wrench Gang*. There is little to like about dams—they trap nutrients, concentrate pollutants, destroy shorelines upstream and down, block genetic flow. They are ugly.

If forced to choose between dams and nuclear stations or an equivalent string of coal plants, I would have the dams. Here, in a vast, young waterscape that nature herself has dammed and redammed a thousand times with her ramparts of glacial ice, perhaps a few walls of concrete that might survive a few hundred years are not so bad.

This is not the pertinent question, however. Rather, we need to question how we spend electricity. A prodigious quantity is used turning bauxite ore into aluminum—the industry that gives this region its economic identity. Aluminum is a fine material for building airplanes; its use in beer cans, lawn chairs, or coffeepots owes more to marketing than to good sense, an invented need. Home heating in Quebec and down the eastern seaboard relies heavily upon electricity, a profligate use akin to cutting butter with a chainsaw.

But I was on holiday . . .

Down at the shore, great numbers of people were enjoying the lake on a simple scale that was refreshing. There were no sprawling hotel estates, no ostentatiously large single-family cottages, no beachfronts turned into strip malls. Instead, there was a bicycle trail, the Véloroute des bleuets, that allowed you to make a complete lap of the lake without ever having to tangle with automobile traffic and connected many small, interesting museums, restaurants, and inns. Visitors lodged in tiny hotels on the low-key commercial streets in the shore towns, in *gîtes,* or in rented bedrooms in residential houses. As in so much of Quebec, there was a firm rejection of the kind of globalized retail outlets and restaurant brands so ubiquitous on the rest of the continent. Loyal Europeans were repeat visitors here.

I found Guy Dufour's travel agency on Saint-Félicien's main street. He was on the telephone when I arrived, so I chitchatted with the receptionist about the hot weather. I was getting more comfortable speaking, or rather more comfortable with the undisguised bemusement my rusty anglophone French produced. Not too many western Canadians came out this way, it seemed. Guy emerged, delighted to see me. Then we were out the door and striding down the street toward a *dépanneur* to provision ourselves for the day. We bought drinks and sandwiches, and Guy got a small bag of the fresh Perron cheddar sold on every counter in the area, made just a few kilometres up the road in Saint-Prime.

"The aged stuff we are sending to England, for one hundred years now," Guy said, proffering the open bag. On first blush I found the cool, rubbery, salty fresh curds unexciting. But by the end of the week, I was buying my own bags at every chance.

We crossed over the bridge spanning the Ashuapmushuan River to Guy's house on the high bank. He lived with his wife and daughter, who were away, and with a noisy poodle, who was home. By my western standards the place was small—a woman I met later told me that if you ever saw an overly large house around, it had to belong to an anglo. Guy's abode possessed the standard Quebecois *piscine* (pool) and an elaborate gazebo. Guy's was the only house on the lake that I entered by the front door—people went to the side or around back. He was busy stuffing our provisions into a cooler and adding more items from his refrigerator, including several brands of American beer. He was cheating time away from work to do this outing, and I thought of how many people had already done the same in order to show me Lakeland through their eyes.

A red car pulled into the drive and the poodle began to bark. The door opened and in came a woman in dark glasses and a one-piece bathing suit covered with a skirt. Her name was Francine

Bouliane. She had been at the table the previous night, though we had not met. She would be joining us for the day. Guy translated briefly as we made introductions, then left us to get acquainted. She spoke no English.

Francine was deeply tanned and looked every inch *une Québécoise*. She was a writer herself, she said, and had had one of her plays produced in her twenties. Francine had a soft, melodious speaking voice and enunciated in a way I found easy to understand. She patiently repeated herself as necessary. She struggled to pronounce my name, which does not roll from French tongues, but persevered, refusing my suggestion to say "Alain."

"Non! Allahn, c'est beau." But when I said I came from "Saskatchewan," her look went blank.

Guy's boat was moored on the bank, a fibreglass runabout with an inboard engine. I helped him open up the canopy and took charge of the dock lines. Getting afloat on the cool water was the perfect antidote to the punishing heat and humidity, and it enlivened us all. Guy opened beers for us before we were ten boat lengths from shore. Earlier he had given me a printed copy of the commentary he used to deliver as tour boat captain. I was grateful he now chose to let the view speak for itself. Francine seemed to be enjoying the liberty and the sun from her seat in the stern port quarter. As for Guy, he seemed to love every minute of life. He steered, kept the fresh cheddar moving, and translated whenever Francine and I reached an impasse. Meanwhile, he fielded a steady string of telephone calls, which Francine and I teased him about a little. Some of them were for my benefit: he was still trying to get me into the zoo gratis. He really was a sweet man.

"Il est bien smart," Francine said, pointing to our skipper.

"Smart?"

"Oui! Ce n'est pas un mot anglais?" Francine explained that *smart*, in local parlance, was used to mean "kind." She was much surprised to learn it had a different meaning in English. This was not the only English word borrowed by the Lac Saint-Jean patois.

The lake was fairly busy with boats and many a one carried a young woman in a bikini on the foredeck. I suppose there are pretty women in small bathing suits in a lot of summer places, but they seemed to sprawl about so much more unselfconsciously in Quebec; I could not discern why, but it was pleasant to research anyway. We rounded a last point and entered the lake proper, a hot wind striking us. Guy pointed to a sandy north shore where he once owned a beautiful cottage. He lost it, along with a lot of money, in a business deal that went sour long ago.

"I forget about the money," he shouted over the wind, "but I still think about the cottage."

With the wind noise, it was doubly difficult to understand Francine, and I had to lean all the way across to hear her when she spoke. Later, I learned my struggle to speak French, to understand her properly, improved Francine's impression of anglophones a good deal. Perhaps this is what prompted her to mention a biography of Pierre Trudeau she was reading. She described herself as a "former separatist" and no fan of Trudeau. But her need to know her own past overrode distaste. Guy, who must have been catching a few words, turned to me and asked for the second time, "You like Pierre Trudeau?" I was just about to open Pandora's box and shout "yes" when his ringing phone saved me.

The silver church spires of Saint-Félicien and Saint-Prime fell behind, and Mashteuiatsh lay ahead. Also known as Pointe-Bleue, pop. 2,015, it is a popular south shore swimming beach and campground, and the only native community in the region, home to the lake Innu people that call themselves Pekuakamiulnuatsh, though I never heard this formidable mouthful pronounced out loud.

Guy's care for his guests reached new levels. After the beer, he was thinking about our bladders. This was kind, for there is nothing worse than having to pee aboard a small boat among people you do not know extremely well. We landed on the crowded public beach. Tour Captain Guy sent Francine and me over the side, declaiming as if Moses to his people: "You will have exactly ten minutes to take a walk. You will find bathrooms at the end of the sand."

We marched off, but the 30°c heat had left me quite desiccated, and something told me Francine was not looking for a loo either.

"Où est-ce qu'on va?" I asked, wondering where we were going.

"J'sais pas, moi," Francine shrugged, and we both had a good laugh. I said that it seemed *le capitain* always had a plan for us. We went for a swim instead. The shallow water was incredibly warm, the bottom colonized by plants I did not recognize. I dove under, following the sunlit, leafy bottom, embraced by the coolness. Guy came in, and we lingered on the strand until the sun began to ease down the hazy, metallic sky.

When we climbed back aboard it was still so hot that a few minutes of flying back toward the river in the breeze dried us. We stopped at a marina to *tanker*, or perhaps *tanquer*, another anglicism meaning "to buy fuel." The boy who ran the pump spilled some gasoline on the boat deck, which he diligently rinsed into the lake with a little water hose just for that purpose.

Back on the pavements of Saint-Félicien, the heat was stifling. Guy tried to steer us to his house, but I vetoed. Too much sun, too much heat, and, above all, too much French. My tank of verbiage was dry, and I felt physically spent. I owed Guy an eloquent thanks I could not muster, so I embraced him instead. Francine drove me back to my car downtown, which was a little awkward in my tired, suddenly mute state.

"T'es fatigué," she said, a statement, not a question. When we stopped, I managed to say how pleasant her company had made the day, or some approximation, and that I hoped we might meet again. In fact, we would. But at that moment, I wanted to only to escape the French language. And to sleep.

Back in Roberval, I had rented half the main floor of a small house just off the high road near a crematorium. The place had been divided down the middle with a wall. On one side lived the owner, Madame Thérèse Gagnon, a slender, dignified grandmother, whom I found at her kitchen table with another guest, a young woman from Switzerland who was spending a three-week holiday there. *La Suissesse*, likely fluent in four languages, was patently shocked by my poor French. I, a Canadian citizen. But my proprietress was very understanding. She explained about keys, about parking, about the air conditioner blowing a fuse if combined with the microwave or hot plate. It was humble, honest lodging. I told Madame Gagnon I had understood everything she said, but that the effort of speaking French all day had left me feeling done in.

"I understand completely," she said in slow French, looking into my eyes. "It is exhausting. I feel exactly like that every time I take a trip to Florida. You will feel better in the morning." She went out through the door in the wall between her place and mine, locking it behind her. And I fell straight into bed though it was still early evening. I could hear Madame Gagnon and *la Suissesse* speaking quietly at her table.

I dreamed of Emma Lake. I was a small boy, swimming in the cool water so clear it was possible to see the whole lake bottom, which teemed with exotic corals. Two old women, with blue hair and wearing cotton shifts, sat on lawn chairs on the sand. They looked like favourite aunts from my dad's side of the family, yet they were speaking French, and so I knew they were figures from a more distant past. Whether friends or foes I did not know. As long as I stayed in the water, they could not reach me. I had no intention of getting out of the lake.

WHEN I opened my eyes, the heat was already stifling and the telephone was ringing. It was Francine Bouliane. It took me forever to understand she was inviting me to spend the day among her family back up on Lac Bouchette. Within the hour, we were speeding up the hills in her car. Francine Bouliane seemed delighted to see me. With great difficulty and sincerity she pronounced the only English syllables I ever heard her speak: "You are my first friend *anglais*."

It was palpably cooler up at Lac Bouchette. Passing the town of that name we turned onto a dirt road. Francine stopped the car and pointed to a street sign that read "Chemin Bouliane." Her ancestors were pioneers on this shore, and the cabins on the slender point ahead all belonged to her family members, all within a few steps of one another. Her own cabin was a humble box with a wickedly sloping particleboard floor, a metal roof, a sleeping loft above the kitchen. Without unpacking them, she threw two bags of groceries into the fridge, drew out two cold beers, and nodded toward the front porch.

"On va balancer?" Yet another new verb for me.

Francine meant we should sit out on her sofa-sized swinging chair on the deck. The point of a cottage, she said, was to do nothing. Swinging to and fro in the shade of the glider's canopy, watching the sun on the water and the cumulus trying to form in the muggy atmosphere, I saw merit in her philosophy. She lit up one of those very long, dark cigarettes, which was surprising because she had not smoked the day before. Even more surprising, when she offered me one, I took it. I had not smoked in years, but this was Quebec.

We received a steady stream of Francine's female relatives, mostly sisters and nieces. An anglo was a novelty on the point, Francine said, maybe a first. One at a time they approached, and each time I stood, hoping formal manners would offset uncouth speech, and smiled like a fool.

The women came and went; we went ourselves to visit the men. Francine's brother, her grown son, and her rheumy-eyed eighty-two-year-old father were sitting on a deck with their wives and girlfriends and grandchildren milling about. Mostly the men did forestry work. Nancy had warned me that it was mostly blue-collar fathers and grandfathers who kept the separatist torch lit—they who could remember labouring under imported English overlords in the old Quebec. But if the Bouliane men held resentments, they showed me none.

Instead, we traded English and French words for the common touchstones of Lakeland: *birch tree, wasp, whitecap, narrows.* When a loon swam by, Francine called it *un canard.* Attempting to set her straight, I found myself making loon calls, to the amusement of all, until a field guide to birds was produced and the loon was found to equal *un huard.* It pleased me that it was onomatopoeic in both tongues. I was asked several times to repeat the English word *tamarack,* which produced big laughs, rhyming as it does with that signature Quebecois curse, *tabernac.*

It was impossible to follow the real patois. When the conversation ran on ahead of me, Francine patiently provided a synopsis. She was as caring a host as Guy had been, and constantly took the pulse of my comfort, intellectual and otherwise. "T'as compris, Allahn?" "T'as faim, Allahn?" "T'es fatigué, Allahn?"

Pierre Trudeau would be interested to know I learned more French in a few days around Lac Saint-Jean than in months living in Montreal. Theorists in second-language acquisition propose that the key ingredients for learners are a comforting milieu in

which to learn and the company of native speakers active in helping the newcomer gain fluency and comprehension.

Francine and I balancing on her porch swing were a neat
political metaphor for the relationship between French and
English Canada, and we each made discoveries. At one point,
Francine had referred to English Canadians as *les autres* ("the
others"). This hit me like a bolt of lighting. So that was what *they*
called *us*. And what did they call themselves? *Nous*, presumably.
Not quite. Francine said that *nous* referred just to her own people,
that is, the people of the lake. Other Quebecois they called *nous
autres* (literally, "our others"). *Les autres* was for everyone else in
the federation.

For her part, Francine learned a few things about Canada
from me. The previous day her apparent confusion about my
place of origin was real: she simply did not know what or where
Saskatchewan was. She had taken me for an Eastern European.
I listed the western provinces in their correct order, noting that
there were significant francophone communities in all of them.
Francine was unimpressed.

She did recall that during the last referendum, she had
watched some Albertans burning the fleur-de-lis on the news. She
could not countenance such a cruelty. I countered that when my
mother saw images of people's houses being carried off by the
great Saguenay Flood of 1996, she had sent a hundred dollars
to the Croix-Rouge (Red Cross) relief effort. From Saskatchewan.

The sun was declining, dragging my speech-forming ability
with it below the horizon as usual. It was time to go. Before leaving, my host took me down to view *les roches de Francine*, a flat
of granite at the end of the point, which had been her personal
refuge as a child growing up. It gave a lovely view north down the
lake. We might inhabit different political jurisdictions, Francine
and I, but we were two citizens of one Lakeland.

I rode into town with Francine and her sister, who were going down to Roberval to watch—*quel horreur!*—a KISS tribute band. I was kindly invited, and kindly demurred. Once again, I was inadequate to the thanks that were owed, and so mute embraces had to serve.

As I approached my door in a near-catatonic state, Madame Gagnon leaned out from hers. She had made tourtière and said I had to have some of the real thing, lake style. *Oh God.* I simply could not muster the appetite for another intake, neither of food nor French. But Madame surmised all from my weary face. "*Non, non! A ta chambre.* I will bring it." I was encircled by kindness. She arrived with a rich, warm plate a minute later. I put it straight into the tiny refrigerator and went to bed before dark, exhausted, for the second day running.

IT WAS not yet 5 AM. Hours remained before the starting pistol, yet a mania had already gripped the office staff, the timers, the medics, the security guards, and the sundry volunteers needed to carry out the running of a major international swimming race. And no one was more gripped than the sleep-deprived *co-ordinatrice*, Marie-Claude Simard. She was speaking laboured English over her shoulder to me, and machine-gun bursts of French to people in the hallways as we passed through race headquarters. She wore a two-way radio headset that interrupted her every fifteen seconds as we made it to the press room.

"You can have some breakfast here." The room contained the only relaxed-looking people in the building: journalists, who were eating a free breakfast from a buffet laid under windows looking over the grey lake, the finish line, and the as yet empty bleachers. Except for me, it was an all-Quebec media contingent. "After, you take the yellow bus for Péribonka," said Marie-Claude. "Do not be late." And she was off again.

Though little known in English Canada, La Traversée internationale du lac Saint-Jean is a Quebecois institution. The first race was held in 1955 with a local field of swimmers, only one of whom completed the crossing. Since then, swimmers from more than thirty countries have competed, and the race has steadily gained in prestige. And there are similar, smaller events around the province. The hope was to establish open-water swimming as an Olympic sport. This must have been gaining ground because the international competitive swimming agency called FINA had sent an American crew to monitor the race and take urine samples—signs of a sport with a future.

The athletes were already gathering by the start line, thirty-two kilometres straight across the lake at Péribonka. Boarding a school bus with me to travel there the long way around were journalists and FINA people in the back, a noisy contingent of boatmen up front. Each swimmer is accompanied across the lake by a small boat; it was a picture of these distinctive red skiffs that first drew my interest in the race. By tradition, most are piloted by First Nations men from Mashteuiatsh, and they were in a boisterous mood, shouting friendly jibes around the bus as we passed the extensive blueberry fields for which the lake is known.

One of the photojournalists was a twenty-year-old named Frédéric. An art-photography student from Montreal, he had been assigned to document from start to finish some kind of public event that embodied Quebec life. We were both just playing journalist for the day, and we became friendly. Over the din of the shouting boatmen, we somehow managed to broach politics, and I recounted my revelation on Pointe-Bouliane concerning the Lac Saint-Jean use of the words *nous, nous autres,* and *les autres.*

These little words had an incendiary effect on Frédéric.

"Ça me dérange!" he hissed, an expression akin to "that pisses me off."

Those were outdated concepts, Frédéric insisted, retained by people forty and up, by old separatists with a chip on their shoulder, especially in rural Quebec. Urbanites his age embraced a wider, multicultural world, he assured me. I did not doubt him. But the heat with which he made his case suggested the old ideas were still very much in play.

We crossed over the tea-coloured Mistassini, one of the many swift rivers that feed the lake, and passed through fertile farmland going into Péribonka. It was this area that served as backdrop for the enduring literary portrait of Lac Saint-Jean, the 1914 novel *Maria Chapdelaine*. Written by Brest-born Louis Hémon, the story follows the title character, a young debutante, over the course of a year as she chooses from among her suitors. Hémon built the story out of his experiences working as a farm hand, and it became a Quebec classic. Maria is the literary embodiment of an underdog province as much as Dark Rosaleen symbolizes an oppressed Ireland.

When we came down to the pier in Péribonka, it was crowded with spectators come to watch the start, undeterred by the grey drizzle. The swimmers emerged on the dock one at a time, introduced by an announcer. The women came first, then the men, each ascending a little arched bridge connecting two sections of the pier, turning and waving. Great partisan shouts went up for the Quebec entrants. The overwhelming favourite among the men was Petar Stoychev of Bulgaria, who had won the previous six years. The women's side was up for grabs.

Frédéric and I closely scrutinized the swimmers, about twenty in all, as they prepared to climb down into the uninviting black water of the marina. Their bodies were coated in varying amounts of rendered fat—whether animal or vegetable I could not tell—as a hedge against the cold of the seven-hour immersion that was about to begin. They wore dark-lens goggles, their race numbers written in black grease on their skin. They descended to a float, plunged in three or four at a time, and swam slowly to the start line. Without delay or fanfare, the start gun fired. As the swimmers departed, one of the men lagged behind for a moment on purpose, mugging for the crowd.

Despite its obscurity as a sport, long open-water swims are a rite of passage across Lakeland. I've swum across Emma Lake twice and driven the support boat for other people on a number of occasions. As everyone who attempts a long swim discovers, it is not the distance but the cold that gets you. The body loses heat to the environment roughly thirty times faster in water than in air. At 21°C in still air, we can survive stark naked indefinitely. In water of the same temperature, most of us would die slowly in the course of one day. Blood chilled in the extremities shocks the heart and disrupts its rhythm. As the water temperature drops, the risks multiply. Consider the Rule of 50: a 50-year-old will have a 50 percent chance of surviving a 50-minute swim in 50°F (10°C) water.

The mid-July temperature of Lac Saint-Jean is 18.5°C, yielding a survival time for an average person of about nine hours—just enough for the crossing. However, age, fitness, training, body-fat ratio, metabolism, and food intake skewed the numbers in the athletes' favour. Still, the significant challenge of the race was the cold itself.

The Royal Canadian Navy arrived at the dock in a large inflatable launch to ferry us out to view the racing action up close. By the time we got aboard and threaded our way out through the flotilla of pleasure craft following the race, the swimmers had already covered an impressive distance. They were making over five kilometres an hour, a brisk walking speed for most people.

In each accompanying red *bateau* was a coach who held up messages on a whiteboard or shouted advice. Already the competitors were consuming fuel. The coach would pour some sweet-looking liquid into a plastic cup, place this in a metal ring fixed to the end of a pole and extend it over the water. In the few seconds that it took to drink a single large gulp, the swimmer would be many metres behind.

The swimmers crawled out across the grey lake, and we turned back for shore. I was glad not to be among them. It was a vaguely horrifying sport: the mental stamina to stare into the burbling murk by the hour, the sensory deprivation, choking on outboard fumes, and swallowing rogue waves. The total prize money for the race was just forty thousand dollars.

The return trip to Roberval was quiet without the boatmen. The media *co-ordinatrice*, Marie-Claude, was aboard and came back to sit with Frédéric and me. Her two-way radio was put away. With the swimmers in the water, her own marathon was nearly accomplished. Slumped in her seat, she told us the story of the last few days, of how the race had almost been cancelled.

Unbeknownst to me behind my second-language veil, a journalistic frenzy had been underway all week following the release of a government environmental report that showed blue-green algae populations were elevated at several test sites on the lake. There were no great blooms, no swimming bans, no immediate danger. But the Quebec media was inspired to run screamer headlines about "toxic cyanobacteria." Many of the international teams almost pulled out of the race.

"The reporters asked the same questions every day. Every day, they write the same story." At first, Marie-Claude was herself alarmed. Were levels of blue-greens enough to harm her competitors? When she learned the truth—that this was a common symptom of an incremental environmental problem, not a threat to life and limb—she expected the media to help calm the waters. Instead, they fanned up a tempest.

I felt sorry for Marie-Claude and regretted the corrosive effects the stories could have, creating fear and hostility on these shores. But once the furor subsided, the Quebec media adopted a more thoughtful approach, publishing clear-minded reports on blue-greens and other lake water quality issues. Lake conservation has since become part of the daily news stream in Quebec.

BACK IN Roberval, I lunched on Madame Gagnon's excellent tourtière, washed her dishes and returned them with my best compliments, took a nap, slogged through French newspaper stories about blue-green algae, had coffee in an outside café. All this time, the swimmers had been in the water.

By afternoon, the finish line at Place de la Traversée was transformed. The stands were packed. Any boat that could float was moored along the vee of race buoys. Though still just out of sight, the swimmers' satellite-fixed positions were shown on the big screens in race headquarters and televisions around the province. The Quebecois Simon Tobin was in close second place, behind Petar Stoychev of Bulgaria. VIPs were being led to front-row seats; the frowning FINA observers hovered over the finish with folded arms. Frédéric was there, shooting pictures.

When the race leaders appeared to the viewers in the stands, a long cheer began. It continued over the last two kilometres, which did not take the swimmers long. The pace had not slackened from the morning. Tobin seemed to be gaining on the champion. He was making it the closest finish in many years, and the crowd was on its feet. But in the last few metres, Stoychev put on an easy burst of speed, actually butterflying across the line to win the race a seventh straight time in 6 hours, 36 minutes, 29 seconds.

Climbing out of the water, the Bulgarian looked as fresh and relaxed as when he had gone in, and was wrapped in a plush robe and surrounded by microphones like an old-fashioned prizefighter. He embraced Tobin, then strode expansively up the gangway and made a turn in front of the crowd.

At 7:03:09, Esther Núñez from Spain crossed and emerged, much like the Bulgarian, looking fresh and joyful, to be similarly wrapped, thronged, and cheered.

But these arrivals were not typical. Most of the swimmers had trouble getting up the ladder, moving like old people or shock victims. They were immediately placed in a chair and interrogated by medics in English. Their mumbled responses belonged to no language. Their skins had a rough, bluish cast, their layers of protective lard worn thin and grey. Their viciously tight goggles, in place for so long, left purple rings round their eyelids that gave them a ghastly expression. It was hard to believe these vanquished did dozens of such swims a year.

Frédéric and I stayed on the docks for some time—not so much to watch the swimmers come ashore as to observe the crowd, to watch the lake people, the *pure laine*, watching themselves.

These Quebecois had a richness of community distinct in North America. I envied them their cohesive, four-hundred-year-old culture, their mature film and television industry, their literary life, their obscure water sports—all geared to their unique tastes. They were complete unto themselves. Theirs was an encompassing world.

And yet it felt small, just there. Glimpsing the Quebecois from this low angle, from down by the lake that symbolized their independence, I sympathized with their perennial hunger for nationhood. At some point, separation is exile, comfortable containment becomes imprisonment, a distinct society feels besieged. If nationhood would make them feel more self-assured, they could have it—though it was doubtful that sufficient sovereignist flame still burned in Frédéric's generation.

Within the straining bounds of this introspective province, Lakeland seemed more solidly real to me than ever. It would outlast Quebec, it would outlast Canada. Its shorelines, the call of its water birds, would still define whatever they might call this place a millennium hence after all the flags had faded, all the champions had been forgotten, even after all the dams had broken. It would remain until the ice that first scoured it into shape moved south again.

A month after I returned home, I received a letter from an old friend from Montreal. She asked how I had spent my summer vacation, and told me how she had spent hers: "Je suis restée particulièrement au Québec. J'aime de plus en plus ma province. Elle donne tant de possibilité . . ."

INTO THE LAKE-LAP OF THE MOUNTAIN

WATERTON LAKES NATIONAL PARK, *Alberta*

Water is the first world.

SUSAN ANDREWS GRACE, *Water Is the First World*

T HERE ARE no lakes in Alberta. Out west you hear this fiction sometimes, usually from people who have migrated to the gloriously endowed province from elsewhere and just have to knock it down a peg. It is true that Alberta is barely grazed by the lake-rich Canadian Shield. It is true that Alberta encompasses some of the driest country in Lakeland.

Overlooked are Alberta's mountain lakes, some of the world's most beautiful, pure, and protected waters. Lake Louise is probably Canada's most renowned lake, its rock-flour turquoise hue instantly recognizable in photos. Moraine Lake, a short hike from Louise, used to be pictured on the verso of the twenty-dollar bank note. Such images are the quintessence of Canada. As a bonus, the high lakes in oil country are generally beyond the snaring reach of automotive pavement, yet nonetheless accessible by some of the world's most scenic, well-tended walking paths.

In mid-September I went west, bound for Waterton Lakes National Park. It is a less travelled corner of the Rocky Mountains than Lake Louise, far off the busy east–west routes through the mountains, tucked into a corner formed by the U.S. border and the Continental Divide. Besides the novelty of seeing it for the first time, it was the only national park in the country named in honour of lakes. Like most of the lakes in the southern Rockies, the outflow from the Watertons finds its way to the Saskatchewan River, which wends its muddy course within three blocks of my house on its way to Lake Winnipeg. Lower Waterton is the first natural lake upstream of my kitchen taps. Lakeland is all plumbed together.

Beyond these enticements, the Rockies of Waterton are said to rise magically straight up out of the prairie, without the preamble of foothills. The Cheyenne called them "rock-on-the-horizon." To test this proposition, I had an altimeter on the front seat. I glanced at it now and then as I drove across the plains, the golden fields in their close-shaved, post-harvest state. By Medicine Hat, it showed a gain of only 150 metres after five hundred westward kilometres. The South Saskatchewan River had changed its stripes, however. Close to its high sources, its waters were not muddy but clear and blue. The highway that turned southwest to Lethbridge skirted the dramatic coulees the river had cut deep into the glacial till. The lakes of Waterton were still far over the horizon, but their waters had transformed the dry land ahead into one of the most agriculturally rich regions in the country.

This region was surveyed for its agricultural potential in 1857 by Captain John Palliser, who famously reported to the British parliament that the area was too arid for settlement. Though his advice was ignored, the driest region of the prairie is known to this day as the Palliser Triangle, and is for the generations who tried to make a living here synonymous with thirst. By 1900, southern Alberta was receiving waves of Mormon emigrants from Utah, who established the first irrigation cooperatives. But capital for waterworks was always short, and Palliser's Triangle was destined to become the Dust Bowl of the Dirty Thirties.

Oil changed all that. Royalty wealth allowed Alberta to construct the most extensive and sophisticated irrigation system in Canada. Virtually all the runoff from the eastern flank of the Rockies is used for power, for feeding cattle, and for growing every high-value produce crop imaginable. Some 65 percent of Canada's irrigation agriculture occurs in Alberta, most of it along this Medicine Hat–Lethbridge corridor. The fields—sugar beets, potatoes, corn—are watered by pivoting spray booms that scribe great circles, turning the landscape into green polka dots when seen from the air. The highway passes food-processing plants, greenhouses, horticulture centres, intensive livestock operations, turf suppliers. It crosses and recrosses the canals of the St. Mary River Irrigation District, the nation's largest, with over two thousand kilometres of waterworks.

All this makes Alberta's downstream neighbours uneasy. Irrigation supplies 40 percent of global food; it is hard to imagine doing without it. But irrigation can severely salt-damage soils, and lack of flow threatens natural watershed ecosystems. By interprovincial agreement, Alberta is entitled to one-half the South Saskatchewan flow; the province of Saskatchewan gets one-half of the remainder; Manitoba takes the dregs. As a dump for treated sewage and urban storm drains, the river needs steady natural flows to dilute the pollutants. Already there is not enough water for all this human want. As for the other downstream species, they are not signatories to any treaty.

The altimeter showed I was rising above such worldly concerns, into the safe cocoon of the national park. As I left Lethbridge, altitude nine hundred metres, a row of mountain peaks suddenly appeared on the apparently dead-flat horizon, just as promised. The prairie did climb another five hundred metres by the Mormon town of Cardston, but the peaks were fifteen hundred metres higher still. It was indeed like coming to a rock wall at the end of the grass, and vaguely ominous. With the setting sun turning them to blue-black silhouettes, the mountains resembled sea waves on a terrible scale, mounting and advancing over the prairie.

Once the peaks eclipsed the blinding sun, colour returned to their shadows, and I could see deer browsing among the willows of the creekbeds leading into the park. The park gate attendant announced that all the local hotel rooms were full. But it was a warm Saturday night, and I had brought a tent. The road climbed along Lower Waterton, just a silver pond, reached across the last spit of prairie, and brought the famous Prince of Wales Hotel into view, pasted against the mountain background, standing lookout over the grassy narrows between Middle and Upper Waterton. The first-quarter harvest moon was up.

Upper Waterton Lake is an arrow-straight, mountain-walled trough ten kilometres long and less than one kilometre wide, straddling the Alberta-Montana border. It was gently played by warm south breezes at that moment, and the moonlight invited an evening swim. A swim would be a rude shock, however, for the lake is ever cold. Waterton, the village, is now mainly a summer resort, though it once had a sizable year-round population. It began as a work camp in 1904 after the first oil well in western Canada came in, now a National Historic Site in nearby Cameron Valley. The town has a resident herd of mule deer. They keep the lawns well trimmed, pose for tourist photographers, and take their ease under trampolines and swing sets. At the campground I got the very last space—a sleeping-bag length from the entrance road and under a glaring yard light. The mild, calm night was inviting, and I went "downtown" to eat at a sidewalk table among cottage owners from Calgary enjoying one of the last weekends of the season, and tourists from Frankfurt and Sydney.

This area became a federal wilderness preserve in 1895. Across the Montana border, which serves as the park's southern boundary, is Glacier National Park, and the two contiguous parks, tied together as Waterton-Glacier International Peace Park, are a UNESCO Biosphere Reserve and a World Heritage Site.

Though dwarfed by other Rocky Mountain parks on both sides of the border, Waterton is, acre for acre, among the most biodiverse. Not only does it straddle mountain and grassland bioregions, it is a collision point for moist, warm Pacific air and dry, cold continental-Arctic air. The weather is wildly variable. Chinooks, the warm, roaring winds that spill over the eastern Rockies, are common. The abrupt weather changes that accompany chinooks are amazing to experience. One record-setting day in January 1962, the temperature in nearby Pincher Creek rose from 19°C below freezing to 22°C above in one hour.

For exercise after dinner, I cycled up to the Prince of Wales Hotel. The entrance road was an inky defile through bush, leading onto the small grass-topped plateau where the hotel commands the view down the lake. Opened in 1927, this was a Canadian railway hotel built by neither of the national railways but by the American Great Northern line. Affluent travellers reached the hotel from the Montana end of the lake aboard the MV *International*—the fine original vessel still sails the same route today. Opened during Prohibition, the hotel was a posh watering hole for thirsty Americans. Like all the great railway hotels, the Prince of Wales is said to be haunted. With its windows full of amber light and milling guests, it looked warm and kindly to me, but I stayed outside, under the Milky Way.

In the few minutes it took to descend to the campground, the famous Waterton wind arrived. For some reason I had brought a tent large enough for a Sicilian family. The great span of nylon flogged like an untrimmed sail. The yard light shone like the sun, the great cottonwood hanging over the tent creaked loudly with every gust, and vehicles rumbled past incessantly. After much preamble, sleep arrived. Seemingly a moment later, I roused, having migrated a whole fathom across the slippery floor toward the tent door. I slid open the zipper and stared up into the stars. The Summer Triangle was long set, and Auriga and Orion were scouting their winter grounds. The Big Dipper stood balanced on the handle. It was the same sky I had seen nearly a year ago at this time, coming ashore in Newfoundland. It had to be early morning. I felt a strange, sleepy euphoria looking up into the star calendar. I had been given another year of sweet life in the heart of this great, mysterious clockwork of nature.

WHILE DRIVING is the default mode for millions of visitors, the Rocky Mountain parks are meant for foot travel. Taking European Alpine tourism as their model, the railway hotels promoted hiking from earliest days. Today, according to my copy of the classic *Canadian Rockies Trail Guide*, there are three thousand kilometres of trail through the twenty thousand square kilometres of protected land within the five national parks of Banff, Jasper, Kootenay, Yoho, and Waterton.

Having rooted mostly in the basement of Lakeland's watersheds, I wanted to climb one of these trails to the other end of the spectrum, to touch—though it sounds like an advertising slogan—the pure mountain source. The highest mountain lakes can indeed approach the purity of distilled water. On high, water is all promise and potential, a reservoir, a stock chemical, an abstract quantum. At some point on the mountainside it consummates union with the earth and life issues forth. It becomes an aquatic ecosystem. I wanted to observe the precise transition from purity to fecundity, to find—if it be not too proud an undertaking—the rung on the ladder where life begins.

Back in high school, a friend and I hiked to a chain of high mountain lakes and camped by one of them just at the tree line.

It was too cold in the shade, too hot in the sun. The waters were as clear as those of a tropical reef, so that, simply standing on the shore, you could see right down to sandy bottom in the middle of the lake. Unlike the tropics, the lake appeared devoid of life: no murk of plankton, no shoreline fringe of bottom plants. The purest lakes are, of course, dead.

As we sat, contradictory evidence swam into view. A full-grown fish moved lazily by. Some kind of trout. Then another disturbed the surface, and another. It seemed impossible that sufficient food could be found in these clear waters, that enough insects lit upon it, to build flesh upon bone. But we had seen the apparition with our own eyes.

I was eager to revisit the high-altitude food web. By telephone, prior to leaving, I had spoken to a most helpful warden who warned me not to delay in getting up to Waterton, as the weather did not take long to go from fall to winter. Indeed, the forecast for the next few days seemed to guarantee snow at altitude. Somehow I forgot to write down the helpful fellow's name. But when I stopped in to the park administrative centre, he was sitting right there at the desk and recognized my voice. Talk about my tax dollars at work!

Derek Tilson resembled a park ranger from an old Disney film, with his perfectly pressed uniform and a wholesome, fresh-air complexion. He had the trim, slight physique of a young man. In fact, he already had thirty-five years at the park and was officially retired, having been called in to help with the high-season rush.

Some 400,000 visitors reached Waterton every year, sharply down from previous decades. It was a familiar story in wilderness parks, Derek said. Travel costs were rising beyond the reach of average families; there were new immigrants for whom the park experience was unfamiliar; the ever-aging baby boomers were aging still more.

But Waterton has stayed relatively quiet for a more basic reason. "If the water was warmer, the pressure on Waterton would
be enormous," Derek said. On a hot summer day, campers will
take a dip in the shallows of Emerald Bay, but they do not linger.
The Waterton Lakes never really warm up, the wild winds make
boating treacherous. Once Derek and his wife had capsized their
sailing kayak, and it was a harrowing ordeal. The snail-slow pace
of life in the resort was thought to be harrowing to Calgarians.

Then there was winter. Hotels have attempted to bring in
convention business in the off-season, but the formidable Waterton wind thwarts civility. It may blow at a hundred kilometres
per hour for days at a time, said Derek. "Anywhere else, and it
would be on the news." And so Wateron goes quietly along its un-
Alberta ways.

Derek recommended that I hike the Carthew-Alderson Trail,
which begins at Cameron Lake on the Montana border, climbs to
a summit, and then steps down a series of small lakes that straddle the tree line. It sounded perfect for the observations I wanted
to make. Though a pelting rain had begun even as we spoke,
Derek thought there might be a clear window early the following
morning. He warned me to not to risk being caught in a whiteout
at the summit. Taking the wrong valley down could result in a
twenty-kilometre forced-march detour through prime grizzly bear
habitat.

Derek was a fount of knowledge and even had a theory on
the mysterious fish I had seen so many years before in that seemingly dead lake. Only the lower Rocky Mountain lakes naturally
supported fish, but many of the higher ones had been artificially
stocked, a practice that ended not many years ago. Before leaving,
he lent me an enormous green binder, a compendium of decades
of government research on the natural and cultural resources of
the park, including fish.

I spent the rest of the day exploring the grassy trails and red rock of the Blakiston Valley. The valley was named for Lieutenant Thomas Blakiston, who led a section of the Palliser Expedition. His company was returning to the prairies via the South Kootenay Pass when, on September 6, 1858, he descended this valley to Waterton Lakes.

Blakiston named the lakes after the eighteenth-century naturalist Charles Waterton. The very emblem of aristocratic eccentricity, Charles Waterton was a stubbornly Catholic Englishman who wore a crewcut in a long-hair era, liked to walk barefoot, and read Latin poetry while perched in the limbs of his estate trees. In 1824, he built a high stone wall around his property to repel poachers—though he gave the townspeople leave to picnic and birdwatch—thereby creating the world's first nature preserve, according to the town council in modern-day Wakefield, England. They further credit him with inventing the bird nesting box, which he placed throughout the estate. Waterton also fought a soapworks company in court for polluting his lake, a first in ecological justice.

Thomas Blakiston, a naturalist in his own right and a contemporary of Charles Darwin, would have seen the valley just as I was seeing it, in a tumult of fall colour: the shimmering gold of the wild grass; the pale, twisted aspen branches still holding deep-green leaves; the ruby hue of the lower mountains under the grey peaks; the flame-orange of the lichen-covered rubbing stones waiting unperturbedly for the bison to return. Over it all sprang rainbows in steady succession, the mountaintops tearing long rents in the cloud and letting the sun strike through to their falling mists. It was improbably picturesque—like a television car commercial.

Blakiston would not have had the road, neither its convenience nor its affront to the natural order. It would be glorious

to arrive in this valley astride a horse like him, but then I would
have needed all summer to get here and might not have come at
all. Our relationship with nature is now postmodern, and our best
course for the future will involve a complexity that even an inno- ·
vator like him could not have conceived.

Anyway, I hoped any conceivable future would still feature
walking. I spent the rest of the day wandering the natural grassland at the foot of the mountains, snooping up the slopes under
the cliffs, taking photos of rainbows and the blood-coloured stone
here called argillite. I can fall into daydream while ambling with
no particular destination, and hours pass. But a familiar pain in
my feet kept me in the moment. I was wearing my old Vasque hikers for the first time since going to Grey Owl's cabin, and they felt
even worse than before. I would have to fix the problem before
the twenty-five-kilometre hike the next day.

Back in the village, I sought out Tamarack Outfitters, est.
1922, one of the oldest businesses in Waterton, catering mainly
to hikers for the last thirty-five years. As I came up the walk on
my complaining legs to seek their counsel, a group of young people was gathered on the benches outside the store. They were all
strikingly tanned, their wooly dreadlocks bleached by the sun.
Their clothing and backpacks were grimy and impressively worn.
Their leg muscles were so developed they reminded me of cartoon superheroes.

It transpired that this group of men and women not long out
of high school had just walked to the Waterton Lakes from the
Mexican border, completing a five-thousand-kilometre through-
hike of the Continental Divide Trail. They were taking a shuttle
back to the United States, to begin the next chapter of their young
lives. I cannot think of a better opening gambit in the sober game
of adulthood than to walk a wild path across one's country. There
is no sure inoculation against a closed mind, against creeping

conservatism, but it was hard to think of such people ever becoming slaves to convention.

The shopkeeper who provided this background information was a woman with a schoolteacher manner. She took only a moment to diagnose my ambulatory discomfort. Plunging a brave hand into one of my still steaming boots, she yanked out a threadbare insole and brandished it before me: "How thick is this, now, maybe a millimetre?" Her authority was formidable, but kindly. She led me past all the fifty-dollar replacement insoles to the ten-dollar ones, which were just as good, she said. My venerable old boots were instantly restored to vessels of comfort.

Having pulled up stakes in the noisy campground, I took shelter at a lovely motel next to Tamarack Outfitters. Of the many roofs under which I had tarried in my journeys through Lakeland, the Bear Mountain Motel deserves particular mention for its simple, sustainable elegance. Built in the early 1960s, the motel had rooms that were blessedly small by today's standards—some North American hotel rooms have bathrooms as large. There was no in-room telephone, which made perfect sense in an era where every guest brings their own. There was no air conditioning, which made sense at 49 degrees north latitude. There was a small television that took its two imperfect signals via antenna—just enough to get the hiking weather forecast. Places like this still exist across the country, but they are being let go, torn down, replaced by properties twice the size and half the simple charm. Bear Mountain was freshly decorated in Rockies pueblo style, and the bed was very fine. As an added *plaisanterie*, the chamber staff were all pink-cheeked Hutterite maidens in polka-dot kerchiefs who sang their Mennonite work songs with great, innocent gusto as they went from room to room, fluffing, tucking and vacuuming.

Delving into the great green binder that Derek Tilson had lent me, I sought any references to Waterton's higher-altitude lakes.

These had undergone their share of heavy-handed "management," with sport angling in mind. Existing species of local fish, like Dolly Varden trout, lake trout, and cutthroat trout, were transplanted up-mountain across natural barriers like falls. Hatchery-raised and genetically similar subspecies like Yellowstone cutthroat trout had been added to wild stocks, and overcompetitive exotics like arctic grayling, rainbow trout, and brook trout introduced.

Such manipulations have permanently altered Waterton's aquatic habitats as they have many places the world over. Native species moved into high lakes without enough food to sustain them effectively wiped out any prey species, then slowly starved. Hybridization with hatchery fish has made the indigenous West-slope cutthroat trout, Montana's state fish, a species at risk.

IT WAS 7:08 AM when I clicked the doors locked and crossed the parking lot to the trailhead. The Carthew-Alderson Trail begins on the shore of Cameron Lake, altitude 1660 metres. The rock face at its southern end belongs to Montana, the ridge above its west shore is part of the Continental Divide. Just as Derek Tilson had predicted, the sky was mostly clear. I hoped to cross the summit into the next valley before the weather closed in, and so get a look at the descending staircase of high lakes I had come to see. A woman was standing on the dock behind a camera on a tripod, facing toward the vista still in dusk. I bid good morning, not much above a whisper. She turned, a pale beauty with thick brown hair, a Dark Rosaleen from an Irish poem. "I am waiting for the light," she said. *Aren't we all.*

Bill Mason observed that it is risky for the artist to portray nature as it really is, whether in books, films, or paintings. For if you dare show it true to life, your audience may go straight to sleep. The human observer demands action, drama, danger, or at least the piquancy of a transient moment. So a mountain photographer

{ 235

awaits the fleeting sidelight of dawn to paint distant cliffs—or the viewer will fail to *see*. Mason admitted his own films made it seem as if the woods were absolutely jumping with bears, deer, wolves. Truth was, it could take him patient weeks to capture such glimpses. In writing of his beloved desert, Edward Abbey said that language was a loose net with which to capture the intricacies of nature, that he could no more get the desert into a book than the fisherman could pull up the sea with his nets. Ultimately we must go ourselves, and let nature work the senses directly. And so if you, patient reader, feel you must now close this page and go into the great living room of the outdoors, I willingly defer.

The trail mounted upward through mature lodgepole pine, switching back half a dozen times, and Cameron Lake soon began to seem a small pool. In their renovated boots my feet found an all-day pace. My mind began to walk trails of its own in the drunkenness of pine scent. Beads of dew gave a diamond glint to the ground. This was all carbon atoms done up in endless sparkling variation. We accept De Beers' corporate assertion that two months' salary will last a lifetime if spent on an engagement ring. Maybe we need some conglomerate to make a monopoly of our diamond wilderness, hoard it in vaults, and so drive its value up. And then sell it back to us. Maybe by this stratagem we would see its worth.

The trail emerged onto a plateau, actually a gentle descent toward Summit Lake. The dew weighed upon the bear grass, the morning sky pink-blue. I stepped on a frozen puddle, the first of the season, then came to the water and its crystalline reflection of the rock. No occlusions here, no discolourations. I sat on a log, steam rising from both the water and my shirt, and tried to compute the probability of this stone, this sky, the trillion cellular stitches that wove them into a living picture. The alpine light had arrived. Somewhere far below, in an atmospheric rapture of the deep, Dark Rosaleen tripped her shutter.

Summit Lake was a misnomer, for the trail continued steeply on. It wore through the last lodgepoles and into the subalpine firs. These small, stubborn grey-barked trees linked arms together like scrappy little rugby men in a scrum. The view was opening up. Across the valley in Montana, the Herbst Glacier clung to a north face of Mount Custer. The ice was a few thin patches of dirty white, and there were similar, unnamed glacial remnants clinging to north faces elsewhere on the American side.

Since there are no glaciers in Waterton itself, this was the closest I would come to the ancient ice. One could think of glaciers as lakes of a special order, diamonds in the sky. Except for their frozen-to-the-bottom state and their gymnastic ability to cling to steep slopes, glaciers are really just high-altitude, ultra-oligotrophic lakes. For that matter, the water-laden atmosphere itself is the greatest lake of all.

The sky's willingness to yield water swings through great extremes in the west, and the Rocky Mountains appear to have been storing less over recent decades. In my lifetime, the ice-fields of the mountains have shrunk visibly, some glaciers losing half their ice mass in the last century. It seems likely the Rocky Mountains will be ice-free in another hundred years. Glaciers are primary reservoirs for the Saskatchewan and other major watersheds, and it would seem a frightening prospect to see them wither to nothing. The natural midsummer flow of glacier-fed rivers has decreased by as much as 84 percent since the early twentieth century. What these days we call climate change appears to be the smoking gun—and we fear we have pulled the trigger with our carbon dioxide emissions.

The truth of our carbon pollution has been difficult to dig out of the complex strata of climate information, for global weather has *always* been in a state of flux. Canada has no normal map of ice cover, having experienced more than fifty glacial-interglacial cycles in the last five million years. The Rocky Mountain glaciers of today appeared only three thousand years ago, during a cold dip in the otherwise warm interglacial of the present Holocene Epoch. As they recede now, some Rockies glaciers reveal the trunks of great trees they entombed millennia ago.

I am tempted to express gratitude for the current climate change crisis, but that would be flippant. Curbing our carbon dioxide emissions, which have such profound effects on global temperature, is a desperate cause. But I cannot help seeing the silver lining. Global warming has ushered in a new era of international cooperation and a flowering of holism in our approach to the biosphere. It reaches across scientific disciplines, flies over national borders. It has brought us to a new era, putting all living things, for the first time in history, on the same side of a practical problem. The earth is Noah's ark. We have finally begun to put a value, expressible in dollars, on natural systems we have hitherto taken for granted. The search for clean energy has been rejuvenated. All of this feels to me more like a renaissance than the End of Days. Having grown up with the certainty of global war, I feel that with global warming we have something like a fighting chance at transcendence.

A clattering brought me out of this hopeful daydream. The trail had left the trees and entered a great bowl of jagged talus. The sound was of two deer traversing the rock high above. The whole slope glinted dully from the dew on the rock, though the individual fragments were a dull red. The mountain light began to play tricks. At some altitude the air achieves a clarity that brings great detail to the eye. With less atmosphere to scatter the light rays, there are fewer visual cues to suggest distance. The double summits of Mount Carthew seemed close enough to touch, though there were still many switchbacks to climb.

Beyond the tree line there were still growing things, low-slung moss campion, *Silene acaulis*. Shaped liked little cushions, the spongy domes retain precious water and serve as heat traps when the sun shines on them. Though a new acquaintance to me, this plant is common around the Northern Hemisphere on mountains and on the tundra, and Derek Tilson told me it is one of his favourites when it blooms in purple flowers. I scanned the slopes for grizzlies, which he said sometimes crossed this pass. This was the open rock where you could quickly lose the trail in heavy snow. But the day was bright, the air completely still, and an hour later I stepped onto the ledge atop the col.

The altitude was 2,300 metres, and the other half of the horizon appeared—360° of blue mountain peaks and bleached cloud tops jumbled together. The summits at each end of the ridge beckoned even higher, but they were farther than they looked, and the weather would not keep long. A high overcast was approaching from the southwest. Meanwhile, there was hardly enough wind to waver a candle—a rare experience on a mountaintop. I sat and ate cheese, an apple, cold chocolate.

At that moment came the call of a great raptor sailing onto the ridge. *Kee-eeh, kee-eeh.* I took it to be a red-tailed hawk. The bird had no need to flap, powering his morning commute from sun-warmed air rising off the mountain. If he chose to dive down the valley, he could be over the Waterton townsite in two minutes. It was eleven o'clock, and I would need the rest of the day to walk that far.

And to pay attention. The valley down which the trail led was a giant's stairway of three paternoster lakes (a term referring to the beads of a rosary), each pouring into the next. Along this path, the water would become progressively richer with life. Here at the summit there was a near-elemental simplicity of air, water, and rock. Not far below was a diverse forest. I was ready to observe precisely the transition. Before leaving the ledge, I tossed a bit of water from my bottle across the summit, as an offering.

Only Upper Carthew Lake was clearly visible as I descended past the severe red pyramid of Mount Alderson's western flank.

The lower valley was full of cloud. In a few minutes, the trail arrived at the shore. And it certainly seemed like the first lake under the roof of heaven. Its perimeter was barren, last winter's dirty snow lying in the shady hollows. What water it contained had come either directly from the sky or run over rock colonized only by traces of moss. Nothing seemed to grow below its dark aqua. Then, as I tracked along its west shore, a small vee disturbed the surface, like the wake of a toy boat, came directly into shore, and dissipated. What devilry was this? There could be *no* fish. This lake had last been stocked in 1929, according to Derek's big green binder, and had to be dead as a doornail. Maybe it was the tiny, troubled ghost of the last starving trout, or some minor mountain spirit. I concluded it could not have been a living creature.

Lower Carthew was only two hundred metres below Upper, but it was another world. This short distance brought the trail into the cloud. Wildly weathered, twisted subalpine fir conspired in the misty crags. The water that seeped along the fissures now fed a dense community of moss leading into the water. Then my phone rang. It was Marlene, just wanting to talk. She had already driven the kids to school, gone to see her herbalist. She had a dream the night before . . . From inside a cloud I listened. I tried to tell her about the tangled boughs of fir, the layer-cake rocks, the swirling mist, the fish ghost. I tried to explain that a cloud was really just a lake in the sky, ultra-oligotrophic. This all made her laugh. Amused by the separateness of our altitudes, our perspectives, we said goodbye. Now, where was I? The trail went on, back and forth across the creek, down through the cloud. A cold breeze was coming upslope, anabatic wind, and it carried a forest scent.

The crag firs increased their ranks, and grasses came on the scene. A few birches had appeared, tamarack, and lodgepoles. Shrubs now spread among them. Chipmunks and voles scurried along the trail often. In a scant few metres of descent from Lower

Carthew, the food web had spread wide, and I thought it best to warn any upwind bears of my presence. "Coming down, coming down," I called into the thickening trees.

Clouds are mostly flat on the bottom—moist air reaches its dew point at a precise altitude—and I stepped down out of them as if descending an attic hatch. Under the cloud the air was much warmer, the sun a pale disk through the veil. I was feeling spent now and needed more food. Still ten kilometres to go.

The last of the three lakes, Alderson, lay under the trail, a roundish cirque fenced by mature forest at one end and a vertical rock face at the other. Seated on a rock beside the trail, you could look straight down into it. With a white ceiling of cloud just overhead and the water a glowing aquamarine hue, it resembled an indoor swimming pool. A submerged shelf of rock extended from the west shore, then plunged away. Though tiny, the lake had to be profoundly deep.

Above the cloud was another clatter of stones. More deer perhaps. The rocks tumbled a long time, then silence, then another slide. It occurred to me that I might chance to see a rock actually fall down through a cloud and into the lake. I ate a round of cheese and the slides grew louder. It was also possible I would receive a projectile to the top of my head, and I considered moving off the scree and out of harm's way. I stayed put through a short lunch, but nothing arrived to ripple the water—or my skull.

After Alderson Lake, the profusion of life forms was too much to track. The thick understory was alternately huckleberry, its small leaves gone tangerine, and thimbleberry with leaves the size of a splayed hand. The bear grass whose blossoms can turn an avalanche slope white in spring retained their showy stalks. The dampening bark of red-osier dogwoods was deep burgundy.

It was starting to rain at last. It was surely snowing heavily on the summit. My feet hurt exquisitely. The trail seemed to run flat, but such mountains confuse the flatlander's eye, and my mashed toes told the truth. Alderson Creek ran ever more furiously in the deep valley below. When had it gathered itself into such a torrent? How had the soil grown so deep and lush? All day I searched for these—what would you call them? Genesis points? I realized with hapless amusement that I had not succeeded in finding a single one with any precision. I had only noted where something previously absent was now present. I wanted to turn and go back up the hill, to zero in on just one of these delicately sewn seams in the fabric of the mountain. But my beaten legs would never accede to such fancies.

Large balsam fir had usurped their subalpine cousins from higher up. Their leathery bark is covered in blisters filled with resin used in numerous folk remedies' first-aid treatments. Circling to the side of a tree hidden from the trail, I glanced guiltily about, drew my knife, and incised one of the blisters. I had no wounds to treat except a little weariness, but the scent of the clear sap was so tonic it instantly lifted my mood. It smelled like a whole summer of fresh air. This tree had done well with its share of water coming off the mountain.

After seven hours of seeing no one, I suddenly spotted the Akamina Parkway across the valley, a car whirring along the pavement. I was now in a dreamy, liquid state, and I resented the intrusion. But then, the road would come in handy for retrieving my truck from the trailhead. And what was this hiking trail under my sore feet but a little highway cut through the wood, the one built exactly like the other, only on a different scale? Was a bridle path better than a turnpike? Was animal motive power superior to motors? Without some kind of easy pathway, many wild places are inaccessible to us. And so some should remain. There are no easy answers to these questions of access to wilderness, any more than the interstices in the web of life can be pinpointed on

a mountainside. It is not easy to apportion the life-giving water
that flows from these magnificent slopes among ourselves, let
alone between us and the rest of the biosphere. I only know that
we must never stop trying to solve this complex division with
elegance and humility. And that the truest essence of our relationship with nature we are more likely to find along narrow
paths than wide ones.

In a few more minutes I came to a chainlink fence and
stepped around it onto a concrete sidewalk. The mule deer rest-
ing on the lawns watched me pass through town, down to the
Bear Mountain Motel and to sleep.

THE LAWNS of Waterton were under a thick wet snow by morning. It was still falling heavily. Only the rocky lower mass of Bear
Mountain was visible. There would be no more views of the
Rocky Mountains this season. It was time to descend back to the
prairies, to go home and rake leaves, hunker down for winter.

Having paid faithful attention to the wild side of a mountain for a time, I felt ready to descend from the sanctity of the
park gate to the messy real world, to return to live among my
own ever-hungry species. With the equanimity that comes from
monastic retreat, I looked kindly on the fruitful farms, these
waterways shepherded into fields, which seemed for the moment
not so different from firs and dogwoods thriving higher up. It was
a marriage banquet of water and earth. Best give thanks for the
bounty.

By the time I reached Cardston, the snow had become wetter
still, and it was already much warmer. I stopped to take a picture
of some ponies by an abandoned house. They seemed not to care
about the cold broadside pelting their calico flanks, seemed to
know the sun would soon melt all this. On the highway, buntings
played daredevil with my speeding metal carriage, alighting upon

the yellow line to take a drink from the wet pavement, then flying up over the hood just in time. After the storm, they would keep moving south, over the mountains and down to their winter range. In a few more minutes, the snow became driving rain. Despite the downpour, the sprinkler heads of the pivot booms continued to water the ever-thirsty fields of southern Alberta.

EPILOGUE

A JOURNEY MAY take you into exile forever, or it may deposit you back at your own front door. Either way, your idea of home is altered by the intervening miles, and events unfold in your absence. In the aftermath of my journeys across Lakeland, I returned to find that my familiar little corner of home at Emma Lake seemed turned upside down.

To begin with, the woman who had brought me to Emma for the first time so many years ago had reached the end of her days. At ninety-two, my adoptive mother Olive was old enough to be my great-grandmother. She should have had both her hips replaced a decade earlier. But she had always hated hospitals and put it off. The inactivity made her progressively weaker, however, and a day came in October when she could no longer stand up. She called me to say, with calm finality, that she was waiting for an ambulance ride over to the hospital. Marlene and I spent two weeks by her bedside. Olive was so enlivened by the steady stream of visitors—she was a profoundly social creature down to the very last—that the visitors themselves could not believe the patient was ill. But she wound down a little further each day, and by the second midnight of November she was gone.

Among a hundred details that had to be considered with the passing of the matriarch was the question of what would become of her cabin. The place on Emma Lake had effectively been mine since my dad had died five years earlier, and Olive's passing should have sealed the transfer. But the little red cottage, source of so much simple pleasure, had begun to hang over me like a weight.

Measured against all the lake country I had seen, the truth about Emma Lake and the Rural Municipality of Lakeland was bitter. These twenty-five square kilometres of water where my journeys had begun—the waters I knew best in all the land and for which I bore direct responsibility—were surrounded by some of the most egregiously bad shoreline development I had seen anywhere in Canada. The problems had only escalated. Mansions continued to replace cabins, traffic increased ashore and afloat. The beleaguered rural municipal government was facing ever more lawsuits from landowners pressing their right to develop new subdivisions. One developer, the descendant of a pioneer family, vowed to clear-cut log his land if he did not receive permission to build.

Certainly there were ways to fight back. As on so many lakes in the country there was a cottage owners' association here opposed to further development. I could see places to put the tool of citizen science to work on Emma Lake. If the future of the Rural Municipality of Lakeland was going to be decided with lawsuits, maybe it was time for the citizens to launch one of their own, backed by citizen-gathered data that the courts could not ignore.

The question was not what to do, but whether I was willing to roll up my sleeves and start. What used to be a place of simple rejuvenation was now fraught with politics. Emma Lake had become an obligation, a suite of problems. The previous summer I had avoided going out on the water because that only improved my view of developments I did not wish to see. On weekends I stayed away altogether because it was just too busy. My kids were beginning to lead lives of their own, and more often I was coming up alone. Having not grown up here, Marlene had never been deeply attached to this lake, had always chafed at its material excess. Perhaps Emma was a lost Eden, a thing of the past. Maybe it was beyond saving. You let go of things like that, don't you?

For the first time in my life, I thought of leaving Emma Lake forever. It was a profoundly disloyal thought. And yet there was a delicious freedom, a lightness of being, imagining it. I recalled the words of my friend Gerry Wilson from Lake of the Woods, about leaving the problems of Lakeland behind and retreating farther into the bush, finding a pure, quiet trout lake a little farther north. In a country this big, you can always push back the frontier with another tank of gas.

I contemplated leaving the Carwin Park road for the last time. Yes, it would be like losing an appendage. But the tidy proceeds from the cabin sale would help cauterize the wound, and maybe I could get myself a little shack on some canoe pond or an old farmhouse on the fringe of the national park. Without a cabin on Carwin to tend, I could spend more time on *real* wilderness lakes, of which I never get enough.

Emma Lake weighed upon my thoughts even as Marlene and I worked to box up the contents of my mom's apartment in the city, gathered up the trappings of a lifetime, and sent them off to the auctioneer. Olive's condominium looked north over the edge of the boreal forest, and I sensed Emma Lake out just beyond the horizon like a question. I thought of how the ice was forming, a bit more each day, and imagined it staying frozen forever, like a piece of Olive's quaint crystal stored away in a box.

WHEN I next saw Emma Lake, it was the dead of winter. A record snow burdened the roofs along the Carwin Park road. Ours was so laden that as I pulled up behind the cabin, I marvelled it had not collapsed. The drifts were past the window bottoms, wrapping the place like a shroud. In the front seat I pulled on my layers of winter plumage, then got out into the cold. I took a pair of skis from the trunk, stepped into the bindings, and slid down the slope of the yard to the lake.

The relentless and majestic seesaw of the seasons sets up a harmonic resonance within each of us, within all plants and animals. Summer brings such Eden to Canadian latitudes it is impossible to believe that a single leaf could ever fall or flower fade. In the triumphant light of June, the cold, pale cast of January seems only theoretical, an ice world from a bleak science fiction novel read long ago. But the leaves do fall; you will gather them up, bury them or burn them in a funeral pyre, and again you will harden yourself to a new regime. And before long you are scraping ice from the windshield of a cranky automobile. Now it is that other world—of sunflowers and bushes full of mating songbirds and buzzing mosquitoes—that seems impossible.

Winter and death are mythologically the same. The Greeks explained the winter as a kind of hostage taking. As the story goes . . . one day by the tree-lined shore of a beautiful lake where it is perpetual spring, young Persephone is picking flowers. Hades rides up from the underworld, nabs the maiden fair, and takes her down, down. Persephone's mother, Demeter, is so frantic over the disappearance that her work suffers. She controls things like growth—of crops in particular—and the world turns bleak without her ministrations. And so begins the first winter. With a tip from Helios, the sun god who sees all, Demeter learns her daughter's whereabouts and entreats Zeus to intervene. He is willing, provided that Persephone does not eat any food of the dead while residing in the underworld. Whether by intent or by Hades' trickery, Persephone does eat several pomegranate seeds in the darkness below. Upon this technicality the seasons hang: Zeus and Hades agree that Persephone will divide her time between two realms, spending one month in the netherworld for each pomegranate seed she has eaten. While she is gone, Demeter's sadness brings winter. Persephone's return is the harbinger of spring.

Winter is the season of introspection and taking stock, which is never comfortable. The lake, mirror of our soul, is frozen, heaving and cracking under the strain of wind, in the dark. Without enough light to plant and plow by, we have too much time on our hands, and idleness is the hardest trial. Our ancestors comforted each other through the long soul-night with talk, storytelling, bow making, sewing another row of beads onto the cultural fabric by tallow light.

In *Walden*, Thoreau devotes several chapters to winter. I think the quiet and solitude of the season suited his frosty temperament. And he was unafraid to delve beneath the frozen mirror. "As I was desirous to recover the long-lost bottom of Walden Pond," writes Thoreau in a chapter called "The Pond in Winter," "I surveyed it carefully, before the ice broke up, early in '46, with compass and chain and sounding line." Thoreau cut some one hundred sounding holes in the ice and drew himself a map of the lake bottom.

I have been obsessively sounding the bottom of Emma Lake for years. Some people pull tarot cards. It pleases me to plumb the depths in this old-fashioned way, to infer the shape of what lies unseen. I entered the shadows of our lakeside shed and found the poleaxe. An auger is a much more efficient tool for piercing lake ice. But neither Thoreau nor I owned one. I took a cracked Zebco fishing reel for a sounding line, found a heavy old Len Thompson Number 2 trout lure with the barbs cut off to use as a sounding lead.

Out on the lake the snow, aided by the wind, had settled under its own weight to a surprising firmness. I skimmed effortlessly out to the middle in a few minutes, stepped out of my skis, and began to chop. Under the fresh snow was a layer of weak, white, air-filled ice, the compacted mass of previous snows. Then began the clear, strong ice of the frozen lake itself. The axe, though dull, went along easily, and I checked my watch. At the rate the chips were flying, I thought fifteen minutes would do.

The cabins, great and small, stood quiet on the shores all around. If anyone was behind their windows, there was no sign. No chimney smoke rose. It was still possible to have Emma Lake to yourself. In the weeks after Olive died, I had floated the idea of selling her cottage with my kids, just to gauge their reactions. Both of them were young adults now, just beginning lives that could lead them far over the horizon. But both of them begged that we hang onto the cabin, that we not disqualify it from their futures, not yet. I remembered how grateful I was that my parents had kept the place long enough for me to rediscover it after that period of youthful wandering was over, when it was time to settle down and define what *home place* really meant.

As the hole deepened, the axe head could not touch bottom before the shaft struck the rim. And so I had to chop out an ever-widening dish. The chips all fell directly back into the hole, requiring frequent clearings. This had to be done by hand on bended knees. Thirty minutes passed. When I had chopped and cleared through half a metre of clear ice with no sign of the end, I was hot and thirsty. I threw off my anorak, drank half the water from my bottle, hefted the axe, and went to it again. Sweat ran heavily under my layers. I was now attempting to chop at a level well below my own feet. The deep bending pulled mercilessly on the hamstrings. The dish was already the size of a large bathtub and resembled a pit mine seen from the air. Agonizingly often I got down into it to clear the chips. I now had the frozen lake at eye level the way a swimmer sees it.

From this odd vantage point, I sighted our red cottage, which seemed to have grown smaller with the years, and suddenly knew I could never turn my back upon it, could not leave stewardship of this lake to someone else while I retreated farther into the bush. As with most tasks, shirking was more painful than doing. Anyway, where would I go? Was there truly an escape? I thought of Doreen Olson, the woman I had met in the Okanagan Valley, who had fled development from Toronto to Vancouver to Penticton before she decided to stand and fight. If Emma Lake wasn't my Penticton, my Alamo, then what was? I knew that the work was mine to do, that my hesitation was mainly just good old-fashioned fear of failure. Activism in an overbuilt place like this could well be a losing battle. Perhaps the Okanagan Valley was a lost cause. Maybe Lake Winnipeg was too far gone. And yet, by such logic, we might as well give up on the whole biosphere. No, the only true failure was not to try at all. In fact, I was generally optimistic that our clever species would stop fouling its own nest with pollutants, would stem the tide of global warming, would push through to a clean-energy paradigm. The sundry problems on other people's lakes seemed solvable. Here on Emma Lake, it was time for me to get past my sense of personal loss and work on the possibilities.

Olive and I had once briefly discussed working with a conservation group to turn our place into some sort of Concept Cabin. It would demonstrate responsible, sustainable resort living right there on Carwin Park. There would be signage, a footpath, a composting toilet. We discussed granting some sort of conservation easement, or placing a covenant on the land against future development, just as Doreen Olson had done with her place in the Okanagan. Land donations and easements were increasingly common in more remote wilderness areas, especially along the boundaries of park reserves. Perhaps they could be used to advantage here in the proximate wilderness. I was not sure of every detail, but I knew the red cabin had not yet reached its full potential. It would do so not by growing larger, but by staying small. Its strength was not its size, but the number of lives it could still touch, the inspiration it could still kindle. It felt like a new start.

Over an hour had passed, and I was just about to give up on my Thoreauesque plumbing when I noticed a warm amber light glowing at the bottom of the pit. The axe made a duller thud as it struck. I got down to clear the chips again and have a good look. The ice was as pretty to behold as cut stone, seemed to glow from within. I stood and delivered what turned out to be the coup de grâce—and the lake began to gurgle in. In less than ten seconds, my icy tub was filled.

The water was the palest shade of green-amber, tinted by the cellular remnants of last season's life. It would be hard to discern the colour at all without the pure whiteness of the surrounding snow with which to compare it. It was summer seen through the ice lens of winter, for such are the living colours, ochre and faint jade, from which things will grow—the broth of life. The little ice tub of water gave the feeling that a small forerunner of the warm season had arrived on the scene. It quivered alive and cast an image of the sky up at me, and I could imagine its heat relative to the surrounding ice even if I could not feel it. This little wound, like a puddle of blood on skin, would congeal quite soon, leaving a small, clear scar. But it gave proof to the life still pulsing underneath. It was a perfect day. In nearly two hours not a single car had disturbed the quiet. Emma Lake was still a beauty, moving warm and sensuous under her white robes.

Cold was penetrating my own perspiration-laden clothing, now that the heavy work was done, and I was famished. There was only the ritual of sounding the bottom. I dropped the red-and-white Len Thompson into the ice tub and down the dark drain hole at its bottom. Down and down. When the nylon line went slack, I pinched it at the water level, then dragged it back out across the snow until the lure emerged like a tiny fish, and paced the length—eleven big steps. The cut I had made was an inverted cone nearly one and a half metres deep. What would that much ice weigh? The weight of the whole sheet of even this one small lake was incomprehensible.

Like most substances, water becomes more dense as it cools. Yet, against all logic, as it reaches a temperature of 4°C, it reverses itself, becoming less dense down to the freezing point. Thus water has the exceedingly strange property that its solid form floats upon its liquid one. If water was a typical compound, all our northern lakes and polar seas would freeze from the bottom up, and would tend to stay that way year-round. Instead, the frozen surface serves as a thermal blanket, inhibiting further freezing below.

The very presence of liquid water on this planet remains a miracle, an amazing statistical anomaly in the known universe. Perhaps the water molecule itself—one hydrogen atom joined to two atoms of oxygen—is Persephone's pomegranate seed, balancing the seasons, life itself, on a fine point. Thoreau had cut one hundred holes in a day on Walden Pond. Well, his ice was thinner than mine, and I was pleasantly exhausted. It was time to go south and leave winter to play itself out a little further. The days were getting longer, the equinox was only a month away, and the sun, Helios, was beginning to come into his own again. It was a promising time of year. The snow would lie white for weeks to come, but it was getting warmer each day. Spring and summer were ahead. Like money in the bank.

I left the cabin and Carwin Park—not for the last time—and followed the road back toward the Christopher Lake townsite and the world. The Yellow Fender was still open. Inside, the café was full of heat, the smell of baking, friendly voices. I ate like a return-ing hunter and caught up on the local news. There was still light in the sky, enough to get back to the city before dark. See you in the spring. Yes. *See you in the spring.*

NOTES

Notes refer to direct quotations only

page #

10   Henry David Thoreau, *Walden* (New York: Time Inc., 1962), p. 184.

35   J. Stan Rowe, *Home Place: Essays on Ecology* (Edmonton:
NeWest Press, 2002).

Sharon Butala, *The Perfection of the Morning: An Apprenticeship
in Nature* (Toronto: HarperCollins, 1994).

36   Bill Mason, *Song of the Paddle: An Illustrated Guide to Wilderness
Camping* (Toronto: Key Porter, 1988).

P.G. Downes, *Sleeping Island: The Story of One Man's Travels in the Great
Barren Lands of the Canadian North* (Saskatoon: Western Producer Prairie
Books, 1988), p. xvi.

46   Grey Owl, *Tales of an Empty Cabin* (London: Lovat Dickson, 1936), p. 274.

47   Ibid.

50   Grey Owl, *Pilgrims of the Wild* (Toronto: Macmillan Company of
Canada, 1968), p. 278.

54   Lovat Dickson, *The Green Leaf: A Tribute to Grey Owl* (London: Lovat
Dickson, 1938), pp. 7 and 13.

55   Grey Owl, *Pilgrims of the Wild*, p. 48.

56   Grey Owl, *Sajo and the Beaver People* (Toronto: General Paperbacks,
1991), p. 16.

249   Henry David Thoreau, *Walden*, p. 284.

The Sacred Balance: Rediscovering Our Place in Nature
by David Suzuki, Amanda McConnell, and Adrienne Mason

An Enchantment of Birds by Richard Cannings

Where the Silence Rings edited by by Wayne Grady

Dark Waters Dancing to a Breeze edited by by Wayne Grady

Wisdom of the Elders by Peter Knudtson and David Suzuki

Rockies: A Natural History by Richard Cannings

Wild Prairie by James R. Page

Prairie: A Natural History by Candace Savage

Tree by David Suzuki and Wayne Grady

*The Sacred Balance: A Visual Celebration
of Our Place in Nature* by David Suzuki and
Amanda McConnell with Maria DeCambra

From Naked Ape to Superspecies
by David Suzuki and Holly Dressel

The David Suzuki Reader by David Suzuki

When the Wild Comes Leaping Up edited by David Suzuki

Good News for a Change by David Suzuki and Holly Dressel

The Last Great Sea by Terry Glavin

Northern Wild edited by David R. Boyd

Greenhouse by Gale E. Christianson

Vanishing Halo by Daniel Gawthrop

Dead Reckoning by Terry Glavin

Delgamuukw by Stan Persky

**DAVID SUZUKI FOUNDATION
CHILDREN'S TITLES**

. . . . .

There's a Barnyard in My Bedroom
by David Suzuki; illustrated by Eugenie Fernandes

Salmon Forest by David Suzuki and
Sarah Ellis; illustrated by Sheena Lott

You Are the Earth by David Suzuki and Kathy Vanderlinden

Eco-Fun by David Suzuki and Kathy Vanderlinden

THE DAVID SUZUKI FOUNDATION

THE DAVID SUZUKI FOUNDATION works through science and education to protect the diversity of nature and our quality of life, now and for the future.

With a goal of achieving sustainability within a generation, the Foundation collaborates with scientists, business and industry, academia, government, and non-governmental organizations. We seek the best research to provide innovative solutions that will help build a clean, competitive economy that does not threaten the natural services that support all life.

The Foundation is a federally registered independent charity that is supported with the help of over fifty thousand individual donors across Canada and around the world.

We invite you to become a member. For more information on how you can support our work, please contact us:

The David Suzuki Foundation
219–2211 West 4th Avenue
Vancouver, B.C.
Canada v6k 4s2
www.davidsuzuki.org
contact@davidsuzuki.org
Tel: 604-732-4228
Fax: 604-732-0752

Checks can be made payable to The David Suzuki Foundation.
All donations are tax-deductible.

Canadian charitable registration: (BN) 12775 6716 RR0001
U.S. charitable registration: #94-3204049